Khomeini, Sade and Me

19/05

About the author

Abnousse Shalmani was born in Tehran in 1977. Her family went into exile in Paris in 1985 where she studied history and became a journalist and short-film maker. With the memoir *Khomeini, Sade and Me,* her first book, she returned to her first great love: literature. *Khomeini, Sade and Me* was originally published in French and has also been translated into Italian and Dutch.

About the translator

Charlotte Coombe is a British literary translator currently based between Morocco and UK. She is particularly interested in translating women writers and is currently working on a collection of short stories by the Mexican author Rosamaría Roffiel. Her translation of *Traces of Sandalwood* by Asha Miró and Anna Soler-Pont was recently published by World Editions.

Abnousse Shalmani

Khomeini, Sade and Me

Translated from the French
by Charlotte Coombe

World Editions

Published in Great Britain in 2016 by World Editions Ltd., London

www.worldeditions.org

Copyright © Editions Grasset & Fasquelle, 2014
English translation copyright © Charlotte Coombe, 2016
Cover design Multitude
Image credit JF Paga © Grasset

The moral rights of the author and translator have been asserted in
accordance with the Copyright, Designs and Patents Act 1988
First published as *Khomeiny, Sade et moi* in France in 2014
by Editions Grasset & Fasquelle
British Library Cataloguing-in-Publication Data
A catalogue record for this book is available on request from
the British Library

ISBN 978-94-6238-051-6

Typeset in Minion Pro

This project has been funded with support from the European
Commission. This publication reflects the views only of the author,
and the Commission cannot be held responsible for any use
which may be made of the information contained herein.

Co-funded by the
Creative Europe Programme
of the European Union

This book has been selected to receive financial assistance from English
PEN's 'PEN Translates' programme, supported by Arts Council England.
English PEN exists to promote literature and our understanding of it,
to uphold writers' freedoms around the world, to campaign against the
persecution and imprisonment of writers for stating their views,
and to promote the friendly co-operation of writers and the free
exchange of ideas. www.englishpen.org

Distribution Europe (except the Netherlands and Belgium):
Turnaround Publisher Services, London
Distribution the Netherlands and Belgium: CB, Culemborg,
the Netherlands

To my father

'I desire the freedom to scorn or mock all religions; the people who gather in some temple to invoke the Eternal in their fashion should be seen as stage actors, whom everyone is permitted to laugh at. If you do not view the religions in these terms, they will reclaim their serious character, and then their importance (…).

I cannot reiterate it often enough: no more gods, Frenchmen, no more gods, if you do not want their catastrophic dominion to quickly plunge you back into the horrors of despotism; but you will destroy them purely by deriding them; all the dangers in their wake will promptly resurface in throngs if you fight them listlessly and take them too seriously. Do not topple their idols in anger; pulverize them while playing, and public opinion will tumble of its own accord.'

Donatien Alphonse François de Sade,
'Frenchmen, some more effort if you wish to become Republicans', in *Philosophy in the Boudoir*[1]

Tehran, 1983

When I was a little girl, I felt a strong desire to get naked in the school playground. It wasn't because of the intense heat: it was an act of provocation. The same kind of provocation that made me play leapfrog in the school mosque. It was physical.

I don't want to wear that thing. It's so ugly! No way! And with the logic that is so unique to children: okay then, but just you wait and see. I'll get my revenge! I will wear that tight, suffocating grey headscarf, but you'll see. And lots of them did see. My arse.

I don't want to wear the veil, but I have to put it on to go to school, and sometimes when I go out in the street, go shopping or see my friends. I do it. But as soon as the bell rings at the end of the day, I take it off. Not just the grey hijab, but also the regulation dress and the equally regulation and equally grey trousers. I hide in the stairwell or take refuge in the toilets, just before my classmates make their way out of the school gates. I take it all off, or sometimes I keep my knickers on, depending on how the mood takes me. Then I ball everything up and stuff it in my schoolbag, and off I go, sprinting at full pelt toward the main gate, dodging the Crows who spring into action at the sight of my naked bottom. I score points: half a point for one Crow dodged, one point for two Crows dodged, three points if a Crow trips up over the hem of her chador*, and so on.

I win every time: they don't know how to run in a chador. I end up in the car that is waiting for me with the driver—who is also the gardener—of the big house in Tehran where my great-aunt and uncle live along with my two younger aunts. My parents live just down the road in an apartment—my father hung on to his independence—but we spend most of our time up at the big house. I put my knickers and white T-shirt back on; there's no point being naked in the car. The driver-gardener will tell on me, I know it. The last time he did that, I chased him round the garden with the watering hose. There is a mutual dislike between us; he hates my cats that live in the garden and ruin all his handiwork; and I hate the fact that he's the only one who doesn't laugh at my crazy naked dash. If he complains—again—to my great-aunt, I swear I'll pull up all the tulips he has just planted.

Why did I find such pleasure in exposing myself time and time again? Above all, it was fun. It is always amusing for a six-year-old child to make adults run around. Those adults

---

* A large cloth worn as a combination head covering, veil, and shawl usually by Muslim women especially in Iran.

in particular, more so than others. Bundled up in their black chadors, the Crow-women chased and hurled themselves at me. It's surprising, the hysteria that a naked child provokes. I had fun, I amused my classmates, I enraged the Crows, and I worried my family. I had become the centre of attention for lots of people; I had become a hero among my schoolmates, even the older ones. And nobody that mattered, not my father, nor my mother, not my aunts nor my uncle had ever punished me for it.

I'm sure they thought I might be slightly unhinged, because each time I was suspended from school I did the same thing again, reducing my mother and the driver-gardener to nervous wrecks. But after witnessing one of my ridiculous chases, my family's laughter outweighed their concerns about my mental health. As the Crow-women carried on with their duties, painting my city and my childhood black, I carried on getting naked.

I wasn't the only one playing that game. Nudity was on everybody's minds, just *before* and *after* the Revolution of the mullahs. To this day I can still hear the questions, the uncertainty and tension over a skirt that revealed too much ankle, or a blouse that was too low-cut for dinner at the So-and-sos'. A full-body inspection was an essential ritual before leaving the house. 'You're crazy! You can't go out *like that!*' was the standard dressing-down you received before you faced the outside world. The morality police and their 'guardians of the Revolution' kept a close watch on every street corner. They scrutinized the men and women passing by, observing them with an unhealthy interest, a self-appointed voyeurism, a systematic ogling, trying to spot the slightest sliver of skin that might have escaped the family's vigilance. The way the Beards and Crows look at you is anything but discreet. Despite firmly advocating the disappearance of the body and insulting anyone who dares to raise their eyes, they let their own eyes wander freely over the terrified crowd, undressing them, in the name of the law.

I did not understand how I was the only one getting naked. Every day I observed the ritual of my mothers and aunts putting on their hijabs and I was revolted: meekly they covered themselves before going out—even though, every time, like some kind of incantation, they cursed Khomeini and all the Beards the world over. But children need heroes. And it would be an understatement to say that the Beards were not exactly heroes for me. My mother and my aunts had not even tried to remove, rip or trample their veils, as I had done when they made me try on the headscarf for the first time. Their lack of revolt was revolting to me.

I do remember one morning, though, when my mother had woken up in a strange, agitated sort of mood. My little brother had just been born and she was totally exhausted. She was holding my hijab in her hand, when suddenly she flung it to the floor and pulled a different scarf out of a drawer. It was bright red with an Indian pattern on it, and moreover it was see-through. She fastened it round my chin. Of course, I did not pass the clothing inspection at the school entrance. I was sent straight home. Though she never used me like that as a form of rebellion ever again, I remember her mischievous smile as she saw me getting out of the car, just twenty minutes after I had left for school. Perhaps she had simply wanted her oldest child at home with her that day, or perhaps it was the absurdity of the swathes of grey covering her little girl that had impulsively made her dress me in red. Either way, I was incredibly proud of my mother that day.

And the men? How did they protect their identities? They didn't! They all looked the same. They didn't dare to bare their arms or legs either, and it was rare to see someone without a moustache or a beard. If women dared to wear a colourful scarf, or men dared to wear a tie, if women wore lipstick or men attempted a flowery Hawaiian shirt, they would swiftly be whisked away to the local police station or to a shop—formerly a tea shop—which was now used as an office by the morality police. There, morality was dealt out to them in the form of shouts and insults. Or worse. But in those cases, you were sent to the cell. A real cell in a real prison. If the Crows and Beards were to be believed, a bare forearm or manicured nails were tantamount to a rejection of God and an act of treason against Ayatollah Khomeini—it was always about him. My bare bottom was therefore a supreme insult, the ultimate act of revolt. Nowadays, although I do understand the mechanism of ultra-contagious fear, I cannot come to terms with it. The ease with which everyone is made to look like everyone else is still a strange source of anxiety for me. What if everyone had taken all their clothes off, like me? What if all the random passers-by in the streets of Tehran had suddenly whipped off all their clothes? Would Khomeini have sent in his army to open fire on a crowd of naked people? The Revolution might have ended right then and there.

The guardians of the Revolution were the lords of the street, and it would have been *impossible* for me to take my clothes off there. They were far tougher than the schoolyard Crows; convinced of their righteousness, victorious. I not only couldn't, because I was always with someone when I went out; but I also didn't need to, because the veil wasn't actually obligatory in the street for little girls under the age of eight. It depended on which neighbourhood you were going to. In the bazaar or the administrative districts my mother always covered my head, while in the more affluent areas of northern Tehran we could leave my hair uncovered. Everybody was obsessed with the body, or rather with the absence of it. Tehran had become just a sea of faces.

My youngest aunt—my favourite one, the one with the ample bust—was in Paris during the Revolution. She returned to Tehran just afterwards, on 'holiday'. For a long time she was the most optimistic of her sisters, before caving in to bitterness too. On the flight back to Tehran, she covered her head. As soon as she got off the plane and came face-to-face with a zealous soldier of the new regime— among the ordinary travellers, baggage handlers, customs officers, the secret and less secret police, hidden agents— she felt naked. She was covered head to toe and remembers how she was sweating in her closed shoes, which were far too hot for wearing in a Tehran summer. Even so, she still felt naked. In the eyes of those 'Mr. and Mrs. Morality' types who were everywhere, her lips were too well-defined, her eyes too almond-shaped, her body too accustomed to moving freely. And for those ambassadors of morality, she was an insult to decency, to religion, to Khomeini. Later on, in the street, in restaurants, and even in the doctors' waiting room, everywhere that—whether you liked it or not—men and women had to be in the same space, and so women had to be covered, she still felt naked. Victimized. She returned to Paris post-haste, where she could even be chatted up without feeling that same naked feeling. For it was that, above all, which led to the veiling of women: pervasive sexual desire.

One of my older cousins told me how he was totally shaken up when as a young man he had inadvertently touched the finger of our first cousin, a girl of thirteen who wore the veil. He had never thought she was beautiful, in fact she was far too young and incredibly pious, but this unexpected contact had aroused something in him. To this day, now as a forty-year-old man living in Europe, he still remembers the sensuality of that little fingertip.

As soon as a man entered the stairwell, the supermarket, the bus, the headmistress's office or the lift, there was always that little gesture which had become automatic: adjusting your headscarf. And of course this gesture caught the eye, fanned the desire. For the majority of veiled Iranian women, it was a form of flirting disguised as extreme piousness. But I know one woman who did not play the game of false modesty. She was a friend of the family, famous for the sensual way she adjusted her headscarf: it was the dance of the seven veils, albeit in reverse, but every bit as mesmerizing. I recently found out that she has remarried for the fourth time in Miami. In 1960s Tehran she had taken over the family business from her father, a pastry chef by trade. She successfully developed the business from a regional to a national level. As a child she had fascinated me, just as she enthralled my father, who would spend entire nights drinking and debating with her. She was easily in her forties and never left the house without make-up on, neither *before* nor *after* the Revolution, and her regulation clothing was such a pale grey that in the sombre streets, all you could see was her. She said she was too old to be afraid. Every time she got arrested, she managed to get herself freed thanks to her numerous contacts. She was not easily deterred. But in 1982 she decided to go to San Diego to join the Iranian community there, living as they did in Tehran before the Revolution. I know that she still plays cards every night, sometimes all night, and that she often has to wake her son up at 4 a.m. to get him to lend her the money to finish her game. I remember how she used to laugh at all the gossip and how she had such vulgar language that my mother would blush before she had even opened her mouth. This friend of the family was the only woman who openly congratulated me for baring my bottom. She leaned in toward my mother and whispered in her ear, 'You should be thrilled to have a daughter like that, despite the poker you and your sisters have up your arses.' This family friend was the only other woman I knew who also exposed herself to people.

On the bus, people avoided looking at each other to get a better look at each other. It was so weird: you should never, and I mean *never*, meet the eye of any unknown man: any man who was not your father, or brother, or husband, or son. Your eyes had to be fixed on the ground. You had only to forget for a moment, to be daydreaming, staring off into space, to accidentally make eye contact with a man, and suddenly you were as ruined as a woman of the nineteenth century would have been for surrendering her virginity to a man out of wedlock. One day, my mother was followed by a man she had inadvertently looked at on the bus. He had taken it as an invitation. The more she fled, the more offended he became. He ended up calling her a whore. My aunt's wonderfully shapely breasts were not to blame for her being sexualized by men. Even I, a mere child, was effectively assigned breasts by the 'old man in black and white' and was seen as a sexual object.

In this context, for a child who was a woman in the eyes of the law, the fact of getting naked symbolized a return to innocence: the exact opposite of the sexual desire caused by the veiling of women. Everybody had started to look out for visible traces of the body in public spaces. In the streets, in cafes, supermarkets, everyone became like furtive animals, constantly keeping an eye on everyone else. The guardians of the Revolution were already redundant.

Paris, 2013

If Ayatollah Khomeini had not decided, one fine day, to politicize his faith, he might have had better things to do than transform little girls into women. Although I was still utterly a child, wearing the veil elevated me to the same level as women. Real women. Women with breasts and hips, with make-up and children. Since they no longer had the right to appear in public, the nape of my neck, my hair, my ankles, and my wrists all suddenly had the same impact as those of *real* women. By covering my head and body in grey, black, brown, or navy (the only colours permitted by law) the 'old man in black and white' decided to stop making the distinction between women of different ages. And it didn't stop there. Little boys and girls were no longer seen as children, but treated as men and women. All of them were swallowed up in the sinister, anonymous crowd, which was supposed to be nothing more than a single shout, a single people, a single faith. How can I describe the complete transformation of both the physical landscape and mental attitudes that took place with the veiling of Tehran? How can I capture that totally unique atmosphere? Even calling on photographs, films or archives that clearly show the *before* and *after*, there is something missing: the feeling. And this feeling, which was an inextricable part of the social landscape after the Revolution, is something shared by us, women and girls, who experienced it from the inside. I allow myself to say *us* because we all disappeared at the same time. All of a sudden there were no more children, adults or teenagers. There were no trendy young men or well-to-do women, good little girls or fine arts students. There were men, and there were women. These days you can see a variety of clothing on the streets of Tehran again. Coloured scarves are permitted—or at least there are no guardians of the Revolution hunting for any wayward lock of hair—and women no longer have to fasten them round their face and under their chin. They drape them lightly over their tinted, blow-dried, styled hair. Tehran does not look the same as it did in my childhood. But *after* the Revolution it was important to hide anything that made you stand out from the crowd. It was dangerous. The bourgeoisie drank alcohol, and had a western and therefore debauched lifestyle; students were bound to be unruly; pretty women out walking in the street could only be whores; men wearing ties must have been traitors to their country; the mother of a family coming out of a supposedly deviant (communist) bookshop instantly became a suspicious element.

In order to instil the Revolution in people's souls as deeply as possible, a reign of total fear was necessary. It was the era of suspicion. There was something in the air that made pedestrians cling to the walls. Quite literally. The street no longer just belonged to the guardians of the Revolution, the militants, and the madmen. Young, charismatic Beards were also suddenly making proclamations in the street, in the midst of the passers-by. The words on everyone's lips—the return of the Shah to stand trial, the liberation of this or that prisoner, the closing of the cinemas, the destruction of the United States, the murder of a famous singer—passed from mouth to mouth until they swelled into a spontaneous demonstration. And if you defected by not chiming in with the crowd, there was always someone nearby ready to cast you a dirty look, and if the words were clearly not coming out of your mouth, that somebody, thrown into a panic by what he was unable to control, would raise his accusing finger and call for your head. Then it was you that everyone was talking about.

Try and picture a crowd of people shouting, sinister, aggressive, and above all, terrified. What made this post-Revolution crowd so dangerous was the fear. Going outside was always risky. Tensions ran so high that even children did not chatter away idly or look around inquisitively, or smile up at whoever walked by. How can I describe the way the veil makes you invisible, makes sure you disappear into the crowd? You no longer exist. Yet the great paradox of the Beards' Revolution of 1979 is that the more women were covered up, the more they were sexualized. The more the crowd swallows you, the more you sink into it, and the less eye contact you have—or worse, physical contact—the more it causes an outpouring of sensuality to which nobody is immune.

My guerrilla nudity as a child shaped me, carved out my personality and sowed the seeds of my future passions. This childish nakedness that would always oppose the veil and the hiding, denial and exclusion of the female body, was something that has obsessed me to this day. There is also a real relationship between Khomeini and me. He embodies everything related to my femininity. I fed Khomeini with my reading and my life choices; I kept him close to me so that I never forgot that morning in February 1979 when an 'old man in black and white' completely turned my life upside down; I know that he is my greatest enemy. Years later, Khomeini is still there. With his swathes of cloth, his black turban, his sexual apartheid. Khomeini lies in wait; he is there in smiles, in a bared breast or in the veil's sinister fabric.

Years later, I realize that getting naked was the only *visible* way of defending myself against Khomeini. I was drowning in grey fabric, and my mouth was sealed shut by the law. Taking my clothes off was my way of showing him that he was way out of line. I was just a little girl. I look back at the images—the archives, but Khomeini has not yet become an archive for me: he is still too alive—and the most striking thing is the long layers of clothing covering him. Several long embroidered robes in fine matching fabrics, and of course the turban, black or white, depending on the genetic standing of the wearer. For only the descendants of Ali are permitted to wear a black turban. Khomeini wore his black turban proudly. Khomeini was the Mahdi: the hidden Imam of Shia Islam who would come to save the Muslims. Many people believed this and many are still convinced of it to this day. The black turban of the sole descendants of the first of the martyrs. Ali and his sons and his descendants. And all the other believers. Iranian Shia Islam is mystical martyrdom. It is beautiful and dangerous. Beautiful inasmuch as it is the culture, but dangerous when it becomes a political slogan, entrenched in law. The Beards of my childhood are there, covered from head to toe. Not content with being covered up, they wanted to see the rest of the world swathed in fabric too. And just as any child pulls off anything that smothers it, I ripped off the fabrics that were suffocating me.

Years later, one morning, there it was: the photo of Aliaa Elmahdy. The nude photo of Aliaa Elmahdy, the Egyptian student who wanted to be free. In stockings and red ballet pumps. No bra, no knickers. She was not yet twenty years old and there was no malice in her nudity. Paradoxically, despite the stockings, despite the flower in her hair, despite the pubic hair and nipples on display, she looked like a little girl. I had already started writing *Khomeini, Sade and Me* three or four months earlier. And there was that photo of Aliaa Elmahdy, right in front of my eyes, as if taking my hand and leading me back through time and space. From the little Iranian girl who got naked to the Egyptian student who gets naked to claim the right to have a body, the female body is always the issue; a body both risqué and at risk.

How a woman's body is perceived is a good indicator of the state of law, equality, and education. Each woman's body carries the history of her country. Looking at that image of Aliaa Elmahdy naked gives me hope. Thirty years later, she hasn't managed to find a better answer to Khomeini either.

Tehran, April 1979

I would never hug my mother—or any other woman—
until she had taken off her grey outdoor clothing. She was
anonymous like the others; she wasn't my mother when she
was covered head to toe in grey. I needed to see her hair
and skin to recognize her. Naturally, I was also afraid of
disappearing—like her—beneath the influence of the veil.
The exact feeling goes back to my second birthday. My
mother had come home and ripped off her headscarf as if
tearing her hair out. She threw the newspaper down on the
table in front of my father, and before he could say anything, my aunts arrived, one after the other, each pulling
off her headscarf, each with a newspaper tucked under her
arm. My father read aloud, and they all kept saying over
and over again, 'We're screwed.' My mother cried. One of
my aunts got drunk with my father and spent the rest of
the night vomiting. My uncles kept very quiet. As communists, it was a worrying time for them. I did not want to be
like my aunts, tearing out their hair and being sick while

making awful noises. I did not want to be like the women that I watched fearfully from the window of my parent's living room, when the ink was barely dry on the new regime's official daily newspaper publishing the new Constitution. It had been voted in, proclaimed, recorded. Religion had just celebrated its unhealthy union with the law. An unnatural marriage that would issue forth a prolific and troubled progeny, from the mountains of Afghanistan to the port of Algiers, the prisons of Tunisia and the poverty-stricken streets of Cairo.

It was 1 April 1979: the date of the referendum that sanctified the Beards as the new government. In an ironic twist of fate, it is also the date of my birthday. Ever since then I have been doomed to share my birthday with that of the proclamation of the Islamic Republic of Iran. I have only three terrible Polaroid pictures—all of them far too dark—of that birthday. That 1 April is the first historical date I can remember. The Islamic Revolution had already deeply affected me as a child by giving me an impressively accurate memory at an early age. I had an uncontrollable urge to visualize and recreate things in my mind because there was too much noise, too much movement, not enough normality, not enough consistency. There was only one thing that was more stable and constant than Khomeini, and that was history.

There were four years between the end of the Shah and when I started to wear the veil. Four years when I still looked like a little girl. Since 1 April 1979 I had known that sooner or later I would have to look like all the others. When the time came for me to go to school and wear the veil, it was tragic in a typically Iranian way, with much sulking, silent tears rolling down my cheeks, my eyes huge and moist. The veil was the end of the world to me. My first historical moment became the litany of my despair.

Perhaps all children of history who are flung out of their everyday lives—by forces that seem sometimes like the wrath of unhappy gods—are more sensitive when it comes to the past. When it comes to history. As if those in exile have an instinctive familiarity with the past. Exiles hold the key to yesterday because they are sealed shut to the future; they are the victims of an almost divine movement that is more powerful than they are; they are unable to imagine a future. Perhaps that is why I find it so easy to travel back in time to be with the likes of Diderot, Sade or Boyer d'Argens: I have always felt close to the past because it is so easy for me to sneak away back into it. The present has its limits; only the past can open the floodgates of hope so you can cling to something that is more solid than your reality. And there is nothing more solid than the historical past. Some call it identity, others integration, and others call it loss of the self. Personally, by studying the past I've found the best way to understand my childhood and to share a common memory with the country I became a part of after exile. I was born several times. Once on that day in April, again when I removed my veil and asserted my nakedness, a third time when I set foot on French soil, and again when I opened a book by Zola and discovered eighteenth-century French libertine literature. Each birth was like the story of a new love. Exiles have huge hearts.

From 1 April 1979 onwards, all dates are indiscriminately etched in my memory. I memorize the markers of Time to reassure myself. Dates are my tranquilizers. There are key dates and there are timeouts, there are glorious, poetic, and terrifying dates. That's how I remember the exact day when *West Side Story*, in the form of a miraculous VHS, burst into my life, or rather into the video player that my mother had saved from the clutches of the morality police by cleverly hiding it inside the mattress. As all the other video players in the building had been taken away by the police, my parents used to connect theirs up to their neighbours' TVs via the fire escape. We therefore had to agree on the evening movie from everybody's VHS collections—quite a meagre selection that arrived in dribs and drabs from the United States, Germany or France via family, or sometimes via the once-thriving black market. I can no longer remember if it was in the clandestine bookshop/grocery store/bar belonging to one of his army friends that my father had found George Chakiris and Natalie Wood, or if it was my American uncle who had sent it via a thousand intermediaries, along with a plethora of chocolates and cinnamon-flavoured chewing gum. But I remember that I jumped around all over the place, dancing and clapping my hands. I was seven years old and I had never seen a musical. I decided to become a dancer: the dancing body was yet another weapon that could be used against Khomeini. Body language is an entrancing, unknown sort of gibberish to the Beards and Crows. They hate it. And so because they wanted to hide everything like that, for no reason other than out of fear, my immediate reaction was to want to put my body on show. I took classical dance lessons but it had nothing to do with red blouses and high heels, ruffled dresses and sensual swaying. From that day onwards, my long-suffering family and friends had to sit through my endless dance routines— whose only redeeming quality was the determination I put into making the enjoyment last as long as possible. As soon as I got home I would rush over to the VCR and put on the film, then I sang and danced along with all the numbers. Or rather, massacred them. The neighbours could not turn on their TV sets without having to endure 'I Feel Pretty' for the gazillionth time.

My passion for dance led to my expulsion from school. Not content with dancing alone, I started a dance troupe with my classmates. We were caught in the middle of a dance show in the school toilets, and I was sent home. My arguments that we were not naked and we were simply practicing a cabaret show only seemed to make things worse. My dance troupe also dumped me in it, unfortunately. The girls cried, saying that I forced them into it. My parents were called in. I still remember the things they were told. According to the headmistress I had a problem that went far beyond disobedience: I was 'possessed', because I had absolutely no modesty. She pushed my parents over the edge by giving them the contact details of an exorcist. I kid you not. That's what a harmless VHS could lead to under the reign of the Beards and Crows.

I have never been able to rank dates in order of importance.

While 1 April 1979 will always be etched indelibly on my mind, 19 March always makes me hum 'Tonight' ... These are the two sides of the same story. My childhood filled my life with contradictions: the anonymization of women and the doomed love affair of Tony and Maria; the invisible body and body language; ugliness and art. And I already knew that one could fight the other.

Paris, 2013

What can you do if the past sticks to your skin like a plaster? Ripping it off might tear your skin. You have to subtly pull at it, neither ignoring it, nor pursuing it. You have to pick carefully around the edges: if I know how to do that, then I will know why, and the past will no longer overwhelm me. There will be no more precise dates, no more *befores* or *afters*. It will be tamed by the power of knowledge. The past became history on 1 April 1979. I decided at that moment that I had not been born in 1977, but in 1979 instead. That is when my first clear memory dates from. I felt like I didn't exist before then because I didn't remember anything before it.

However, the irony of this power struggle is that the Beards are also obsessed with the past. In their desire to impose their ancient prejudices, they have the same compulsion to go back, to return to earlier times, the times of the prophet and his victories, the times of the conquests of Islam, which was an empire. They want to go back in time, to repeat the course of history, back to where they think they can control it.

Here we are, the Beards and me, face-to-face, quarrelling over a shred of memory, over a historical reference, to stall for time. Perhaps the difference between us is that I am looking for something to understand and they are looking for something to emulate. Perhaps they are stuck in a past that they feel is reassuring, and that's why they want to cling on to it as long as possible. Because—and this is certain—one day, modernity will conquer all. While we wait, we must help those who want to carve little niches of modernity into the labyrinth of prejudices and we must look to the past—and not just Islam's past. We must provide the keys that break the code, that open up new pathways and enable us to stick two fingers up at the Beards. I think I have one of these keys, which I discovered in the past, in the heart of history. The French Revolution must have had a heart.

We are face-to-face, the Beards and me, and I have a burning desire to show them my arse and shout at them that their identity is not in the distant past they appear to be stuck in. That their truth is here, today, in the change that begins with dusting off faith before hiding it away inside—where it belongs—and occupying the public space. Not just with bodies, but with words as well. Dirty words.

Here we are in confrontation, the Beards and me, face-to-face; each of us is waiting for the other to lower their eyes. But I have already lowered mine and they did not suspect a thing. I lowered mine to read the words of a book, a book born out of my imagination and my disobedience. I won the first round. And ever since that day, I have outwitted them in the stare-down. I looked down, and without them suspecting anything, I read. I won the most important battle of all: that of art against stupidity. I read. There is yet another irony. The first order of the Revelation, the first words uttered by the angel Gabriel to Muhammad who heard him, were: *Read. In the name of your Lord, read.* It's crystal clear. I did as I was told, but I purposefully chose the wrong book.

I did not leave the Iran of my childhood unarmed. This desire to rummage about in the past, to understand it, is perhaps the best weapon for fighting all of the world's Khomeinis. It is crucial to study history, but one can only shed light on history by studying mores and private life. Having knowledge of social organization, relationships with death and with the body, knowing how men see women and how women see men, means never taking the easy route of prejudice. Taking the details into account helps you to pre-empt. And to talk less bullshit. I will never forgive Michel Foucault for supporting the Beards rather than the nasty Shah. Even though Michel Foucault was obliged by his political choices to support a movement of supposed emancipation of the masses against Western domination, and the acculturation that entails, he screwed up. He knew nothing about the moral fabric that held Iranian society together, he knew nothing of the Beards' horrifying lack of culture and he neatly forgot that Iran had never been colonized. He did not even try to understand what Iranian society was all about and why Khomeini should not have any part in it. It was possible to be against the Shah's dictatorship without falling into the arms of the Beards, just as it is possible to be against Islamism without being a xenophobe. But to achieve that, you need to know what you are talking about and exactly what you are fighting for.

What I am fighting against is a series of prejudices that imprison women under the veil, which is just the visible part of her inner prison. I am fighting against the Beards and Crows who see a dangerously powerful woman in every little girl. I am fighting against anything that submits women—and men—to the dictatorship of the eye. I am fighting against the *awrah** to reduce its sphere of damage to the minimum—to its appropriate size, which is no bigger than a fig leaf. I am not fighting against men or women but against concepts, unhealthy traditions, and the violence of prejudice.

We must accept that moral history is intimately linked with political history. It is not a question of reducing history to important dates and important men, nor to stories of intimacy, but about exposing the things that connect them. History is linked with human relations: how we make love, how we eat, whether we close our door or not, how we pray, how we take drugs, how we fantasize, how we sleep

---

* The Arabic word *Awrah* is a term used within Islam that denotes the intimate parts of the body, for both men and women, which must be covered with clothing. Exposing the awrah is unlawful in Islam and is regarded as sin.

with one another. Khomeini is nothing more than a concept that I turn over and over in my mind as if trying to unravel the mystery. He ceased to be a man a long time ago. Understanding how that man got there, understanding what was so relevant in the things he said that it resonated so strongly in the Persian psyche and still does, even thirty years later. That is what will prevent him from being reborn again and again, *ad infinitum*. An interest in human interaction is what is lacking in all intellectuals, who feel they are superior to men they know nothing about. It is in that dimension that one witnesses women unable to remove their veils without breaking the dictatorship of fathers. And mothers.

Tehran, 1979–1985

Of the six conscious years that I spent in Tehran after the Revolution, between the ages of two and eight, I have terrible memories of women. No man ever made me suffer like the Crow-women of my childhood. I still hold it against them. If a woman so much as raises an eyebrow and tries to say that another woman is a whore, I get angry. Sometimes I cry, sometimes I snap. Either way, it is always the Crow-women of my childhood who come back to me. I will never forgive them.

The first was an enthusiastic activist, with crazy, aggressive eyes and clinical movements. She stridently vilified any woman who didn't wear the veil. The Revolution was underway and the Left were still cheerfully demonstrating, always in the company of the Beards and Crows. It was all about being against the Shah (who was an absolute dictator), against the Savak (the political police who tortured with a vengeance) and against censorship (which was widespread). The Beards and the communists joined forces to bring down the worst of the monarchs. Very soon it became clear that women should wear the veil during the demonstrations, as they were now clamouring for Khomeini to return (he was in exile in France). The Revolution succeeded in achieving a reign of fear by using fanatical Crow-women like her to constantly accuse and debase women while making them feel guilty. The fact that it took my mother and aunts until that day to realize that their leftist Revolution was at a serious impasse, never ceases to amaze me. They had to wait for hysteria beneath black veils to notice that for some time already, democratic ideals had ceased to exist in that hateful crowd, fuelled by its vibrant nationalism, screaming out their hatred for anything that wasn't pain and ugliness. It was a crowd of martyrs already preparing themselves to send their children to the front line. That Crow-woman made me fear the crowd. Nobody in the family took part in the demonstrations against the Shah any more, as they came to understand, thanks to my first Crow-woman, that their long hoped-for Revolution had passed by under their noses.

There was another one, the 'moral supervisor' of the playground. She loathed me for getting naked every time I was out of her sight (following several successive nude episodes, she began to come and find me at the door of my classroom and escort me to my waiting car). One morning she noticed that my nails were too long. Hygiene was an obsession of the Islamic Revolution. Some vague history of purity and whiteness. Every morning all of the students would line up to have the cleanliness of their hands and the decency of their Islamic garb checked. I have always hated white. Nothing frightens me more than a deserted snow-covered plain. That day in May, the 'moral supervisor' was overjoyed to find my nails were too long, as this gave her an excuse to take me to the infirmary and cut them right down to the quick until they bled. That day was the first time I saw her smile. I was so surprised by the smile that I even forgot the pain. She was fired but then rehired—she knew a lot of important Beards—but this torture scene rang alarm bells with my parents. They knew that I could never live in Iran. I wasn't able to adapt, I didn't want to look like everyone else; I wanted to be naked. By cutting my nails to the quick, that Crow shaped my parents' destiny.

There was another one who grabbed my mother's arm and kept calling her a whore because her headscarf was not covering her hair properly. My mother couldn't give a damn, since she was holding me in her arms and I was crying because I had mumps. My mother—consumed by that absolute love that affects some mothers more than others—only cared about one thing: getting me to the doctor. The three guardians of the Revolution, including the Crow-woman, had arrived at the precise moment that my mother, holding me in her arms, her headscarf askew, came rushing out of the house to jump in a taxi. The Crow grabbed her roughly by the arm. My mother couldn't care less, but she ended up at the police station where a charming Beard phoned my father and told him to come and pick up his 'whore of a wife'. That Crow-woman made me love whores. The way she shouted made me realize how a whore can be delicate and sensitive. She taught me never to use the term 'whore' to insult a prostitute. To that woman, I owe my attraction to the great courtesans of the eighteenth century, the horizontal beauties of the Second Empire and the Belle Époque. I owe my passion for Ninon de l'Enclos to that Crow-woman.

There was also a cousin of my parents who became a Crow because she was ugly. The Revolution gave her the chance to turn her ugliness into a strength. She was the first in the family to wear the chador; she was the first to feel the change coming and the only one who stopped associating with future undesirables such as writers, singers, journalists or even the seamstress who used to visit us who had married a German. She was the only one who adapted perfectly to the new era that was dawning. She met her husband at one of the demonstrations. Her ugliness was a measure of her purity and he quickly married her. Even quicker still, he became the head of the Basij* in his neighbourhood, then of his district, and finally he ended up in an important international position. The ugly woman became rich and respectable and took her role as a 'muse of the Beards' very seriously. The last memory I have of her is very specific: it took place in her huge house, which was devoid of any decoration; white, sad, immense. Inside it, our voices echoed. We were visiting her precisely because she was a threat to us. They explained to me a thousand times that I shouldn't

* (The name of) a volunteer militia founded in Iran in 1979.

say anything about the wine my father made at home (and even less about how I crushed the grapes under my feet as I recited my lessons), and that I shouldn't take off my head-scarf—or my dress for that matter—and that I definitely should not recite the funny anti-Beard ditty that my father had made me learn by heart to liven up the dull evenings. I should keep quiet and most importantly, never answer a question with anything other than a saintly smile. As soon as we arrived we were separated into two groups: men and women. Sitting with the women and feeling utterly bored, and despite being forbidden to say anything, I dared to ask for some colouring pencils and paper so that I could do some drawing. Big mistake! The ugly cousin told me that we should not draw human figures. I replied that I only drew cats. This was true. She refused to believe me. I asked again, and promised, hand on my heart, to only draw cats. I prom-ised that I would hide under the table, behind the sofa, in the toilets, if I could just draw some cats. She flatly refused. I was a whisker away from kneeling down and making the sign of the cross—I was a big fan of making the sign of the cross ever since I had discovered the film *The Song of Bernadette,* which was on TV every Christmas—when my mother told me to sit down, casting me a dark look. The cousin took the opportunity to stop me from asking again, by assuring me that God saw everything, everywhere. I wish she hadn't said that! I already knew that God did not exist because my father did not believe in him, but I had never considered the idea that God might be everywhere and might be able to see everything. I did not say another word. But when I went to the toilet, I couldn't help thinking that God was watching me. It was paralysing, yet liberating. That same Crow-cousin later sent the morality police round to my parents' house and forced my father to burn a bathtub full of banned books, or else they would send him to prison. It was the most difficult experience of his life. My mother was screaming that books would be the death of us—they had already got my brother imprisoned under the Shah—and that I would never see them again, and I would have to look after my little brother. She forbade me from continuing to love books. That Crow-cousin taught me that God was everywhere and that I should stop looking for him and just leave him the hell alone.

One day—and this memory could be real, or fantasy recreated later by the combined forces of memory and fear—there were hundreds of Crow-women (and Beards as well) passing by, holding the charred body of a prostitute above their heads. Demonstrators had locked some prostitutes inside one of Tehran's brothels and set fire to it. They waited for the bodies to be roasted alive and then they passed them out over their heads, with hands stretched to the sky; the hands of people who in normal times would be incapable of hurting a fly. I still don't know if this is a memory recreated from a photo by Abbas, or if I really saw it. My mother remembers the scene but doesn't know—or doesn't want to know—if I was with her that day. I think I remember it perfectly—as if I had experienced it, with the smells, the exact blue of the sky, the noise, and the blackened corpse frozen in an almost absurd defensive position, blending with the black chadors. Sometimes I close my eyes and it is the photo taken by Abbas, the same setting, the same depth of field, the same faces that come to mind. Those Crow-women—who thought that God and the Revolution were in danger as long as the city's prostitutes were still breathing—were no longer women. They condemned themselves by trotting along proudly with the tortured corpse of their liberty held high above them. Whether I saw this rabid hatred of the female body with my own eyes or whether I recreated it after seeing the photography of Abbas is of little importance: either way, that sequence of the Revolution was real, those murders were collective, and the joy that followed the procession of the corpses was chilling. The Crow-women taught me that you should never place your confidence in morality, that it is often just an excuse for letting women be killed.

There was one more Crow, the one who I thought would be the last in my life. She was a Crow-soldier. She was responsible for the female body searches at Tehran airport. She had black hairs sprouting from her chin, which she sported proudly like a symbol of her virtue. She had searched me roughly and with a look of utter disgust on her face because we were leaving for Paris, in the West, or in other words, we were jumping ship. She did not ask questions; she barked them. And when, spitting with rage, she asked my mother why we were leaving to be with 'foreigners' when the country was at war, my trembling mother replied with her eyes fixed on the ground that we were going to visit her sisters who were studying there. The

Crow-soldier asked if they were married. My mother told her they weren't, and the Crow lost it: it was a disgrace to leave girls alone in a city full of vice, it was shameful to let them prostitute themselves and my mother would never have enough tears to wash away the shame that had been brought on our family. Then the Crow-soldier pointed at me and asked my mother the million-dollar question: 'Do you want a whore for a daughter?' *Voila.* I was already a whore, and Paris was an immense brothel where my aunts plied their trade. The Crow continued to hurl insults about foreign lands, Paris, whores, my aunts, our cowardice, her own greatness, until another Crow-solider cut her short by asking her to hurry things up a bit. It was over. There would never be any more Crow-women in my life. There would only be whores. And perhaps this was the sole reason why I left the country of my birth, the paternal grandparents and cousins that I loved so deeply, without a single tear or regret. I knew that I would not see them again right away, not even in a month or in two years. I knew that something was lost, there in that unfriendly airport. But there was a promise: there would never be any more Crows making me cover my head. That Crow-soldier, who should have been the last, taught me that Crows know no borders. And that they often have hairy chins.

Paris, 2013

When Atatürk or Bourguiba wanted to demonstrate a break with the past and modernize and secularize power, they decided to lift the veil for women. Atatürk prohibited it, pure and simple, while Bourguiba put words into action by removing the veils of the women he met during his walkabouts. What they wanted was to bring women into the public arena and allow desegregation, which is so inherent to modernity. There is TV footage showing an eloquent Nasser, before an audience of uproarious Egyptians, making fun of the Muslim Brotherhood who wants to impose the veil on all women. He wonders how this could ever happen seeing that the leader of the Muslim Brotherhood could not even impose it on his own daughter! Gone are the days when, among Muslims, we could laugh about the veil. These days, since September 11 and the sudden significance that Islam and Muslims gained in the eyes of the world, no one laughs any more. Neither Muslims nor anyone else.

A trivial 'It's hard being loved by jerks', uttered by a

gently caricatured Muhammad caused such a backlash that you have to wonder about the mental health of the angry Beards. But you have only to see the reaction of the Taliban, which is disproportionate to say the least, when faced with a marriage ceremony containing music and dancing—they kill the guests—to realize that Islam is so afraid of losing its identity, of dissolving into democracy, into modernity, into the West, into everything that is not familiar or inscribed in their Quranic past—even though it is so outdated, so unliveable in this day and age—that it focuses on the fear of the image it portrays.

It is a prejudice that has become law and which in turn imprisons women in the black fabrics that conceal them. According to them, we cannot imagine the damage that the nape of a woman's neck can cause. The Hadith* say that one of the prophet's companions noticed that when men and women were gathered together beneath the tent where the dinner in Medina was hosted, there was dangerous promiscuity. Hands brushed, women looked at men who were not a brother or a husband. How could temptation be resisted? Immediately, Muhammad decided to separate the men and women when they ate dinner. And for everything else as well. As if the veil was not enough. Why did it not occur to any of Muhammad's guests or even to him that it is possible for a man to look at a woman who is not his sister, mother,

---

* A collection of traditions containing sayings of the prophet Muhammad which, with accounts of his daily practice (the Sunna), constitute the major source of guidance for Muslims apart from the Quran.

or daughter, without wanting to screw her? That would have been too simple. Instead, they took it to the extreme: men shall not look at any woman apart from their wives, sisters, daughters or mothers. When you really think about, it is so hyperbolic, so delusional: it's like emptying your house of all its appliances just to avoid a domestic accident.

In the end, it doesn't really matter whether or not the Quran tells women to wear the veil. As soon as the issue comes up, the focus shifts to the famous suras, or chapters of the Quran, 33:59 and 24:30–1. Is something lost in translation? According to some, they tell us, 'You should', according to others, 'You have no choice'. In any case, Muhammad was not the first one to come up with the idea of women veiling their heads. Some Catholic women cover their heads out of respect when they enter churches, and certain Orthodox Jewish women rarely take off their wigs. What is specific to Islam is that it imposes the veil from morning to night. Wearing a headscarf is something that is immediately associated with Islam. This was one of the first measures implemented by the Beards when they came to power. It was the most visible way to give Islam a recognisable presence. There are no images better known or more bandied about than the striking pictures of the women of the Iranian Revolution in their black chadors, gun in hand; or the more *modern* images of the blue-caged women under the Taliban. Look for the veil. The veil is political Islam. It is the border between private and public, taken to its absolute extreme.

Years later, when I was studying women's history at

university, I was fascinated by this issue. The private versus the public sphere, or women's historical boundaries. The border that women learn to cross in order to be equal to men. The border between the closed (i.e. protected) domain, and the open (i.e. dangerous) domain. It's simple: over the centuries, women have always had to struggle to access the public domain. Their voices, their bodies must form part of it in order to have rights. It's simple: women excluded from the public domain have no rights. No legal existence. What I found unbearable as a child was suddenly being excluded from the public arena. And not just physically: I was grey like the walls, grey like all the others, but I was also excluded as a voice. I no longer had the right to speak. Just like all the other women.

There is really a very simple relationship between the headscarf and modernity, and it is this: they do not belong together. They do not mix. The headscarf is the enemy of modernity. You could show me a thousand veiled women of all ages and make them repeat that they feel free, that they feel happy wearing the veil. I would not believe them. They may be heads of business, feminists, politicians, biologists, writers, engineers, potential Nobel Prize winners, but they are still women marked by the stigma of being women. With their veils, they are toting millennia of abuse, inferiority, and contempt. They cover themselves to hide their shame. Their professional success will never change the ingrained mentality that drives them: a woman who does not wear the veil is a godless woman, offered up for all to look at. And above all, offered up to predators, i.e.

men. Men, who are forgiven by women for everything, just because they are men, like the prophet. A man is not guilty of raping a woman if she is not wearing the veil. A woman without a veil is a provocation. She doesn't even need to wear a miniskirt or a plunging neckline; she is provocative simply by being *uncovered*. Laugh, laugh in my face as a child imprisoned under the Islamic veil, history will prove you wrong: the veil is more than just a veil.

Tehran, 1981–1985

I remember the sheer panic I caused my parents on account of my uncontrollable outspokenness. As a child in Tehran and later on in Paris, before every dinner, every lunch, birthday, concert, or wedding where I would come into contact with Iranians, my mother and father told me all the things that I shouldn't say or do in front of them. I didn't get why I couldn't say that we ate pork, when we had always eaten pork in front of the same friends and never mentioned it. I didn't understand why I shouldn't say my clothes were from Paris—my aunts were students there—because everyone could see that they weren't living in Tehran! I didn't understand why, in Paris, I shouldn't say that my aunts were my aunts. I have never understood and still don't. Just like I didn't understand why, at their father's funeral, my aunts insisted on saying that he had built a mosque in the city where he was born. He was neither a believer nor practicing, and if he did build a mosque, it was only so that the Beards would leave him alone. There were no political police in Paris watching my family, and among the few people at the funeral, there was nobody who was even the slightest bit 'shady'. But you never know. We had to pull the veil tightly over our heads. Like burning a specific incense to protect against the evil eye whenever good news was celebrated, when the family gathered together, or at births and weddings. The evil eye—the eye of envy, of ill will—was everywhere and we had to protect ourselves at all times. The battle against the eye was constant.

In the same way that the body became so shameful that it had to be covered up, life became so shameful that it had to be covered up with lies. Only close family, not even close friends—but is it even possible to have close friends under these circumstances?—knew the truth. Just as the veil covered the head, appearances masked reality. And just as I couldn't bear the swathes of dark fabric, I couldn't bear the lies. Every child knows that you say the truth out loud but lies are whispered. Our life must have been a lie then, seeing as we hid it from those who must have been, in comparison, the true ones—the Beards and Crows. My father tried in vain to explain to me the concepts of compromise, dictatorship, resistance, discretion, but I wasn't old enough to understand political and human subtleties, and I wasn't inclined to listen to my father preaching about passive cohabitation. So I forged on, declaring out loud all the things that made us different from others, to rid us of the lie, and causing mini-catastrophes in my wake. I ended up letting slip in class that my father made his own wine— because the teacher wanted us to believe that alcohol was the devil's creation—and my parents received a visit from the guardians of the Revolution; my father had to throw away all his carefully accumulated reserves. Another time at a dinner that was crucial to my uncle's business, I said with glowing pride that my London aunt was living with an English student—who I imagined to be tall and blond, with a top hat and a cane. This was enough to make one chaste, religious friend of the family choke on her dinner at the impropriety of it all. I told my classmates that we had spent the day at the beach and that we had swum in bathing suits—without noticing that the headmistress's daughter was listening attentively—and the quiet secluded beach which my family and friends always used to go to was raided by the morality police.

In several photos you can see my father sitting next to me, his fingers pinched together, looking down, as if trying to make me understand everything I had to keep quiet about. And me, frowning, pouting, staring at my father's pinched fingers, not having any of it. He was no fool; he knew that at the slightest opportunity I would launch into a description of our everyday life. So he negotiated as best he could: perhaps I could just say it all quietly. But I would rather say nothing at all, than whisper. Because the whispering terrified me. The impression that everything was being said *piano* made the confinement of the veil even more unbearable. I wanted to shout. My mother often recounts how I used to hurl myself at my youngest aunt, hitting her because she refused to repeat out loud whatever it was she had just whispered in my father's ear. To this day I still hate whispering, but I no longer lash out.

After the outbreak of the war, after the arrests of the communists—who were freed by the Revolution, then re-imprisoned, or even executed by the Islamic Republic— after the departures of forced exiles, friends became scarce. However, it was during this dark time—because everybody was afraid—that for a short while, the surveillance of the eye stopped. Inside. Between the reassuring walls, inside, everything could be said, done, or thought. We had added some foliage and replanted the tall trees. Inside, it was the skin, hair, smells, and bosoms of my aunts. Outside, it was lies, secrets, whispers, and shadows. It was the outside that had to be conquered. It was not about a six-year-old girl starting a Revolution, changing mentalities by getting naked. It was simply about laughing and making people run around. About transporting life (which was inside) to school (which was outside).

I remember, as all Iranians do, the parties *after* the Revolution. Those who wanted to could get together to drink banned alcohol, listen to banned music, ogle at inappropriate necklines, children and adults alike. All those Iranians remember the parties behind the blacked-out windows. It was excessive; it was noisy. People laughed more, sang more, drank more, and talked more openly than at any party before or since. I was only six, seven, eight years old, but it was wonderful. Everyone was declaring their eternal love and friendship. It was the first and last time I saw my family and friends freed from the power of the eye. It was during that sad, uncertain time—and only during that time—that

I saw how much they wanted to put their deepest fears and most hidden feelings into words. Perhaps it was the unique atmosphere of those parties that we feared would be the last—close friends were being arrested every day and some never came back—that affected me so strongly that ever since, I have felt the need to put everything into words and lay my feelings bare. My family continued to live in the grip of the eye—after the parties and in exile—but I was never able to accept it. The deeply cultural aspect of the eye was not ingrained in my psyche. I shunned it by taking off my clothes. But before exile and before things returned to normal, in the big house in Tehran—whose garden had fourteen cherry trees and was home to about twenty cats— the parties continued, despite the Beards and the Crows and the Eye.

Increasingly they were *goodbye parties*, as we used to call them then. There was something hopeless about those goodbye parties. They knew that they would never see those childhood friends again: the Stalinist students who muddled Gorky with Soviet politics; the friends they met in their youth in the army, in their first job, or at a friend's wedding; the fierce competitors for a husband who became friends once they were wives; the children of friends who would no longer remember their names once they were scattered between Paris, London, Berlin, Frankfurt, and San Diego. Despite their promises and cheery words, they knew that they would lose all of their memories. It was a time of goodbyes and a time of rebellion. Because they felt rebellious, these men and women who went on drinking;

drinking more than they ever had *before* the Revolution but never as much as they would *after*.

I often find myself—while my parents remain silent, their thoughts drifting to another place that has eluded them— thinking of their friends before exile. They have never seen them since. Perhaps it was precisely because they knew they wouldn't, that they talked so freely to one another in those last days in Tehran. There was nothing to lose. Wasn't everyone's reputation screwed anyway? They were already clandestine in their own country. I remember my mother— who was so timid when her sisters were around—suddenly bursting into song in her beautiful voice, which she had never dared to do before. I remember my aunt (the youngest but one), who always used to paint in secret but who never showed her works (even to this day) to anyone but a few close relations, spontaneously giving her paintings to people she liked and would certainly never see again. I remember my father and my uncles, the male members of the family only by marriage (and future sources of contention) in a family of women, who, only during those nights and never since, linked arms as they drank vodka and laughed at their Stalinist mistakes and the democratic ideals of my father—which had, all the same, prevented him from joining in with the Beards. I remember that those nights were the last time I was happy to be surrounded— protected—by my family. Never again would there be that feeling of complicity, and even less so of solidarity. Those parties were the swan song of my family, of our *joie de vivre*, our nonconformist attitude, our laughter.

That unique atmosphere, the sounds of the party, the abundant laughter and tears ... I felt the overwhelming urge for them to spill over into school, where everything was all whispering and uniformity. I didn't understand that not everyone, when they left school, or the office, or department stores, or taxis, went home to put on music, call their friends, and throw a party. Every time my classmates told their parents about my escapades or told them stories about my family parties that had become legendary, I lost a new friend—gained and then lost, in one fell swoop.

In the end I would have given in, but my father had no intention of seeing me turn soft. I could find fulfilment elsewhere. Somewhere I would not need to get naked in order to feel like a little girl. It took a great deal of courage for him to make that decision. A lot of love and a touch of idealism. My father did not want me to look like Iranian women. He definitely did not want to see me storming the public square, either—he is too reserved and still profoundly Iranian—but in the end, in Paris nobody would rebuke his daughter for talking too much. Like a boy. And in Paris, there were women, real women, with a brain and a destiny. With a future.

Paris, 2013

Since the early conquests of Islam, texts refer to the issue of *looking like* a Muslim. What matters to a Muslim is being instantly recognisable as such and being distinguishable from a non-Muslim. Being immediately recognisable is about controlling the other's gaze, protecting oneself from it, diverting it. All of this comes from much further back, from a tradition older than the Quran and which eats away at social relations.

Etymologically, the *awrah* is the act of 'piercing the eye'. In Islam the *awrah* defines all that is obscene and should be covered up. In general, for men this is everything from the top of the chest to the knee, and for women, the entire body apart from the face and hands (even the feet for some, but not for all). The *awrah* is everything that should be covered for reasons of modesty. The problem is that modesty is such a catch-all phrase that everything ends up being covered. The eye becomes enemy number one. The evil eye is in everyone's eyes.

The *awrah* can kill too. It is the eye that kills—in the literal sense—those who have no shame. It's the *awrah* that places a veil over the obviously obscene body of the women, but not just that. Clinical studies have shown that women who are forced to wear the veil have reported the hallucination of being possessed by a powerful eye. An eye that sticks to their skin or passes through them. An eye that sees without being seen. The eye that imprisons them; that they cannot fight because it is invisible. This obsession with the *awrah* has such a strong presence in Eastern societies that it has become part of its DNA. The *awrah* is the plague of the East. It's not just about avoiding looking at the body to prevent attraction. It's not just about what should be concealed from the eyes of anyone who is not a Muslim woman, or a father, brother, husband or son. The *awrah* dictates a series of social codes and human rules that prevent any intimacy or sincerity. The scope of what must be covered and reserved for private (hidden) life is so vast that the public sphere is reduced to an absolute minimum. So why would women want to conquer it? Why change what is going on outside, when life is fine between your own walls, within your own family? And is it all worth it, especially if it means sacrificing your holy reputation?

Inside/Outside. Private/Public. All space is divided up according to precise rules that designate borders between genders, between worlds. All Iranians are, above all, potential schizophrenics. From childhood they are taught according to a set of rules that apply on the one hand to the outside, and on the other to the inside. Every time I am with my family and someone from outside the family comes into the room, everyone changes. Smiles miraculously appear, and the intonations of voices soften. It's sickening. My childhood reflex surfaces: I want to show my arse. I want to say everything I shouldn't. I want to release what is stifling us all: the inability to express our true feelings and the reality of our lives. The result is always the same: it's incredibly suffocating.

The fear of others looking at you is an inner trauma that imprisons you. To defend yourself you must attack someone else, someone who is more visible, whose attitude is more conspicuous. Someone who can be used as a scapegoat; the famous whore.

Malayer – Tehran – Paris

My mother was born into a family of seven children in a town in the province of Hamadan. Six girls and a boy. My mother and her sisters were sacrificed in favour of their brother, who was everything. He was bright, he was epileptic; he was their mother's favourite. This brother was a militant communist who became part of the forbidden party. He trafficked books—necessary to the future aborted Revolution. He was arrested, imprisoned, and tortured. My grandmother fell ill and let herself die because, with her son in prison, there was nothing keeping her here on earth. She left behind six daughters. The youngest was ten years old. But what was a ten-year-old girl worth, compared to a boy?

My uncle was still in prison when I was a child, and my mother and my aunts used to take me to visit him. There was a reason for this: I was a pretty little girl and I entertained the guards so that my mother and my aunts could spend more time with their brother on the other side of the bars. I thought he was a very great man. It was only later that I learned that my uncle terrorized his sisters. He was so authoritarian that he hit them if they dared to question his decisions. He was an atheist Beard. He refused to let my mother pin up a picture of the heart-throb Alain Delon in her room—'What are you, a whore?'; he refused to let his sisters wear make-up—they wore make-up in secret anyway, and took it off before they went home; he would not let one of his sisters continue her medical studies so he could marry her off—which he did; he decided what they all read—my mother, who adored literature, had cut out the pages of a Hegel book to hide her own novels inside; he chose the studies that suited each one—they all followed his suggestions, except my mother, who wanted to be a hairdresser, and got slapped for it, 'What are you, a whore?' and who ended up studying biology even though she hated studying and in the end forgot everything and did not learn much. He used to rifle through their bedrooms and would throw away any perfumes he found, as well as love letters and dresses that were too eye-catching. If he had not been imprisoned, one of them would not have been able to go to London to study, nor the other three to Paris. Although the episode of his imprisonment was a tragedy, which finished off his mother, and led to a series of major events including my parents' marriage (as my uncle had been a close friend of my father's when they were young), the fact remains that his absence was a good thing for my sisters. My uncle was released by the Beards' Revolution. He was no longer a Stalinist after that. He abandoned the Revolution and politics altogether. He became a journalist and translator of scientific books.

He is still just as bright. He is the only one of my mother's family who still lives in Iran. His sisters, living in Paris, San Francisco, and San Diego, still worship him.

During one of his rare visits to Paris, at the time when he was still as important to me as he was to them, and he used to discuss cinema and literature with me while drinking litres of bourbon, I was surprised to see my great-aunt, who was fifty, slip on a shapeless T-shirt underneath her low-cut dress. When I asked her about it, she rolled her eyes toward her brother. I didn't understand and I went on about it. In the end she verbalized that roll of the eyes: she told me the T-shirt was so as not to shock her brother, who actually seemed as if he couldn't care less about whether or not his older sister wore a T-shirt under the too-sexy dress. After this discovery, which kept bothering me, I questioned each of his sisters at length and they told me in great detail about their childhood and adolescence under their brother's thumb. They had not forgotten it, but it was out of the question to talk about it with him, or to clear the air. That was the past. But their past weighed on my shoulders, too. So I wanted to know.

I found out that just as I was taken along to the prison to distract the guards, my youngest aunt had also been used by her older brother to divert attention away from him while he engaged in the trafficking of banned books. He took her out for ice cream, using the opportunity to leave a parcel of books behind, where another comrade would come to take his seat, accompanied by another little girl who loved rosewater ice cream. I learned that sister number four—

who was smarter than the others—did everything in her power to flee from Tehran and her brother, but also from her sisters. She chose London instead of Paris, and although she hated talking about it, she let slip a few sentences that showed how afraid she was of her brother. She was not afraid of being beaten—he did not do that, or rarely, and only when accompanied by 'What are you, a whore?'—but she was afraid of being forced to marry or being dragged against her will into a political struggle which she alone knew was a lost cause. She had fled. And I keep thinking about how sad it is to have no choice other than to flee.

My uncle married twice. He had two children from his first marriage. My uncle gave his eldest daughter a Western upbringing, and his son is an artist who is sure to be the talk of the town. He no longer imprisons women within traditions, but sets them free. Which is a good thing for my cousins. What I cannot forgive him for is the raw pain my mother still feels as a result of his brutality. While my uncle has enjoyed the luxury of seeing all his mistakes forgiven, his sisters still bear the scars of his blinkered authority. And they still love him with a love so absolute it makes me want to beat it out of them, to make them forget. As if, because he was a man, he could not be guilty of anything, and being women, his sisters were condemned to accept their messed-up childhood forever.

I never got the chance to see my uncle again in Tehran, due to family quarrels that had created a permanent rift. I would have liked to ask him some questions. I would have liked him to explain to me. I would have liked him to tell me how he could have been such a tyrant, how he got everyone to forgive him without even asking for forgiveness, and to talk to me as an equal without taking gender into account. The brother who was the favourite of his mother and sisters. The brother who was simply 'lucky' to be born a man in a family of women. My family's tangled web of issues all stems from the sisters' childhood. Six girls, unloved, and looked down upon, whose greatest mistake was being born female.

If there had been more boys, my family would not have been so unhappy. Even though nobody says it out loud, everyone thinks so. My grandmother—who I never knew—was a mournful and definitely depressed woman. The consequences for my sisters were the same: they turned into complete pessimists. They are almost entirely incapable of trusting in others or in the future. All of them, that is, except my mother—and perhaps the second to youngest sister who is so sensitive it's scary. My mother was born in the wrong place: between the only brother and the most beautiful of the sisters. The two most beloved siblings. She was wedged between the hope that only a male can bring, and beauty, which is the only ticket to happiness when you are born female. She was shattered emotionally and spent the rest of her life trying to be loved without ever believing that it was possible. My mother was a tomboy; she was resourceful and funny. Nobody ever took her seriously and when the family needed to be fed, after her brother was imprisoned, she was the one who gave up the studies she hated to work as a secretary. She paid for all of her sisters' studies, put food on the table for her mother while her father was off seeking his fortune—he succeeded after the death of his wife, and the family moved to Tehran—turned away romantic suitors, and never received any thanks in return.

Years later in Paris, when my mother did nothing but suffer and things were going terribly wrong, her brother did not call her. Ever. And when her brother's children were in Paris, my mother was not allowed to see them. It was decided that my parents should live in the provinces to avoid any temptation. What could have driven her sisters to hide her away like that, and my mother to accept it? Shame. The shame that people in Tehran were calling her a failure in Paris. Her apartment was too small, her profession too humiliating—being a 'childminder' was not exactly a sign of success in the eyes of Tehran's bourgeoisie—and her beauty had faded. My mother, who is as ashamed of her career as her sisters are, is nevertheless the only one who has always worked and the only one who has always been independent. She is talented: a true creator, capable of renovating a shabby living room, or sewing a beautiful evening dress, or making dresses for my few dolls out of old knickers, or skilfully cutting everyone in my family's hair. My mother, who is the heroine of a novel, complex and extravagant, has never been anything but a hopeless failure in the eyes of my family.

I have an awful memory of my childhood in which my mother, caught between the strong, flamboyant personalities of her sisters, was reduced to being little more than 'mummy 1'. My other aunts were 'mummy 2', 'mummy 3', 'mummy 4', and so on. I found a cassette tape on which my mother recorded me singing a childish nursery rhyme. By way of encouragement she asks me to make an effort, not to please my father, but my aunts. Do it again for your aunt. Do it again to make your aunts happy. My mother is the prime example of the result of poor education in Iran: full of hang-ups, lonely. There is not a trace of malice in her and she has fully absorbed all the prohibitions, absurdities, and limitations linked to her gender. Unlike her sisters, she never mastered the hypocrisy that allowed her to live her life in spite of everything, covertly. My mother knew, however, that something was wrong with her life. She knew that she was incapable of making a decision without consulting her sisters. She felt an unease that she did not want to pass on to me. So she tried to raise me in total freedom, while showering me with love—a hefty burden when the day came for her to live her own life. She wanted me to be as free as her brother was able to be, while she worried about my provocative nature. She wanted me to be as beautiful as her sister was, while she worried that I attracted too much attention.

All throughout my childhood and even later, my aunts wanted me to believe that my father didn't love me, that he preferred boys. Why? Simply because they didn't like men. They didn't like women much either, but men were the enemy. They had heard that they were *just* women so many times, they had lost so much by being women, that they only liked girls. And they hardly even liked them.

It is tempting to take my revenge here. It is tempting to voice my anger about all the things I blame my mother's sisters for. It is my mother that prevents me from doing so; her absolute love for her sisters, her inability to live without them. Although they are the proof that there is something very wrong with the education of women in the land of the Beards—even before they came to power—I have to hold myself back, to come back to Khomeini and not say all the things that broke me, all the things that isolated my mother and made my father suffer. And yet. My anger now is outweighed by the love I had—and which, almost despite myself, I still have for them. They populated my childhood with their black hair, their heightened femininity, their laughter, and their love. They loved me and I loved them. But love was not enough when we faced the harshness of exile. The love of my aunts evaporated when I fought for the independence that they still reproach me for. It is still something I cannot forgive: abandoning a woman so vulnerable, so naive, so full of love. My mother.

I know now that my father loved me, even if I doubted it during my sullen teenage years in exile. The fact that 'my mothers' tried so hard to alienate me from my father is simply just another symptom of their childhood trauma of being girls. I was only seven and they were worried about me damaging my eyes by reading, having opinions on everything—all I did was emulate my father; they worried about me announcing at weddings, when they asked the little girls if they dreamed about getting married and how many children they wanted, that I wanted to be a naked dancer, and that having a big pregnant belly was gross. They wanted me to be the image of them, indoors, wary of men—and women—hidden away and in a good marriage. All my father wanted was for me to be a woman. And when he said 'woman', he was thinking of Simone de Beauvoir. Unmarried, childless, rebellious. The worst nightmare of my 'mothers': no marriage, no children, no security. During my childhood I saw my aunts as strong women, when they were really just hard-nosed. They had received no love from anyone, especially their parents, and it was as if they had shrivelled up inside, giving up any possibility of finding happiness in the arms of a man or by gaining their freedom. Years later, when I was over thirty, and suffering from a severe lack of inspiration, I confided in my youngest aunt. Years later, the only answer she could give me was, 'You know what you *really* need? What could bring you back down to earth and stop you looking for artistic inspiration that you clearly don't have, seeing as you haven't made any money yet? You should have a child! And then you'll have more chance of hanging on to a man, too.' I felt sick. It was perhaps from that moment on that I knew what 'living your life' really meant. And I was grateful to my father.

Tehran – Paris

I have often wondered how I might have turned out if it hadn't been for my father. Without the education he gave me. What would have happened if my father hadn't won against 'my mothers'. He chose to bring me up without the traditional limitations of my gender. Being a girl should not alter my choices. It was not about being a tomboy—not exactly—but he didn't want me to hear that 'Girls don't do that.' You should sit up straight, not because you're a girl, but because it's polite. You mustn't raise your voice, not because you're a girl, but because we don't make ourselves heard by shouting. Keep your cool, not because you're a girl, but because we aren't savages. That's why I flinch whenever I hear mothers my age saying the exact opposite to their daughters. To future women. My father was considered something of an eccentric in Iran. I remember a lot of shouting went on about the outspokenness that my father instilled in me. He shouldn't let me do that. It was as if I was defending myself ... like a man! Even within my family they were shocked. They were afraid I would become mad, hysterical, homosexual, asocial. When my father decided to let me read Zola at the age of twelve, we were already living in Paris, but it took no less than two family meetings, full of arguments that made the walls shake, for me to be allowed to do so. My mother and the family—liberal and atheist maybe, but narrow-minded all the same—feared that I would lose all my feminine sensitivity. Zola would kill the woman in me. The way people imagined—up until the mid-twentieth century in the West and even elsewhere these days—that sport would destroy women's reproductive systems.

My father is a mystery. How did he end up that way, in the context in which he was raised? How could he be my uncle's best friend without sharing his Stalinist opinions or his contempt for women? How could he see it as so obvious that a woman was equal to a man and deserved the same access to knowledge, without discrimination?

My father says it is as much due to his own father as it is to literature. He spent all his pocket money on books. From the age of ten he had decided to read, every summer, the entire works of a different classic author. Methodical and passionate, he was discovering Tolstoy and Flaubert while children his own age were buying sweets and chasing footballs about. My paternal grandfather was not an intellectual. He was not much of a reader. He was born in northern Iran, poor and practically illiterate. In Tehran he became a technician in the telephony industry, which was in its infancy then, and gradually he earned enough money to get married and build his house. He never imposed anything on anyone. He discussed anything and everything. People loved him because he was incapable of judging anyone. He was the firmest believer of the family and yet he was the first to laugh out loud when I told him about my bare-bottom dash. He was very self-assured and loved a rebel. I remember once when another of his granddaughters was complaining how she had not managed to get into university, he simply replied: attack them where they are least expecting it. So she gave up literature and switched to engineering. The head of the faculty was so surprised to see a woman appear before him—barely a year after the Revolution, when women didn't even dare to blink—that he enrolled her on the spot.

My almost illiterate grandfather put the house and all his money in his wife's name. By way of an example. To show that he did not make any distinction between men and women. He had a girl and a boy, who he wanted to be equal. All decisions were made collectively. There was no *pater familias* in my father's childhood. My father replicated the same system: all decisions—from the most mundane to the most serious—were made after discussing them with my mother and later with us, the children. My father had never respected anything but democracy, and only enlightened tyranny could save our family.

He told me how when he was young, one evening he had announced his atheism to his father. His father was a practicing Sufi, a respected wise man—in other words, a mystical Muslim, who does not judge, who does not condemn, who

71

couldn't care less about veiling women or eating pork or drinking wine, but who takes God very seriously—a true believer, in short. My father said to his father: I don't believe in God. My grandfather did not seem surprised or hurt. He replied to his eight-year-old son, who had chosen a different path to his, 'Your cross will not be any harder or easier to bear than mine.' My father would tell me exactly the same thing if I were to tell him I believed in God.

I gave my father a nickname (even though I was already well over twenty years old by then): Super Tolerance Man. He tolerates all the pettiness and weaknesses, all the tears, all the shouting. In his life, with regard to everyone—even the worst of my aunts—he has always strictly applied his understanding of life's mediocrities. There was no discussion, he never said like so many others do, 'Oh you know what I'm like, you know I'm a tolerant person.' When someone points it out to him, he opens his eyes wider than usual, says 'Really?' and looks down at the book in his lap. It comes naturally to my father to tolerate foolishness, discontent, and low blows. I hated him for that sometimes and loved him for it often. But it is never easy for any child to be able to make their father react so little. He listened, he made suggestions, he entered into debate, but no decision was ever final, no logic was ever imposed. He gave us the freedom not to *do* whatever we wanted, but the freedom to *reflect* on whatever we wanted. As a teenager, that was hell.

I fell in love with books so early on because of watching my father. For as long as I can remember, I have always pictured my father with books around him. I wanted to emulate him. I used to take a pile of books—even though I didn't know how to read yet—and would trail around after him, so I could sit next to him and pretend to read. When we started going to bookshops, I wanted books with lots of letters and hardly any pictures. I wanted my father to love me and I realized early on that he especially loved books. If I wanted to be a writer, it's because my father loved reading. He loved the cinema and theatre as well. But books were all the time, every day, everywhere.

In the chemistry laboratory where he worked, his superior was a woman. She fascinated me because she was the only 'old woman' around me who was married but didn't have children. She would come round to our house for dinner and I remember that like clockwork, the following day, my mother would cry after talking to one of her sisters on the phone. They didn't like my father's boss. They were scared of her. She was too much of a dubious character, because she was too free with her choices and her body. In the eyes of my mother and my aunts, she was obviously an 'easy lay'—do I need to clarify everything that expression implied? It tells us that sleeping with someone is hard, giving your body to someone else is so hard that women who seem to enjoy it must be dangerous. If I wanted to be independent, it's because my father only respected women who made other women cry. I saw her again once, in Paris. She was passing through—she lived in Stockholm and was the head of a prestigious lab—and I was fourteen. She was interested in me. I told her how she had fascinated me as a child. So far, it was all going swimmingly. And then, just as adults have to ask the obligatory 'So, what do you do?' question, she asked me, the teenager, what I wanted to do in the future. When I told her I wanted to be a writer, she smiled, 'You should become a doctor or an engineer first. As a woman, writing is a lazy choice.' She preferred my brother who was a genius at maths. Women always end up disappointing me.

I do not rail against men, I rail against the Beards. Against all the Beards. And the Crows, too. I owe too much to my father and grandfather to do them the injustice of thinking that all men are Beards. But in all women, there is always the temptation to be a Crow.

Paris, 2013

I cannot say it better than Olympe de Gouges. I can only, a good few centuries later, echo her questions and her frustrations. How is it possible for women to raise men like that? Why on earth are they the first ones to give men the weapons that will destroy them tomorrow? Olympe de Gouges made members of the Constituent Assembly visit the Hôtel-Dieu hospital and showed them dying women giving birth to boys, who when they became men, would hold their nose as they passed them by. She demanded the opening of maternity wards and promoted hygiene to save lives. The lives of many women, of future mothers. She urged men to respect those who brought them into this world. Women rarely forgive: mothers always. I find it really hard watching mothers with their sons. It's amazing how they forget everything that made them suffer, everything that got in the way of their careers, all those things for which they blamed their hordes of mother-in-laws. They raise their little boy to be a cynical knight and a woman-crusher. But to get revenge on whom?

On those who did not love them enough? It's awful when a woman becomes mother to a man. It's as if it suddenly becomes normal for a girl to have to keep her legs together and for a little boy to be able to fart at the dinner table. I hear the same nonsense today in France as I used to in Tehran. I remember the remark of one elegant Iranian woman, who was shocked by my verbal diarrhoea as a seven-year-old girl. She turned to my father and said, annoyed, 'She's too intelligent. You should rein that in before it's too late.' I remember a thirty-something mother, one of those hip Parisian types, who, to stop her five-year-old son from crying, calmly dealt him this blow: 'You're not going to whine like a girl, are you?' And how is he supposed to have any respect, in twenty years' time, for a whiner? What surprises me is that we are surprised. What surprises me is that a French woman, a literary critic, an independent woman in her fifties and a mother to boot, should interrupt me while I was talking about my harrowing discovery of Hemingway, and without skipping a beat, say, 'But really! Hemingway is literature for men! Of course you don't understand anything in it!' as if she was talking to a peasant who had just arrived from Tehran in babouches*. But no, my dear lady, Hemingway is simply good literature, and nobody wears babouches in Iran. And if I cannot understand challenge, faith or self-sacrifice, then I am just plain stupid. My gender has nothing to do with it. For better or for worse. You

* A heelless slipper, typically in oriental style.

should read Hemingway to girls but you shouldn't necessarily make boys play with Barbie dolls. How can Eastern mothers carry on keeping their daughters in strict gender separation? How can they even consider drumming into their daughters the very principles that have poisoned their whole lives? The thing that governs this transfer of attitudes from mother to daughter is fear. The man is the one who owns. The one who feeds. The one you cannot live without. Without a man, there is only misery. Where can women find the strength, the points of reference, even the idea of giving their daughters independence? They are trapped in a social and political system which enslaves them to a greater or lesser extent, but which always enslaves them to men. Sometimes mothers must think that there is no greater danger for their daughters than that of desiring independence. They saw what happened to those who chose another path. Women who are not even welcome in their own families. The dread. Being frowned upon. Always the eye. Being looked down on. The eye again. Sometimes, things can go even further. A father might lose a position because of his daughter's desire for independence.

The issue here is not about higher education. Women study in Saudi Arabia, Iran and Morocco—although it is mainly women from the upper classes who attend university. Saudi or Qatari women study in London or Paris. Therefore, these women have access to knowledge and get to experience co-education. But they perpetuate this handing down of attitudes. Once they graduate, sometimes they use their degree, sometimes they don't. But *it all* depends on the husband. Or the father. Or the brother. There are varying degrees of *it all*, depending on the country (in Saudi Arabia or in Afghanistan, it really means 'all', while in Iran, Morocco, and Tunisia not as much, but a bit too much even so—for the moment). There are still so many contradictory examples. But one fact is certain: those who study are still nobodies. Lesser beings than men. And mothers continue to feed the prejudices that are embedded a little deeper with each new generation. I have heard countless times how unhappy they were, mothers who brought girls into the world. They knew very well what was going to happen to them. A boy, not only is he more loyal—there it is, that myth that all girls are disloyal because their whole education pushes them toward starting their own family, yet we blame them for doing it, even so—but he will always be less trouble. A boy is easier; there are fewer limitations and fewer principles to drill into him. A girl is a victim as soon as she is born. She needs to be protected all her life. Teach her moderation; think about marrying her off from a young age. Above all, we have to tell her what a shitty life she is doomed to, just like her mother and grandmother before her. In the hope that she stays in line. She may be educated, sure, she may have lived abroad, sure, but she should not enjoy applying what she has learned in books and foreign cities to her own life. She should not taste freedom; she will only be left with a bad taste in her mouth when she comes back home.

It would only be fair to fathers to acknowledge, for once, the well-deserved role they play in the liberation of their daughters. My friend's mother, an intelligent and well-travelled sixty-year-old woman, born in Morocco to a French family, who had lived in Sub-Saharan Africa and had friends all over the world, always tells me how important her father was to her. The same goes for so many of her Eastern and African female friends, who today are all liberated women, activists. A father who breaks with tradition to give his daughter as many opportunities as his son is an assurance for all women to never believe they are worth less than a man. If the early dialogue in your life took place on equal terms with the first man in your life, then you have every chance of being proud of your gender as well as never thinking that men are the only guilty party. Having open, equal communication with your father means never being a victim.

Tehran, 1983–1985

When the time came for me to go to school and I had to have my regulatory uniform fitted, it was a tearful occasion. I had to wear it and I had to go to school. But as soon as my mother wasn't looking I added a red brooch to my shirt, I hid jangling bracelets under my long sleeves, I spilled milk on my trousers, hoping I could wear just the shirt. I made cigarette burns in the headscarf, I hid my uniform under the dirty laundry in the hope that my mother's cleaning mania would save me from having to wear grey. Once, I went as far as going off to school in a pair of clogs. It was hell for my mother. I was unbearable. It's amazing how much patience mothers are capable of. And although my mother went absolutely mad, just once—chasing me around our long dining-room table, throwing everything she could at me: plates, glasses, vases—she was a veritable Mother Courage, putting up with the antics of a child who always managed to give her the slip.

The school that I knew for two years in Tehran could

not exactly be described as ringing with the laughter of children. It was too orderly, too silent, too strict, and too anonymous for children. Neither was it like the boarding school in Truffaut's *Zero for Conduct*. Because the feeling of confinement was not just at school; it was in the street, on your TV screen, in the conversations of adults. It was not a question of opening the classroom windows to breathe. The air outside was just as putrid. The Revolution was not quite over and war had already begun. Children are just as susceptible as others to the environment. There was danger in the air and it was a chance for the mullahs to establish themselves even more. Dictatorships are upheld from the nursery upwards. And laughter, so honest, contagious, and liberating, is always the primary enemy. Dictatorships like nothing better than whispers, deserted streets, and muted playgrounds. It was a school with the knowledge sucked out of it; silence was enforced; we got marks for 'morality' and were forced to thank the 'old man in black and white' for saving us from hell. It was not school as I would come to know it in Paris. But by that time, it was too late: I could no longer be a little girl.

School for me meant very few friends (my real friends were my German cousins and my female neighbour) and lots of teachers, who were all women, apart from one.

My female teachers all blurred into one. They were identical in their black headscarves, with their black chadors over the top when they left the classroom and might run into a man. The handwriting teacher was perhaps slightly kinder than the others, as she let us take off our headscarves when

81

the heat was too unbearable. Maybe this is just a false memory I invented to soften the image of the school in my mind. They were all so cruel that the atmosphere was tainted by it. There were the eyes, constantly moving, looking for a sin to flush out; there were the vicious gestures, the ruler smacking down on the desktop, the hand violently yanking a headscarf into place; it was an educational choice, which involved erasing all gentleness and compassion. As if, by being so cold and sullen, my teachers proved the greatness of their souls.

How could they believe so adamantly that a smile or a tender gesture was a terrorist act against the Islamic Republic? They were emotionally maladjusted, unhappy, and frustrated. They put us through what they had suffered throughout their lives: being a woman and having to make amends for it.

The one man at the school was a 'religious studies' teacher. He taught us the lessons of the Quran—a sort of catechism that consisted of us repeating that we must be modest and clean. It was the most boring lesson and the only one where all my classmates agreed with me: it was rubbish. He was monotonous, standing there so still that he looked like a wax doll. This teacher, Mr. 'Clean-Your-Hands', when I was eight years old, in response to my incessant questioning about why women had to wear the veil, replied tersely, 'Because you women are dangerous objects.' It was both contemptuous and life-saving for me. His voice still echoes in my ears. His voice reminds me that you have to be vigilant if you are born a woman. His voice and his haughty conviction always make me hold my head up high. He distinctly told me that everything was my fault. If *I* had to be covered, it was to avoid *him* running into danger. What was so striking about this man was how convinced he was.

Mr. Clean-Your-Hands already had an issue with my mania for dissecting insects. My father had given me a microscope as a gift. Ever since, any insects that fell into my clutches were immediately dissected. It was fascinating and informative. I even decided to do a presentation on my dissection discoveries, rather than recounting the life of Ali, the son of the prophet, and the founder of Shia Islam. But Mr. Clean-Your-Hands interrupted me, calling me a murderer. I was thwarting God's plans and intervening in the equilibrium of the universe by killing innocent animals. Despite his dandruff and greasy comb-over, his hands folded, immobile, resting on his belly; despite his dull eyes always fixed on the floor or lifted to heaven, but never on us; despite everything that was repulsive about this man, he hit a nerve when he called me a murderer. It made me sick thinking about it. How could I accept that I was a murderer of innocent insects? I was so ashamed that I didn't even dare talk to my father about it. I was eight years old and I was a murderer because I killed God's insects. *But* I was also God, because I disrupted his plans by acting as Him. I got over it in the end, preferring to be God than a murderer, since apparently I could be one or the other, according to the wonderfully paradoxical speech of my teacher, Mr. Clean-Your-Hands. So I carried on dissecting insects, delighting in the pain I was causing my only teacher of the opposite sex, whose lessons never taught me anything.

What motivated Mr. Clean-Your-Hands in his pedagogy of woman-bashing? He praised us for being future brides that were modest, clean, and yet educated. We must know how to read and write so that we can support our father, our husband, our brother. But he found us dangerous. Perhaps there, in that admission of weakness, is the key to escaping the fixed pattern in which tradition has locked up women. I am eight years old and I make him that scared? With my hair, my little wrists and ankles, I scare a man who is so much older? Scare him to the point that I must blend into the background and even then, he won't dare to look at me? Then what? Do I have superpowers? Do all women have superpowers? But if so, why do they accept being hidden away so meekly under the veil? Although this question bothered me all my life, I only partly resolved it later on, in Paris, when the 'veil issue' tore society and the political classes apart. Until that day came, I was sure of only one thing: I had a superpower that nobody knew about.

Tehran, 1984–1985

When the Revolution freed my uncle from Evin Prison, the family had not had time to celebrate its reunion, before the Iran-Iraq war began. It was only a slight shock to me as a child, as in the beginning, nothing much changed. Then an uncle who was an architect was called to the front to design the shelters for the glorious soldiers, and everyone was afraid. But most importantly, there were already whisperings about children. I listened at doors—it's the only way to keep informed in Iran—and from hiding in the shadows, I learned that there were children in the war. They recruited kids of eight, sometimes as young as six, and dressed them up in soldiers' uniform. They photographed them, so as to leave behind a prestigious memory for their parents. And then they sent them out into the minefields ahead of the more experienced soldiers, which the Revolution so desperately needed. The families would then recover the 'pieces' of their children—that was the exact term used by my parents: 'pieces'—which had the supreme honour of being buried in the martyrs' cemetery, where the fountain bubbles over with the (fake) blood of thousand-year-old martyrs. The mothers were proud in the knowledge that their martyred sons were in paradise, and the fathers boasted about the sacrifice they had made. They were the blessed of the blessed. Although I was scared, just for a moment—hiding in the corridor, listening to my terrified parents whispering—of being taken away by the Beards to the minefields, I suddenly remembered that I was just a girl and that no Beard would dare to touch me with his hands, let alone carry me away, even if it was to leave me on the minefields. I was spared because I was a girl, but I could not stop thinking about all those children in pieces. I immediately tried out the experience by dismembering my dolls into several pieces, but it seemed too horrible to do that to real humans. Although I dismembered ants, flies, worms, spiders, they still didn't look anything like children. Although I had seen bloodied faces, dislocated arms, broken legs, and slashed torsos in the streets during the Revolution, although they were covered in blood, they moved, they shouted, they cried ... and they were still in one piece. Although I was used to violence, the death of a child still seemed impossible to me as a child, and the possibility of a body in pieces, even more impossible. I thought that only old people died. The others were just temporarily wounded. There was nothing that a plaster, a spoonful of medicine or a kiss couldn't make better. A bloody knee was not serious—skin grows back, or losing an eye—that surely must grow back, too.

A few days after this discovery, I witnessed an *Ashura* procession—my parents had managed to prevent me from seeing the spectacle until that day. We were late leaving for the Caspian sea and family farm, and we got caught in the midst of the men cutting their skulls open—just enough to stay alive but make enough blood pour out to prove their faith—others lashing their own backs with whips, all of them screaming. Their clothes were so ripped that they were practically naked. While my parents decided what to do—my mother wanted to stop me from seeing it, my father disagreed, fearing my imagination more than anything—I had plenty of time to see everything anyway. I didn't say anything. I didn't ask any questions. Nobody asked me any questions but my father succinctly explained that these men were flagellating themselves in memory of a certain Hussein who they had not been able to protect, and were punishing themselves by beating themselves and chanting 'Hussein was murdered! Hussein was murdered!' I was only half listening. An idea began to grow in my mind. I got it into my head that the human body could not be broken into pieces! The proof was there, with those men hitting themselves so much that their blood spurted out of them onto the car windshield, yet they remained intact, whole. It was a lie on the part of the 'old man in black and white' to make grown-ups afraid. My parents and the other grown-ups must not have known this; they were always getting it wrong. I mean, hadn't they told me that after the Shah everyone would be happier? They were still being taken in by the Beards—they believed that children could be cut into pieces. It wasn't even true.

The dramatic *Ashura* procession also provided me with a new solution to the problem of the veil. The following morning, I appeared at breakfast with my clothes and veil slashed to pieces with a knife—feeling pretty happy about my stroke of genius. If you had to slash your clothes in order to get the right to walk around almost naked, I was prepared to do it. Everyone breathed a sigh of relief: the sight of the blood and violence had not traumatized me more than that. They punished me for having destroyed my dress, which came from Paris and was very expensive; I was not allowed cherries for the whole day and my horse remained in the stables.

The war ended up being the Revolution but worse. Nothing had really changed, except that some of my older cousins who had disappeared came back and then left again. Nothing remarkable happened except that the Beards were even more on edge than before, and every day in the playground we had to say a prayer for the soldiers who were fighting for us. Laughter was already long gone from the streets of Tehran: the war only accentuated the sadness of the streets and the ravaged faces of the passers-by; women were already ugly under their rags, they had not worn make-up for a long time; but now it was fashionable to have eyes rubbed red from crying for their country. Some of them would rub their eyes with onions before they went out to do their meagre shopping. It was worse than nonsense. The whole country was in mourning. The biggest tragedy however was the television. The biggest tragedy for me, that is. There was nothing on except the endless sermons and deranged TV news that praised the Iraqi losses and paraded the great leaders, and equally great Iranian soldiers, across our TV screens. This was war, and as happens with all wars, things went from bad to worse.

Life became difficult because we had to make provisions, for fear of going without. The Iranians who railed against Khomeini the religious fanatic were seduced by Khomeini the political end, who reawakened the Great Persia in the hearts of Iranians. My parents lost lots of friends. And the war launched by the moustachioed one helped to strengthen the Revolution of the Beards. The world reorganized itself around the war. Although the war began shortly after the Revolution, I only really saw it after the War of the Cities. From 1984 onwards, the bombing began from both sides. Windows had already been blacked out for parties but now it had to be like that as soon as night fell. Everyone shrunk into themselves. A year passed beneath the bombing. Everything became so menacing that the world began to whisper. Before night fell, there was always a suffocating feeling of nostalgia in the air. It was the fear of not seeing another day. The War of the Cities was Guernica resurrected each night. Creating panic, laying out the lifeless bodies in sight of civilians, was depressing enough to ensure a victory. The morale of the soldiers was built up behind the scenes. Despite the bombs and fears, the Revolution was too close, the atmosphere too electric for people not to support the war. It was all we talked about and there was nothing more mesmerizing than the fear of dying in your bed, at night, beneath the bombs. It was definitely not the time to fight Khomeini, the Beards or the Crows. It was the time for defending yourself against death, which hovered ever closer. Everyone kowtowed to that priority. The arrests continued and the guardians of the Revolution had no intention of letting up. And the Iranians hated the moustachioed one more than the Bearded one. So we simply had to silence the opposition, as the bombs went on falling. Although they fell frequently, they were much less traumatic for me as a child than Khomeini's veil.

Because, thanks to my mother, the fear of the bombs was eradicated by a tube of lipstick. The big family house's shelter—which also housed neighbours, for above all my family loved to be loved—was comfortable, and most importantly, to reach it you had to cross the garden level, which had never been built, and which was the size and had the wall decor of a ballroom. An endless ballroom that my great-aunt had wanted and the construction of which had been interrupted by the arrival of the Beards. You had to cross the entire length of this ballroom where a ball would never be held, before you reached the cellar, whose thick carpet and soft sofas allowed you to wait for the iron storm to pass. For me, that crossing became a secret passage from one world to another. Because before you reached the cellar, you had to prepare yourself. As if you were going to a ball.

It is here that I should pay homage to the eye—for once. To keeping up appearances. To the fear of tarnishing her reputation that motivated my mother and still drives her to this day, just as it drives all the women in the family, and the men too—although to a lesser extent. A soon as they sounded the alert, often in the middle of the night, the first thing my mother did was dress us up in our best clothes. I was even allowed to wear lipstick. In my mother's eyes, it was essential for our bodies to be well dressed. She feared the eyes of others more than the bombs of the moustachioed one. No air raid siren, no bombardment, no cry was stronger than the pleasure of waking up in the middle of the night and *getting dressed up* and going downstairs to find our friends. And soon there was laughter; there were games, funny stories. Better than that: nobody thought about covering anyone's head. Although my family was always dressed up, this was not the case for the others, who in their sleepy state had just chucked on whatever clothes came to hand. It was chaotic and cheerful. We always stood out in our surroundings, but my mother was happy. And I was allowed to stay up. After a neighbouring building collapsed, however, nobody thought about telling funny stories any more to laugh off the fear. There was a terrible, deafening noise. Then we didn't hear anything else. A silent panic descended. That night, even I, who always refused to cry when everyone else was sad, couldn't hold back the tears. I realized that I would never again see my classmate with the hair as blonde as a field of wheat who always argued with me, or that woman—so beautiful even beneath the veil—who had to make herself look ugly before going out so as to avoid the guardians of the Revolution. No other tragedy affected us as much as that one. The bombs went on falling but it was never as close as this again. We continued to get dressed up to take refuge in the shelters and nobody had their hair or shoulders covered. But the children didn't run any more, and the adults no longer nudged their neighbours before telling a dirty joke that made us children laugh, even though we didn't understand it.

The war transformed the Beards into heroes. They were legitimized in all their decisions. Criticizing the Islamic Republic meant betraying your country, your blood, God, your father and your mother. The awful thing about war is that it transforms nations into police regimes. Exaltation conceals the fear hiding within. Women tied their headscarves tighter. I stopped getting naked. It was no longer worth trying to fight. I knew, as everyone else did, that the Beards and Crows had won. And despite the discretion exercised by my parents when they planned our departure— especially with regards to me, as they feared my obsession with always telling the truth—I knew that we were going to leave. For once, however, I didn't say anything. I didn't even want to. There was a lot of silence in the last six months, despite the air raid sirens and bombings.

One afternoon while I was out with my parents at the department store, an air raid warning siren threw all the customers, their eyes dark-ringed from sleepless nights, into a panic. We lost my father in the chaos of the moving crowd, everyone rushing to the exits. We were already in the shelter on the pavement opposite when a bomb exploded inside. It was a homemade bomb, often the deadliest kind, made by amateurs who miscalculate the force of their resentment. This homemade bomb left one person dead and twenty wounded. My father was no longer in sight. My mother was in tears, passers-by were curious, the guardians of the Revolution were at work. Dry-eyed, I searched for my father. He appeared behind us. He was alive and in one piece. I had never had such a desire to leave Tehran and the Beards as in that moment, as I found the clammy hand and impenetrable face of my father. My mother dried her tears and my father suggested we go and try to find some black-market bananas—since the war began, there had been a shortage of bananas. The hope of finding those unobtainable bananas was perhaps the best way of shaking off the fear that gripped us. It was the fragility of Tehran, the smoke of the unpredictable fires breaking out, the furtive glances, and the general feeling of imminent danger that made me want to leave, and consumed me, as the urge to get naked left me.

There were still parties but the laughter had been silenced. I knew that something was rupturing in my parents' life, and that I was vaguely responsible. I couldn't stand being under the Beards and because my father had decided, and my aunts were already in Paris, we had to leave. Even today, although I forgive myself without any hesitation for making the Crows chase after me and for telling stories about the real life we lived, I always find it hard to forgive myself for having rushed my parents into exile. I'm sure they would have gone anyway. Perhaps. But even as a little girl, I heard my parents talking—as always, I was hiding in the corridor—and they often said, shaking their heads, that I was not completely Iranian. There was something in me that had broken free from my environment. Sometimes children believe in their childhood enough to pursue it later in adult life.

The Crow-woman who had cut my nails down to the quick had gone to the front as a nurse. She had gone the day after the general mobilization. Every day in the school playground, before the daily prayer, her name was barked out on the list of glorious fighters against the moustachioed Iraqis. One morning, her name had been moved on to a different list: the list of the glorious martyrs who had fallen so that faith, the Revolution, and the Ayatollah Khomeini might live on. There weren't even any more enemies to fight. They fell of their own accord. The day before we left Tehran there were not many friends left; it was sad and empty. It really was time to leave.

My childhood may well have been full of blood and tears, but above all it was an education in freedom. It was during my childhood that I learned that there is not a lot you can do when you are imprisoned. We had to break free. It is impossible to negotiate one's freedom. We choose it and we take it. The fact that I never experienced fear when faced with the Beards and Crows (the fear came later and was traumatic enough for me to look for new, sharper weapons), meant that I was spared from one of the biggest dangers: putting your enemy on a pedestal. Khomeini was nothing more than an ogre out of the most gruesome fairy tales. All we needed to do to make him vanish was to wave a tube of lipstick around.

Paris, 2013

Perhaps the war had affected me more than I admitted. Perhaps I was still afraid of the child-soldiers in pieces. Because although I had denied—by decreeing it impossible—the link between the children in pieces and death, it remained such a powerful memory that the feelings associated with it instantly came flooding back to me. In the meantime, I had learned that it was possible for a body— even a child's—to be in pieces. I was a child with a vivid imagination—through luck and parental encouragement— and moreover I was also a bit of a loner, the key ingredient for creating any solid inner universe. By telling myself stories I built a world where the bodies of men remained intact. I didn't just want to grow up, I wanted to understand, feel, and even forget. Perhaps I needed to add a bit of colour to my childhood and that was only possible by appreciating the particular traits of my cultural background.

I had to wait until I was twenty-eight to finally make sense of my parents' whispered dialogue and understand that it had seeped into me more than I had ever admitted. This was proved by the fact that I was missing something vital to my understanding. I did not know it until I discovered the *Ta'ziyeh*, which was only possible in Paris, thanks to the programming of the Theatre de la Bastille, which is so fond of eye-opening ethnocultural works. Suffice to say that Abbas Kiarostami's *Ta'ziyeh* ticked all the right boxes. I went with my father and my first—and only—Iranian friend in Paris, who was in love with me and who I could never manage to muster the same feelings for because he was Iranian and because nothing had been fully settled yet with Khomeini. The *Ta'ziyeh* is the *Iliad* and the *Odyssey* of the Shiites, telling the mythological birth of the martyr Hussein, the son of Ali, the grandson of Muhammad, and the third of the imams. The *Ta'ziyeh*—very long, very melodramatic, very tearful—is based on the last battle of Karbala when the *son of* was killed in atrocious conditions by those who would become the Sunnis, after wandering in the desert for ten days with his defeated army. Kiarostami uses a genius theatrical set-up which simultaneously enables action (the play) and reaction (the audience): three screens face you; on the left and right, on two large screens in black and white, are the audience of the *Ta'ziyeh*, women on one side, men on the other—obviously since the Revolution men and women are separated in the stands—and in the middle, a small screen where the *Ta'ziyeh* takes place in colour. The set-up means that you can follow, live, the faces and bodies of the audience, the emotions that grip them throughout the show. They eat, they call out, they suffer, they drink tea, they cry, they shout, they drink tea, they let themselves go. Men and women alike—children of the same categories—cry, moan, and beat their chests and heads passionately at the high points of the tragedy of the *son of.* It was poignant. Perhaps I'd never understood Iran so well, and I thank art—once again—for helping us so powerfully to reach the truth.

All that pretence of unhappiness, the screeching and over-the-top gestures that I could not bear among Iranians, made sense in that intentionally trendy room in a hip Parisian theatre, through the staging of an Iranian filmmaker involved in European film festivals, who perhaps delivered the truest of his works there. I'm being serious: being brought up inside it, in that huge melee of bad feelings, of unnecessary sacrifices—which pay cash in paradise—that masquerade of death becoming life, that enjoyment when faced with agony, that joy in loss ... Shit! Iranians really need to be loved! And they suffer in their bodies so much. As if the body will only stop weighing them down when they are dead. It's poetic, sure, but it is definitely heavy going! Kiarostami's *Ta'ziyeh* not only spoke to me about martyred children but also about the body. The body in the *Ta'ziyeh* is the reminder of the first of the martyrs that condemns you to experience the body in horror. In the drama of Hussein, who founded Shia Islam, the body suffers for ten days in the desert, without water, without hope, then there is the capture and slaughter and finally the decapitation. But that's not all: there are still the widow of Hussein and his children who have to undergo the sadism of Yazid—the victorious Umayyad imam—on the remains of their husband and father. It is this intolerable violation of the body, which is seen as the receptacle of all suffering, that is the foundation of Shia Islam. That is why every year during the first ten days of the month of Muharram, so as to never forget this martyred body, Iranians relive the suffering of Hussein with endless processions where people's bodies are subjected to self-flagellation, with the *Ta'ziyeh* as the culmination. It is not insignificant that the spectators of the *Ta'ziyeh*, captivated and covered—by veils and long shirts, with only their faces and hands visible—react so physically to the drama that they know off by heart: their hands raised in imitation, striking their heads and their chests. As the end draws nearer, the tears get louder. The spectators are perfectly united in this celebration of bodily suffering. It is a chilling fervour. What it showed me was the reason *why* they covered the body: he had lost the war one day in October 680 and had been punished for it ever since. If Hussein, grandson of Muhammad, had betrayed him with his body, then what about our bodies? It is better to accept that the body is just a (dirty) problem of the living, until deliverance by death, or better still, by martyrdom.

Yet the *Ta'ziyeh* is the only officially approved form of dramatic art in all of Islam. It is fascinating and rich, mystical and profound. Because martyrdom was also born out of Islamic mysticism, which does not exist among the Sunnis. The Sufis—with the highest form of mysticism—are full of magic, ambiguous belief, messiah, absurd revelation, ironic tales, laughter, dance, and music. The bright side of the dark force, somehow. The best and worst of the same venom. Since the *Ta'ziyeh,* I have so clearly understood the difference between faith and culture that I am able to be interested in my cultural origins once again, without fearing that Khomeini will suddenly jump out and attack me as I turn the page of a harmless novel.

Paris, 1985–1986

We had the early morning departure, the goodbyes. We had to be careful not to overdo it, we were pretending we were going on holiday after all—we didn't want to be seen as traitors, to be seen as leaving for good. Yet we were actually leaving for good. And during the journey came that strange, unreal moment when the stewardess told us that alcohol was permitted and that headscarves could be removed. It was over. As simple as that. We were no longer flying over Iranian air space. There was nothing more to say. It was finished just as it had begun. In a neutral voice. With a mundane sentence.

The family was back together and although everyone was relieved to be safely in Paris, nobody was fooled. My aunts' apartment was small, and deceit lurked beneath the poorly trimmed beards. I felt like everything was going to fall apart but I didn't have time to hang around. The TV was on and there was Madonna, swaying her hips, her breasts spilling out over the top of a black corset. She looked you straight in the eye and nothing could stop her. She was a woman, she was erotic, and she was powerful. I could not manage to separate her body from her power. After more than a year of seeing the Beards preaching on the TV screen, Madonna absolutely blew me away. I had never seen anything like it. She was the body that went with the voice that announced the end of the headscarf. Madonna gave me a weapon: pride. It was no longer about getting naked; it was about being proud of being a woman—even with clothes on. I went on to love Madonna for a long time. I didn't care about going to her concerts or buying her albums: I wasn't a fan. No, it was her music videos I loved, her arrests and her crucifixes. I liked her provocative actions—childish and obvious perhaps, but provocative nonetheless—which she thrust in the face of prudishness. Every time she appeared, the Beards shuddered. She was my heroine when I was eight. All she had to do, to live without shame, was to dance. She made the people who raised their arms to throw stones at her and stop her seem ridiculous, because after all, she was just a pop singer. But she was visible. And from far away.

I was a little girl who preferred nudity to the regulation uniform of the Islamic Republic of Iran and now I suddenly found myself in Paris, where there was no longer the need to remove any headscarf: I was lost. There was no more reserve ammunition. There was nothing to fight against. It was boring. But there was Madonna. She was there to give me mental ammunition after I discovered that there were women, in Paris, in France, who voluntarily wore the headscarf.

It was on the metro. I squeezed my mother's hand so hard that it was blue for a week after. I panicked. That headscarf had no right being there. What is a Crow doing on the Paris metro? Is she following me? Doesn't she have a choice? I mean really! Who, in France, in Paris, could force a woman to cover her head? There are only whores in Paris! There are bare heads, girls and boys sitting next to one another in cafes and short skirts, and Madonna calling us to action! You might laugh at me for thinking this, but don't laugh too much. I was only eight years old and I had come to Paris with the promise that there would be no Beards or Crows. There would be men and women and children, and nobody would mind about me being a woman, ever again. With this promise etched in my heart, I saw my first Parisian Crow. It was an intense shock. I had not accomplished anything. I had been betrayed. My father had lied to me. It was as if the Crow-woman, the playground's very own 'master of morality', who died in the bombing at the front, had come back to life. There she was with her pathological inability to smile and her wrinkles of bitterness even though she probably wasn't even thirty years old yet. She would still be there, later, in another playground, and she would only be twelve years old. And even later still, in a hospital waiting room, demanding to be examined by a woman doctor. And even later again on the TV screen, in the form of mothers coming out of a court, baying for blood, shouting that their sons were innocent and that they hadn't raped anyone, because the 'anyone' was a girl and was nothing but a whore. Of course, this reincarnated Crow-woman in front of us cast my mother and my aunts a heavily reproachful look, full of contempt. They were too colourful, too scantily dressed and therefore they were voluntarily offering themselves up to general lechery, in her eyes, in the eyes of the first Crow-woman I saw on the Paris metro. There would always be a Crow-woman in my life.

So what did I do? I pinned up women's bodies all over the walls of my bedroom. As soon as I saw a slither of body in a magazine, or an expensive book (whichever!), I ripped out the page and up on the wall she went. I was no longer baring my bottom—that didn't interest me any more—but instead I was pinning up nude women on my walls. I remember mothers coming to pick up their children from our house—children who still had inoffensive posters of horses on their walls. Their eyes widened when they came into my room. They looked at my mother, desperately seeking an explanation, and my mother gave them the Iranian treatment; in other words, she acted as if it were nothing and then attempted to distract them with a charming, 'Would you like a cup of tea?,' and above all whisked them away from me as quickly as possible. She could see that my mouth was already wide open and desperate to give them the correct explanation: 'It's like garlic for vampires, it repels the Beards.' I don't know if they got it. Most of them never said anything. They didn't even laugh to try and hide their embarrassment. They just thought I was weird. Only one of the mothers had a different reaction. Or any reaction at all, in fact. She had lived in Algeria and Syria with her Brazil-ian businessman husband. She had remarried a Frenchman the second time round and was free, in the sense that you could really see it. She was remarkable with her jewellery, her tastefully dyed blonde hair, and her tendency to get her lovely legs out. She looked me in the eye, placed her hand on my head, then ruffling my hair she whispered, 'Poor little girl.'

She was mistaken. She had not understood at all. She thought I had been traumatized by the war and by men, when in fact I had just found the best remedy for countering the Beards. She told my mother later that she understood the *deep-seated* reasons for my precocious homosexuality. Men must *deeply* disgust me, because I must have seen terrible things. Perhaps even my father ... That was when my mother switched off. She did not speak French that well and was genuinely wondering why her daughter was a homosexual because of her husband, who had a problem with women. My mother is always very bashful when it comes to anything to do with sex. Imagining her faced with an imposing blonde lady making a perfectly delivered speech at her, punctuated only by the words my mother could grasp in French—which were: *homosexual, husband, sex* and *daughter*—to this day still makes me chuckle. Later my mother told us that at first she thought that the blonde was announcing that she was gay, then that she had slept with her husband and another woman—at the same time—then that she thought my father was homosexual, and finally that *I* was homosexual. It was at that moment that my mother offered her another cup of tea, with a smile so innocent and open that the remarkable mother realized my mother was

giving her the brush-off. This mother was so convinced—
she suffered from that incurable disease, curiosity—that in
the end she met with my father. He explained to her that I
was neither homosexual, nor precocious, nor traumatized
by men. I just needed to exploit the freedom of expression
that I had found in exile. I had lived surrounded by women
walled up inside their fabric and now I was celebrating the
newly found beauty of women's bodies. I think the remarkable woman found us all a bit odd. In fact that is what she
said after the conversation with my father: what an odd
family. And she added: I knew *their kind, back there*. Algeria and Syria don't have much to do with Iran, but anyway,
you know? It's kind of the same, right? And then that was
it. She knew. She no longer came to fetch her daughter from
my room with nudes all over the walls. Her daughter wasn't
allowed to come and see me. Then she left for California
with her second husband. She didn't understand anything.
She had lived in Brazil, Algeria, and Syria, but she just carried her convictions with her from place to place. She had
not learned anything, reflected on anything, observed anything. I wonder what she would have said if she had seen
my father giving me a first edition of *Thérèse the Philosopher* for my eighteenth birthday. She probably would have
alerted social services. What a remarkable idiot.

Every time we had Iranian friends over, we had to change
costumes and change the decor. I had to cover the walls of
my bedroom and put on a dress that was not *me* at all. And
I could not mention that I wanted to be a writer. Especially

not that. I should like pastel landscapes and wear a dress with a pink bow and want to be a doctor or an engineer. To keep our *reputation* intact. Which only meant something among the vague Iranian community that we were barely part of, and increasingly less so over the years, and now hardly at all. I did not completely understand how my love of black dresses and my desire to write could make me a whore in the eyes of Iranians, but the link seemed completely logical to my mother. That *my* reputation *in Tehran* could matter to my mother *in Paris*, is an equation I can't solve. The eye knows no borders. That is where the veil is, nestled in this mass of contradictions, which includes the need to uphold one's reputation. The veil is just the visible face of a freedom made impossible. Of course, just as I had absolutely refused to wear the veil, I refused the pink bow and the insipid landscapes. I swore I would get naked— again—if my mother forced me to place a veil—again—over my life. I promised her that I wouldn't tell people I wanted to write, but that I wanted to make the career leap straight to becoming a whore, just to make things clear right from the start. Anyway, it was the same thing: writers and whores are paid to turn people on. And nothing turns people on more than the imagination. My mother gave in to the force of my words. My mother had a vague understanding that I was free because of words. But those words got stuck in her throat.

Madonna was incredibly invigorating for a child of eight who had just landed, fresh from a city of headscarves.

Like all exiles, I needed to understand the place where I had actually landed. In short, I needed to fall in love with France to become French. My father made me learn French by opening *Les Misérables* in front of me. It wasn't so much a reading exercise, as a painstaking study, word by word, sentence by sentence. But it was a good move by my father. I already loved words in Persian; I was going to love words in French. The melody of the French language was going to be instilled in me, day after day, and I would understand, even if it was slowly and with much difficulty, that the key to a good story is making you eager to find out what happens next. In order to follow the adventures of Jean Valjean I learned the melody of the language very quickly. It is obvious to say that Victor Hugo is a great writer. And he is a great writer because he knew better than anyone how to portray the whole gamut of human reactions. Whether you are Chinese, Iranian, Peruvian or English, you can easily identify with his characters. The reader couldn't care less about the setting; what they care about is seeing themselves in his writing, living and reacting. Eager to find out their own ending, they all turn the same pages with the same sense of excitement. The only accessible way for all people to learn how to live in a new country, in a new culture, is to appropriate its words. I don't think you can be happy in a country if you do not share the language. I owe my love of the French language to Victor Hugo. He was also my passport to real life, which eventually came knocking on my door. Openly. There was no need to hide any more.

Although it took many months of hard work to even

pronounce the French word for frog, '*grenouille*', the words very rapidly strung themselves together and before I knew it, I was thinking in French. Fast-forward another three years and I was dreaming only in French. I lost my mother tongue very quickly. Hugo was most certainly to blame. But above all it was Khomeini. Persian was too linked with Tehran and the Beards, and my parents kept telling me— to convince themselves—that we were never going back to Tehran and that I had to learn France by heart. It took me a long time to find the beauty in my mother tongue again, but I was never again able to read and write in Persian.

French literature saved me from isolation. I constructed a new memory for myself, and that memory was supposed to protect me from all the Beards of the world. Madonna provided the body and words did the rest. After Hugo, there were other novelists who held my hand while I was learning. Women's bodies were no longer a problem. Nothing had to be hidden. I was overjoyed to see Madonna getting arrested coming out of concerts with a smile on her face, knowing that whatever happened, she had won. And I read so that I could be something more than just a provocation. Other people's words looked after me. But I found it difficult to put myself in the shoes of the heroines. Thérèse Raquin was not exactly a good example to follow, and neither Emma Bovary, Gervaise nor Rachel resonated with me as much as the heroes I loved: the Rubemprés, the Sorels, the Duroys. The first French heroines I had known were Fantine and Cosette ... Needless to say, I much preferred playing at being Jean Valjean. I wanted to conquer the world—or Paris at least—and certainly not get married to just anyone! However, I was a bit short on women. I had not met Merteuil yet. But I no longer doubted the power of literature, or the heroes of novels.

It came as no surprise then, that my chosen topic for the first presentation I had to give in my final year of elementary school was entitled, 'Queens of France'. My father was called in: there was not enough reference material *at my level* for me to do my presentation. My father offered to help me sort through the reference material for adults but the teacher, who looked sceptical when he heard my father's strong accent, would prefer that I chose a topic on his list. Everything was arranged and I was assigned the topic of 'Reproduction'. No kidding. I can still picture myself now, traumatizing my classmates with the stages of birth. My parents liked a job well done. They made me photocopy—in colour, thank you very much—each specific stage of birth. The images were taken from a library book for eight-to twelve-year-olds. At my level. I still have the cardboard folder containing my first presentation. It is quite frankly ... disgusting. There is no other word for it. I can see myself in front of my class, embarrassed but serious, speaking loudly and clearly—as I had been taught to do—and reciting off by heart what I had spent days writing in my rough French. Using a ruler, I helpfully pointed out the gradual colourful stages all the way from dilation to birth. The teacher was feeling as uncomfortable as his pupils; he could never have imagined the level of detail I would go into, with my six horribly realistic drawings. He seriously regretted not letting me do my Queens of France.

I kept on discovering that although there were still Crows after me, there weren't many women to help me fight them. I was expecting to study women. I wanted examples. In books and in history. I read the chapter at the end of the school book which covered women's history (which had all the time periods summarized in one chapter) so many times that I knew it off by heart. I was furious to see that here, too, women were hidden.

I found an intimate pseudo-diary from when I was ten years old, where I wrote that I wanted to be Madonna AND Émile Zola. Up to the age of thirteen, I was convinced that Émile Zola was a woman. Émile sounded too much like Emily to my novice ears. But it was certainly not an innocent mistake to turn Zola into a woman. I desperately needed to.

Paris, 2013

Little girls lack strong female role models. This is one of the reasons why I didn't get along with other little girls. There is no point beating about the bush with laws and parades: the fact is that it is more difficult for a girl to envisage herself as Napoleon than it is for a boy. Today in the West, we debate about whether it is discriminatory or not to differentiate between married women and other women. It was suddenly decided that it *is*—following a pretty surrealist debate—and the term '*mademoiselle*' disappeared from administrative documents. It is already ridiculous to consider the marital status of women as a form of discrimination, because whether married or single, the status of women already condemns them. For some, it is 'Miss' that is discriminatory, for others, it is 'Mrs'. But girls still go shopping on Saturdays while the boys watch football. It's heartbreaking. The law establishes parity and yet everyone is surprised when women aren't queuing up to appear on the electoral rolls.

Yet it wouldn't take much: just make a bit more room for women in school textbooks. Although women are present in history, they are not found in the books designed to educate future citizens. How can a little girl want to be in politics when she grows up if she has never encountered historical female role models? Would it really be so unwholesome to introduce Olympe de Gouges, Madeleine Pelletier or Ninon de Lenclos into the school curriculum? Must Simone de Beauvoir and Marie Curie be the only references when we talk to schoolchildren about 'famous women'? Are there really *no* other women we can add to this list to raise the level of diversity of the little cherubs? They do exist, and they are powerful women. Marguerite Durand, Jane Dieulafoy, Mary Wollstonecraft, Hannah Arendt, Alexandra David-Néel, Berty Albrecht, and Madame du Châtelet, but also all the others: Marie de Régnier, Laura de Noailles, Carson McCullers, Mary Shelley, Gerda Taro, Germaine Tillion, Madame d'Épinay, Alexandra Kollontaï. Not to mention Eleanor of Aquitaine, Marie de Medici, Anne of Austria, Catherine II, Diane, Queen Christina, etc. I mean seriously, enough's enough: apart from Lucie Aubrac—known above all for her wildly romantic approach to saving *her husband* from the clutches of the Gestapo—and who has the honour of being a famous figure of the resistance, where are the rest of them? Only reassuring, loving, and gentle women are allowed to enter the collective memory. Someone like Hubertine Auclert, to whom we owe the first tax-related strike which was launched with the slogan, 'I do not vote, I do not pay', gets people's backs up. Her logic, her militancy, and her anger all jar with the historical landscape taught in the Republic's schools, which prefers Madame Roland or Julie Récamier, who are briefly studied for their *salons* and the famous company they kept. This is despite the fact that her contemporaries caricatured Madame Roland in the guise of the real interior minister—which was her husband's official position. But again, what is taught can be summarized as: 'Madame Roland, Muse des Girondins'. Why don't they study her political texts? The Dutch athlete Fanny Blankers-Koen who has achieved no less than sixteen world records in eight different events and who was also married and the mother of two children, has become a celebrity under the name of the 'flying housewife' ... It is so crazy, all this effort of imagination to make sure we never forget that a woman, even an Olympic champion, is still a housewife first and foremost. Even when women *are* represented, they are detached from their real powers and influences. Women pose prettily in the pages that are supposed to tell us about the French Revolution. It is hard to imagine them really taking part in the country's affairs. Instead of worrying about whether women's marital status is discriminatory, we need to take a good look at the content of our school books!

In every field—as the time-honoured expression goes—there are women who can be role models, examples and ways forward for girls who are finding it hard to envisage themselves as Danton or de Gaulle. How can women seriously think that without education or culture it is possible to hope for more female politicians? How can we want to have power, exercise any authority, when absolutely nothing in our cultural and educational environment invites us to do so?

The neo-feminists are passing laws to protect women from sexual harassment—which actually only victimize them further—forgetting that all you need is to be self-confident enough and sufficiently aware of your femininity to knee any assailant in the balls. Careful! I'm not saying that women who are victims of compulsive stalkers, detestable rapists (all rapists are detestable) or ignorant brutes, do not deserve our compassion. They are victims. But it is pointless trying to deal with this issue through legislation alone, washing our hands of education and culture, which are the keys to everything. Men will carry on pushing up against their secretaries in the lift so they can touch their bums, and women will carry on hesitating before they alert the hierarchy, and will have a breakdown before they get to court—if they even get to court. A woman who is as proud of her femininity as a man is of his manhood would never allow a man to harass her—however high up in the hierarchy he is. Freedom can be learned. So can independence ...

Paris, 1985–1988

It would not be fair to reduce my early years in Paris, between the ages of eight and twelve, to a multitude of books and an unknown language which became my only means of expression. There was a feeling in the air that I can still remember so well. It was linked to sound: it was muffled. I didn't understand what was being said on the streets, or what was being said on the television. At first, I only knew how to read.

It was not unpleasant but it did accentuate the bubble we were living in. We were still very much Iranians; we weren't fully aware of exile and its scope. From June to September 1985, I learned French with Victor Hugo and my father, and I discovered the Parisian streets with my mother, by walking around aimlessly. I was not educated yet; there were my parents, my aunts and uncles, my young cousins, exiled friends of the family and the television. At first I enjoyed hearing without understanding, letting my imagination do the rest. Then it became infuriating. So I learned faster. But for two long years, even after school, there was always something unclear about the sound. I had to concentrate really hard to remove the filter that prevented me from hearing clearly. It was also at this time that my myopia was diagnosed. But I was in such a hazy sound environment that it took a while for me to notice that my eyes had gone blurry too.

When I try to picture a sharp image of that time, every-thing is fuzzy. I remember school, my year of CLIN class (classes for children of immigrants where we learned French while trying to remain at the level of the official curriculum, before joining a *real* class) and then when I went into Year 5 and started school like the rest of the other French children. I remember winning prizes for my achievements in French; I remember my teacher coming over for dinner with my parents several times. I remember games in the playground with my classmates who did not understand why I wore such *bourgeois* dresses in such a working class neighbour-hood. I remember running as fast as the boys and the scraps I used to get into. I had a tendency to react with my fists when I didn't understand something. I remember that there was another Iranian at my school, his friends were friends with my parents, and his task was to 'look after me'. I remember him taking a lot of blows that were destined for me—years later, I saw him again, studying medicine, so pretentious and still so Iranian: he could (proudly) dis-tinguish the whores from the women who were marriage material. He married marriage material, a woman who has a significant communication problem, in that she never says anything. I remember dreaming a lot, and starting a novel—which I still have in a drawer somewhere—which I wrote on the blue typewriter that my father gave me. I had taken all my family members and given them a French past and destiny. I still remember the opening line: 'I was born on 1 April 1977 in a family doomed to failure'—I already had a sense of tragedy. Once upon a time, there were six sisters and a brother who lived in Brittany and dramatic events led them into exile ... to Paris, after the grandmother died and the brother was released from prison. The brother was a regionalist, of course, and that's why he was in prison. His best friend, a lonely and misunderstood poet (my father), fell in love with one of the regionalist's sisters, the funniest and the most tomboyish (my mother), who married him against everyone's wishes, without ever believing in his love. The plot centred on the discovery of Paris and on the breakup of the family, narrated by Apolline, the ten-year-old narrator, who was my French doppelganger. I remember that I gave Apolline the character traits of Scarlett O'Hara, my first movie heroine, who was free and independent and succeeding—financially—all by herself against other women (mostly) and against men (a little less). A pain in the neck, perhaps; lacking morals and friends. She was me down to a tee.

I have images and memories, but everything is like a blurry photograph. Words (the ones I deciphered in books and the ones I wrote) are the only things that are precisely defined. It shows how much I lived inside my own head. There were also so many questions to ask and it became clear the answers were no longer going to be found in the adult camp. They had no more of a clue how to eat snails than I did. It was not just hard to adapt, it was also difficult to understand. A normal event like Mother's Day was proof that *we were still on the outside*. We did not know about it—perhaps in 1985, advertising was not as hysterical and my parents were as clueless as I was—and come Monday morning in the school playground, I was the only one who hadn't given my mother some perfume, a tea towel, a skirt or a teapot. I came home absolutely distraught, feeling even more left out than usual, and I blurted it all out in tears to my father. After thinking for a moment, my father told me that it was a celebration established by Marshal Pétain, who was the enemy of General de Gaulle, who was our hero (my father was eleven or twelve years old when de Gaulle carried out a state visit to Tehran and remembers it perfectly as he was one of the schoolchildren assembled to welcome the General's arrival). I went back to school in a warlike mood, hurling insults at all my classmates: Fascists! Traitors! Murderers! Not a great way to go about making friends, although everybody neglected to tell me that. We never celebrated Pétain's Mother's Day again, after my parents were called in about the fight that had ensued in the playground.

There were also a number of TV comedy programmes such as *La Classe* and *Collaricocoshow* that were real culture shocks. I shared my family's consternation at this supposedly popular French humour. I didn't understand much, and laughed even less. I found it stupid. Or perhaps it was because my father found it stupid. Whatever the case, I was impervious to it; I much preferred drama. On the other hand, what really knocked me for six, and which I greedily looked for, was the female body. Every other programme seemed to have naked women in it. It would be dinner time and millions of French people would gather in front of their TV sets to watch naked women. It was absolutely free and that was what shocked and delighted me. Seeing my blatant fascination—my mouth open wide in a question that I never dared to ask, sitting so still I was almost contorted— my parents decided that I should not see naked women's bodies any more. And of course there was such awkwardness on everybody's part that I didn't even try to negotiate. But in the end it was worse to turn off the TV or send me to my room. These 'free bodies' populated my evenings. I didn't understand and didn't dare to ask: the two breasts of trauma. The breasts and buttocks of women were present everywhere—including on my bedroom walls—but although nobody had a problem with my father showing me *Once Upon a Time in America, Boccaccio 70* or the series *Duel au Soleil,* it was out of the question to let me watch Mylène Farmer music videos. As if the body should only be visible—for a child—in a purportedly intelligent context. I came to the conclusion that everyone was as confused as me, and women's bodies never ceased to obsess me, to seek me out, to open me up, to motivate me, to inspire me. None of that helped me to make friends, nor helped my (increasingly floundering) parents and I to understand one another.

Books were the only things that were solid; everything

else was poorly defined, crappy, and unreal. It was as if I was cut off from the real world. It was definitely not Iran any more, but it was not France yet either. It was clear that we had everything still to learn and we were very alone, and that my mother and her sisters would never like each other again. Raised voices became a daily occurrence. The members of my family talked to one another less and less, and shouted more and more. I retreated into myself even more but I was not unhappy. I was learning in my own little corner. But it is impossible to stay in a bubble. Everything was too rough since our exile; nothing seemed anchored down. Then suddenly everything became clear. Nothing would ever be out of focus again. That was the day my maternal grandfather tried to kiss me on the lips, grabbing my face between his two withered hands. I was nine years old and it was a rude awakening. All my education, all my reading, all my fears compelled my leg to shoot upwards, thrusting my knee into his crotch. The feeble old man crumpled on the floor in front of me, clutching his crotch with his trembling hands. I got up and left my room, where he was supposed to be having a nap and I had gone to look for a book. Of course I was looking for a book, what else would I be doing? I was home alone with him. He didn't dare come out of my room before my parents and aunts got home.

I don't know how I had known to hit him right there, where I couldn't lose. Perhaps some image from a film (I watched a lot of films); perhaps simply because I was a woman and he was just a man and nature could only direct my knee toward his balls. I don't know where the reflex came from but it saved me. Not only was I never ashamed of the incident, but he also never dared to look at me again after that, while I scornfully looked down on him—it was part of my 'princess in exile' attitude that I adopted most of the time. I did not tell anyone about it at the time. I thought about telling my father but everything was already very complicated and very noisy. Plus my grandfather didn't have long left. Plus my aunts wouldn't have believed me. I was a good twenty-five years old before I confided in my father. He told me that I had done what was best: to defend myself and not say anything about it. There was a hint of pride in his smile, but our debilitating prudishness brought the conversation to an end there. Then he told me about my grandfather: that he had wanted to remarry after my grandmother died but that his daughters had stopped him. They wanted their mother to remain the only one who had been in his bed. He had suffered a lot. Toward the end of his life—during the time he had pounced on me—he used to throw his dinner around and he could no longer sleep. He must have been thinking about the women he could have married. This intimate information was common knowledge only because his daughters had the habit of rifling through his rubbish bins. It was only a small consolation, but it reaffirmed what I thought: he had serious issues. I told the story to one of my aunts, the youngest one who I felt closest to. I've never known if she believed me or not. And honestly, I never really cared.

My grandfather died two years later and I got to see my mother and my aunts no longer plucking their eyebrows, no longer putting on make-up, no longer smiling. But either because they grew tired of it, or because Paris did not allow for that kind of tastelessness, or because there were too many other problems, after ten days everything went back to normal. It was only my mother who managed to carry on mourning for a good month. My mother is a great martyr; in fact it is pretty much her *raison d'être*. She lives for others. Above all her sisters and her children. Then all the others, the strangers. To protect us, the family decided—against the advice of my father, but he was alone in his opinion—that we should hide the death of our grandfather from all the children, including me. We were all aged between five and eleven. The women wore black even though they hated black, and wept as they chopped the courgettes; the men wore pensive expressions—they were trying to work out how to get their hands on the rest of the money—the children cried and wondered why everyone was acting so strangely, and my father looked on at all this, smiling beneath his moustache. I went up to him and said, 'He's dead.' My father nodded in confirmation. Ever since, we have always wondered how one of my cousins never twigged what was going on (he was six at the time). The death was so obvious. To this day he still thinks that his grandfather, who would be at least a hundred years old now, is away on a business trip. He also doesn't know that his mother had a first husband. Communication is sparse in our family. In that particular branch of it, the lack of communication verges on the absurd. So, imagine it: me, the bigmouth, already a self-proclaimed 'French writer' without actually being able to write a single sentence free of errors, breaking the silence by suddenly announcing that Grandfather had tried to stick his tongue in my mouth. It was impossible. Even I knew that. I didn't care: I had floored a man. Grandfather or not, there was no difference between a man and a woman. Absolute equality. You attack me, man or not, I will take you down, woman or not. Nothing could ever strip me of this certainty. I had finally put into practice everything that had happened in my life up until that day in June. And I felt like I was avenging my mother and her sisters. Because the presence of my grandfather meant that they had to play the prude, they had to drape a shawl around their shoulders and sneak off to smoke in the kitchen. Which was absolutely ridiculous, seeing as the apartment had a balcony running along the length of it, and a few minutes after they disappeared, wisps of smoke would drift in, straight up my grandfather's nostrils. Everyone saw it but everyone pretended not to. I hated that. I wanted to light a cigarette right under his nose. Then there was the time he caught two of his youngest daughters on a Parisian cafe terrace, cigarette in hand, sipping an innocent Monaco ... What a drama. Blown out of all proportion. After that everyone made a point of drinking lemonade with grenadine at every family lunch to prove to him that there was no alcohol in it. I hate grenadine. And why did it even matter, seeing as everyone was drinking wine at the table in front of him, including him, first and foremost? It's because it happened outside the house. In front of others. It would never end. The Parisian eye seemed to affect them as much as the one that pervaded Iran. Kneeing him in the balls was also my way of avenging the stupid status quo that kept my mother and her sisters under the moral domination of a patriarch who had not been right in the head since the exile and who imagined he could satisfy his desire, whatever that meant, with a nine-year-old girl. Iran would die with him. Written like that, things seemed simple. But it wasn't easy. There was no frame of reference any more; I had floored my grandfather and I didn't even feel guilty. I discovered that I was alone, but not really: I had my books, and books cannot betray you.

It was also clear that my freedom—i.e. my body—was still subject to debate by my parents. There was always an issue over the length of skirt I should wear to school, or those yellow earrings, or the dress with the low-cut back that my mother had given me, or boys' birthday parties versus girls' birthday parties, or lip gloss, or whether I was allowed to go to the public library on my own. Just as war was declared in the family, my body also became a source of family tension. Whenever my parents were arguing, my mother encouraged me to wear backless dresses, and when all was well again my mother shouted that it was out of the question to go out *dressed like that*. It was as if they had decided that my culture was my father's issue, and my body was my mother's and aunts' domain. They wanted me to look pretty—I never really was, between the age of twelve and sixteen—and they wanted me dressed and coiffed to suit their tastes. It was a cruel pastime. There is nothing meaner than dressing up an ugly teenage girl in pretty clothes. My body needed black and subtle, and my mother gave me pink jumpers that immediately added twenty kilos and were a perfect colour match for my acne. On our arrival in France I had stopped classical dance, swimming, and horse riding, the direct result of which was that I piled on the pounds. Add to this the fact that I started my period at the age of just nine and a half, and you can imagine the result. I was sporting boobs that were too big for my age, too much body hair far too early, and pink dresses. I looked at least fifteen, with a child's face and little girlie dresses.

But in the end, the result was the same: I didn't like myself and this body, which did not belong to me, did not suit me. I had been naked so often as a child that I liked my body more than anything else at that time. When I became a woman I lost my connection with my body. I did not know what getting your period meant. When I came out of the toilet and whispered to my mother that I had 'blood diarrhoea' I saw her eyes darken. She got up and went to find my father who very seriously and scientifically explained everything to me. It wasn't embarrassing, it was terrifying. Well, that was it, I was a woman. In other words, I could procreate. Brilliant! I was in absolute shock. I had barely got the headscarf off and now they were probably going to stick children inside my womb. Whatever next? Swapping one prison for another, condemned to always be a woman. And nothing else. I tell myself these days that if my grandfather had tried to kiss me on the lips as the chubby teenager I had become, I would have been significantly more traumatized. He would have piled shame on top of shame, and the disgust would have been too much to bear. But as a little girl, I really loved and enjoyed my body and had never been afraid.

I remember thinking about how women were targeted from all sides. The blow could come from inside or from outside; I was surrounded! There was always something to differentiate me from men and remind me that I was a woman. Ultimately, in Tehran and in Paris, I was a woman. I remember being especially concerned with finding out whether it was all women who got their periods or if it was just Iranian women. That was the only point that my father managed to reassure me on. As for the rest of it, well, I had to deal with my body which seemed to be bursting out all over the place, and the bars of my prison that were becoming ever more visible.

Paris, February – March 1989

1989 was an important year. It actually started back in '88. But strangely I don't remember the beginnings of the Rushdie affair. How can my memory, which is usually so vivid, have erased the appearance of Rushdie in the public arena? Perhaps Salman Rushdie needed to gravitate closer to Khomeini in order to grab my attention. Only ten years had passed since the 'old man in black and white' had died, and he was all the more present now that I realized what he had done—with the dexterity of a black magician—to my family. In exile my family disappeared. There was no longer a family in the sense of a refuge. There was no more solidarity or generosity and even less love. It was no longer about preserving what had been laboriously saved—some money and a bit of love—but instead it became about doing everything to pocket it all, at the expense of others. Clans formed, terrible things were said, there was permanent shouting, and my beloved uncle, who was like a grandfather to me, looked my father in the eye, pointed at me as

I stood in front of the door about to leave for school, and swore on *my* life to pay him back the next day. My father, who still had a heart and valued literature over money, wrote him a cheque. He didn't see his money again until ten years later. Nobody ever mentioned it. My father waited. My family fled. Meanwhile, we were hungry and nobody came to our rescue. My parents were torn apart, and they tore each other apart, and still tear each other apart; they paid a high price for this domestic war which was incited by Khomeini himself. It therefore seemed natural not to have heard about Rushdie until February 1989. After that, everything becomes clear. I was not yet twelve and the 'old man in black and white' issued his *fatwa* against Salman Rushdie. Sentenced to death for stringing words together. What happened to me at that time was that words turned to speech. Speech for me, as a child, was *Les Misérables* and *Madonna*. And it was *The Satanic Verses*.

Since our arrival in France, watching the TV evening news had become our mandatory pre-dinner ritual. As the war went on in our home country, my parents were highly sensitive and needed to keep up with the news, follow operations, to reassure themselves that exile had been the right choice. I would sit with them, like an adult, to follow the news from my homeland, which affected me less and less. After the war, the habit remained. The *fatwa* broadcast by Khomeini was the opening item on the news one evening. For once, it was not about the war. Or it was: it was the war on our doorstep. Again. But we did not know it yet. My mother started screaming that she couldn't take

Khomeini any longer, how he had brought shame to Paris now too, while I asked—also shouting, so as to be heard above my mother—who Fatwa was and why he wanted to kill the author with the funny eyebrows. My father tried to answer all of us, and my mother decreed that from now on, whenever anyone asked where we were from, we should say we were of Armenian origin. She did just that, from the very next morning onwards. I never did it. I carried on being Iranian while my mother was Armenian. She kept it up until Iran became more respectable in the eyes of her social circle—in other words, the day when in the film *Syriana*, George Clooney said a few words in Farsi, insulting an Arab for not knowing the Persian language. We are eternally grateful to George Clooney, *Persepolis*, Shirin Ebadi, *Reading Lolita in Iran* and *A Separation*, for bringing my mother back to her true origins after years of exile in Armenia. As for me, I carried on being Iranian, if only to make it clear that I was the most legitimate and important living enemy of Khomeini. I was still a child deep down. Although I now preferred reading and writing to playing with dolls, I still thought that Khomeini was aware of my existence. I had to show him what I was capable of, which was being his absolute enemy every day. The same way I had decided that Salman Rushdie was my new best friend, even before I had read any of his novels. Childhood is great for that: you make lasting, quality friendships and enemies that are just as tenacious. As a child, I could not possibly have understood that they had no idea of my existence. One had put a veil on me; the other had written me a long letter—in the form of a novel. That was enough to form real relationships.

What I understood the first time I read Rushdie's book can be summed up as follows: not a lot. Although I made a real effort to read the book, I didn't have the means of understanding it yet. Neither the vocabulary, nor the intellectual baggage. Whatever I did understand, I understood because my father explained it to me. It is the story of two men (from India originally) who survive a terrorist attack and who take opposite paths: surreal paths, symbolic paths. One transforms into the devil—physically—and one takes on the personality of an archangel and can no longer sleep because in his dreams he lives out the life of the prophet Muhammad. They reflect on exile and identity, going through their lives with their heads full of questions and meetings that show the diversity of feelings and the power of emotions over prejudice and tradition. All in a baroque style—according to my father. At the heart of this tale, there is a question, a dash of imagination, a crazy assumption, which sent all the Beards into a frenzy. The question examines the *real* Satanic Verses. It is a story based on sources reported by, among others, Tabari. It talks about Muhammad before the *Hijra*, when Satan was supposed to have appeared to the prophet in the guise of an angel and led him by the nose. Things were quickly restored and Muhammad managed to receive the whole Revelation without Satan meddling in it again. This gets Salman Rushdie *thinking*: what if Satan had never been flushed out and the entire Revelation had been falsified by the devil? An improbable question, a childish question, an absurd question:

what if we lived elsewhere? What if my mother was not my real mother? What if I was a princess kidnapped by the commoners for a ransom? The refrain of 'what if' is a fascinating little game for children and for adults who write. Rewriting history, examining all the variations of the same action, scrolling through all the accounts and discovering a thousand possible versions. Rushdie's ultimate crime was therefore imagining and making a work of fiction. It has nothing religious about it; it is not a theological treatise. There is nothing insulting in a work of fiction that is nothing but a mirage of reality: the world of *what if*.

However, that is not what drove the Beards and Crows mad. It was speaking out that upset them. Freedom of speech. Saying things. Out loud. But Salman Rushdie had written it. He did not have the right to write, to speak, to change history, to poke fun at them, to twist their logic. To open up. Rushdie had opened his mouth. It was only logical that I should immediately fall in love with him. I had been prepared for it since childhood. He was doing exactly what I wanted to do for the rest of my life. I wanted to open doors, slam others shut, flush out the absurd from under the veil of logic, make fun of truths that are little more than kinds of prejudice, jump out of the window, flash my bottom at priests. Rushdie had my full admiration even before I became familiar with his words. Censorship was rife everywhere, and I suffered with him, as I had suffered when my father had to burn the books he loved, so as to avoid prison. The book as an object, the action of writing, the patience of reading; these were to become my weapons. Those weapons were much more powerful than getting naked. Yet—and this is why I chose books—they provoked the same disproportionate and pathological reaction.

Until Rushdie came along I had only known and respected dead writers. Salman Rushdie was part of the present. My present! There were two of us; it was the beginnings of an army on the march!

Until Rushdie—despite the Crows and Beards I passed in the street—I was convinced that all the French were on the side of *The Satanic Verses*. I would never have believed someone if they had told me they didn't like Isabelle Adjani's speech when she received the Cesar for Best Actress. I mean, personally, I had cried. I wouldn't let anyone dislike her. She was even more beautiful than Madonna, plus she loved reading. 'To will is to disagree; not to submit; to dissent.' Pause. Then: 'Salman Rushdie, writer.' Pause. Then finally: '*The Satanic Verses*.' It still gives me goose bumps and brings a tear to my eye. The fact that she specified: *writer*, that's what gives me the chills. Salman Rushdie: a man of imagination. I was proud to be French. Especially since Adjani was not totally. But the worst was yet to come. I was the only Iranian in my college. My college was located in a working-class neighbourhood and it was mainly North Africans who were educated there. The worst part was that I did not know that Khomeini could be loved, in Paris, by kids my age. In the spring of 1989, I overheard some college student saying that Rushdie was a son-of-a-bitch. I heard classmates, who were usually quite temperate, swearing that they would kill him if he were standing there in front of them. I heard them saying that I should be ashamed to own that book. After March 1989, Adjani also became a whore. She deserved to die. I was seething, I was distraught and, worse, I had learned to keep my mouth shut so I didn't lose the few friends I had made. What the Beards had failed to do—to shut me up, make me keep my head down and make me feel ashamed—my classmates achieved with ease. I'm not really sure how they managed to shut me up. I had been warned, but it had never happened to me before: I was afraid. For the first time in my life I was scared. In Tehran, my classmates laughed at my naked escapades and the misery I put the Crows through in the playground. Even though they reported everything back to their parents, who then forbade them from seeing me, at least they went on applauding me in the school playground. In Paris, I could never have imagined children telling me that they would kill a man for a crime of imagination. I was deeply convinced that we were all French. It's silly: it meant that we were protected. Nobody had warned me that the Beards could cause damage in places other than Iran. It was traumatic enough to shut me up.

However, on 4 June 1989—another historical date that I immediately filed away in my mind—my father woke me at dawn to tell me that Khomeini was dead. It was over. I felt joy, as if justice had been restored. Even if it was not going to change our exile, or our memories, or even the Beards. It was something else: the proof that he was mortal. Therefore human. Therefore prone to error. Sounds silly, doesn't it? But there were so many people who doubted that he was mortal, and from that moment on I could silence them.

No sooner had I arrived at school than my classmates started offering me their condolences for the death of my president. *My* president. I felt the same rage rising up in me as when I had ripped off all my clothes and launched my assault on the playground and its Crows. I didn't even talk. I just hit. I hit the first person I found in front of me. I got hit too. But I dealt a lot of blows. Although I had not been able to respond to the diatribe against Rushdie out of fear—paralysed as I was and surrounded by enemies I didn't understand—this time I couldn't let it go. Condolences! In Paris! From kids my own age! It was just too much. I hit. I lashed out, and I do not regret it, even to this day. My parents were called in; I stood up for myself, I wanted *them* to be punished and ... In the end it was I who had to say sorry. My parents reacted in the typical way of exiles: they kept a low profile. I had to apologize because I was not in my own country, because I had to prove myself, because I had to adapt. But in my mind I was already French; I didn't understand what they meant. I was right; I was sure of it. It was they who wanted to kill the imagination and offer me their condolences! I was really pissed off with my father. Not only had he lied to me—Beards and Crows did exist in Paris and they were my own age, too—but he also made me apologize to the morons who wanted to put me back under the veil. That he didn't understand that and just kept telling me that we must respect everyone's opinions ... I felt absolutely screwed over and alone. But I was not about to give up. I apologized, swallowed my anger, took a new stack of books out of my father's library and went on reading. It took a few months before I stopped fearing my classmates, who wanted to stick a knife in Rushdie's heart. *The Satanic Verses* stayed on my bedside table for a long time, until I managed to read and understand the full scope of it. By that time I was seventeen, and had read a fair amount of libertine literature.

Paris, September 1989

There may have been Crows on the Paris metro, but I never imagined coming across a girl my own age who was a consenting Crow. It was in October 1989. The summer had been studious and Parisian, and going back to school was liberating. Finally! I was going to see people other than my family, other than Iranians. I loved school. I loved learning and every day I couldn't help but learn something new. But that particular start of the year was marked by the media debut of the veil in my French life. Everything had begun in June 1989 but when we went back to school that year, everything really escalated. I found out that girls of thirteen wanted to wear the veil at school. Seriously. I still didn't understand how a woman could wake up in the morning and cover her head in black and proudly justify it—referring to God, her faith, her family—and it was happening again, but this time with an extra racist angle to it. It drove me crazy. And everyone fell into the trap: being opposed to the veil meant you were against Muslims and against

Arabs. It meant you were a racist. In other words, the word that made us tremble as a family. It was a word that was slipped into conversations in a whisper. A neighbour could be racist, a cashier, or the caretaker's wife. For me, a racist was someone who wanted to send me back under the veil, back to Tehran. I kept asking my father why Malek Boutih, who was French like us, wanted barely pubescent girls to wear headscarves on the grounds that those who wanted them to take them off, were 'suspicious'. I was 'suspicious' in the eyes of Malek Boutih and I didn't understand why. He spoke of wanting to put Islam in a 'ghetto'. In a 'ghetto'! But we came from the ghetto! That was in Tehran, and it was like a prison. Refusing the discrimination of the veil, is that racism? I was confused. Religion has no place being on the streets, it is only acceptable indoors, in the intimacy of faith. Outdoors, nobody should have religion. I was confused: if the French were fighting for teenagers to be able to wear the veil, what would happen to me? Where could I hide? It was painful. I listened to the news, I listened to my parents, I listened to a French neighbour who had been invited over for an evening drink—and while my parents drank wine with her and ate slices of *saucisson*—she tried to get herself off the hook by saying how she wasn't a racist. That she completely understood if I wanted to wear the headscarf at school because it was important for me to be proud of my culture. I was so disturbed that my father had to take me by the arm and drag me a safe distance away from the neighbour. She thought I had been moved by her openness. My mother did not set her straight and cut some more slices of dried sausage. They were just as lost as me; none of us knew what to say to people who wanted to see us wearing the trappings of a political regime that was not even our own culture. I didn't understand why I would never have the right to be free.

Since October 1989 I have always had to justify myself on the subject of the veil. As soon as it became clear that I was of Iranian origin—and it was impossible to escape it, my name gave away my origin—the first question was—and still is—always about the veil. For or against? Against, of course, but ... I often saw—and at the age of twelve, having lived in exile for only four years, I was very oversensitive to the reactions of the French—disappointment, or even disgust in the eyes of those who expected to see me defending my cultural origins. As if by denouncing the black veil of the obscurants, I was saying that Iran was shit. And if I tried to explain the difference between my religious origins and my cultural origins, I quickly realized that approach was way too complicated. So I put up with the 'suspicious' looks; comments such as 'Don't you feel like you are going against your nature?'—and the stupidity of those who confuse cults with culture. Politics with religion. Proselytism with faith. I realized I couldn't hang out with the practicing Muslims, or the French who wished I was one. I was caught between what seemed to me to be a regression—little girls wearing the veil—and what was essential to independence—the freedom of the body. I knew that there was a link—in addition to the bare bottom of my childhood—but I didn't have enough knowledge to explain to those guilty of colonization that the veil was not just a harmless piece of fabric that racists took advantage of to throw out the Arabs. I tried to tell them about my childhood, to explain to them that the veil is damaging; that the veil imposes too much sexuality on a child; that the veil is nothing but a dangerous weapon in the hands of manipulative and narrow-minded politicians. But it is very difficult to explain that we can tear up the veil without destroying the body it is covering. I was twelve and I already knew that I was going to be lonely because I was incapable of making people understand. The veil was the worst period of my childhood and had now become the number one problem in France, where I was supposed to have escaped from that very veil. Those in exile believe even more firmly in the virtues of their adopted country than its historical inhabitants tend to. I believed in them more than anyone. Victor Hugo was by my side and France would prove me right one day. Victor Hugo would have refused the veil just as he would have refused racism. He would have written about how a woman loses her personality under the veil and how the other 'uncovered' women lose their virtues. Everything is a matter of scale and if the woman wearing the veil is virtuous, then the uncovered woman must therefore be a whore. That's the way it is. Go on, do the antiracist song and dance, that's the way it is, and that's how it always will be. Since October 1989 and still to this day, the veil has always been there and it really gets on my nerves.

The veil is a young mother, born in France, who after a BA in History at the University of Paris VII, with a three-year-old son and a baby girl in her arms, looks me in the eye and says that her son will never treat a woman badly ... if she wears the veil. However, judging by my outfit, she wouldn't be surprised if 'something happened to me'. Her eyes light up. She is sure of herself. She is convinced that her daughter deserves to be treated like a common whore if, later on, despite all her education, she refuses to wear the veil. Like me.

The veil is a local shopkeeper, smiling and shapely, born in Algeria, schooled in France, who loves to chat, and who between a few friendly neighbourly comments casually throws into the conversation that she used to be *like me*. That she used to walk around naked. *Like me*. In her eyes I am naked because I am not wearing the veil. In her eyes, I am as naked as I was as a child in the playground.

The veil is the cousin of a Tunisian friend, born and raised in Paris, who has a baby girl even though they diagnosed her as infertile, and suddenly believes in divine intervention when she finally gives birth. So she starts wearing the veil, which rapidly transforms into a full veil, while her husband cultivates his beard and prejudices. She celebrates her daughter's birthdays without singing and without laughter. She never takes her daughter's photo. Her little miracle is not allowed to draw faces, so she is banned from drawing altogether. Her daughter is three years old and she has never seen her mother's hair. Her daughter, her miracle, her divine intervention, is a poor child who lives in darkness.

The veil is a young Tunisian man, handsome and friendly, dating a French woman who converted to Islam and who does not (yet) wear the veil. It is a young man who is a sweet-heart and he tells me—without a moment's hesitation—that his mother did not obtain French nationality because she wears the veil. Nothing to do with the fact that after twenty years in France she doesn't speak the language, of course. He adds that wearing the veil is a matter of respect—even though he would never force his future wife to wear it. But if he's so proud of his mother wearing it, then how will his future wife be able to accept not wearing it, if she wants him to respect her? When I ask why, he tells me that it's about women's necks, which arouse a desire in men that they cannot control. When I cite myself as an example, hav-ing swanned around with my neck uncovered for so many years, surrounded by men, and to whom nothing salacious, dirty, or unwholesome has happened because of my neck, he replies that not all women are like me. Some simply have to wear it because they do not know how to restrain themselves. The young man looked down and ended the conversation with, 'Well you're not really a girl, you know. You're sort of more like a man.'

So, no, women who wear the veil are not like other women. On their bodies they display all of the dark hours of women's history. They are collaborators. They throw their inferiorities back in my face and urge me to get back in my box, where I and my uncovered hair belong. A whore. I always find veiled women condescending. As if they are the ones in the know. In their eyes, you're the messed up one. So when the law is on the side of prejudice, the danger to a woman is huge. Finding herself suddenly reduced to this woman's body, this criminal object, she rewrites herself to save herself. She sews an inner veil that covers her entire psyche and enables her to survive beneath the real veil. If she were not fully convinced that the veil conceals her shamefulness, she would not be able to survive.

Paris, 2013

I don't know why, but it's my fault. It's my fault if a man desires me. Whatever the situation, it's my fault. I probably don't need to remind you of the rapes, in Iran or elsewhere, where it's the raped woman who is tried and punished for incitement to rape; which is logical if you think that a man is free from moral and social constraints if he is provoked. It's absurd but there is a crude logic to it. That woman might be a girl on her own in a taxi at night or a student strolling in the streets smiling too much, or a tired woman who falls asleep on a bus where there are only men left on board and her headscarf has slipped. You mustn't push your luck. It is a strange notion of living together where each person is allowed to become a predator. Without guilt. The woman is there to be guilty for two. What kind of faith makes women so dangerous to men?

Of course all religions (Buddhist no less than Shiite or Sunni Muslim, or Jewish, or Catholic, or Protestant, or Mormon) have imprisoned women in a shroud of prejudice. All religions have tried to control the woman's body. All religions impose restrictions on women in the name of God and often *out of respect* for Him. The woman is always subject to more prohibitions than men and that goes for all religions. So be it. But I don't care. I have read and reread wonderfully intelligent and erudite texts on religions. Yet my need to demand more from my Shia Muslim ancestors has not lessened. The fact that I was born into an atheist family and I have chosen atheism does not give me any less right to understand what happened to me, in the streets of the country where I was born and where most of my family grew up. You can call it psycho-genealogy, or intellectual masturbation or even another viewpoint on our skewed relationship with Islam post-September 11. An unhealthy relationship, distorted by the (justifiable) fear of feeding the monster that is xenophobia. I want to understand why the Beards go crazy at the sight of a nipple and why they have lost their sense of humour. I want to understand why women are so badly represented, so unloved, so poorly regarded in Islamic countries more than anywhere else.

After all, what is so awful about me that they want to cover me up? What's wrong with me?

Women are repeatedly told in Islam that they are dangerous. They are repeatedly told that there is no worse misfortune for a man than a woman. There is no text where the woman's unworthiness, weakness or deceit are not referenced. Muhammad's *favourite* wife, Aisha, told women that the best kind of woman is one who does not speak ill of anyone and who refrains from deceiving men. One that has no concerns other than being willing to please her husband and to watch dutifully over her family. The Prophet added a subtle metaphor to this: 'The woman is a toy, whoever takes her let him care for her (or do not lose her).'[2] The Quran is clear-cut on the matter: 'the deception of women is very great'[3] (12/28). Mothers go as far as warning their sons-in-law of the misfortunes that await them if they don't train their wives. They advise them to always give them a regular humping. It's the only way to control your woman. From this the great thinkers have deduced that flesh has much more significance in Islam than in Christianity. In the sanctuary of the bridal chamber, anything goes. And much more. The woman in Islam is always inferior to the man. She is a thing. She is passive. She does not talk, she does not refuse, she does not deceive; she remains transparent in the eyes of the world. There is no worse crime for a woman than to be seen.

There is nothing more effective than myths. It is the famous command: you have to go back to the texts. All right. So I go back to the texts. And what jumps out at me, is that women are dangerous. Women must be hidden. As I reread, a doubt surfaces: where are the first women? The women of the founding myths? And suddenly, an observation: there is no Mary in Islam. And no Mary Magdalene either. Well, not really. They exist but they are not easy to find. You have to look hard. You have to dig. As if to prevent women from being able to access a memory that would justify equality and rights, women have simply disappeared from the mythology. There are always plenty of references to Aisha, who rode a horse and did not wear the veil. But Fatimah, the favourite daughter of Muhammad—who had only female descendants—almost disappeared beneath the glory of her husband, Ali, her father's cousin and the first Shiite. Moreover, neither Fatimah nor Aisha, nor any other founding woman appears in the ancient texts. They are cited sometimes, in the *Hadith*: Aisha said such-and-such because Muhammad told it to her; Fatimah said such-and-such because her father told it to her.

The Quran has kept in Sarah and Mary—respectively cited twice (under the name of 'Abraham's wife') and thirty-four times (she is the only woman mentioned by name)—but it has erased the mother and wives of the first Muslim. It took me a while to find the mother, at least. The mother of Ishmael: the first Muslim, according to Muhammadan ancestry. Ishmael's mother would have been the first female Muslim. Muslims therefore date back to the father, the famous Abraham—who is cited seventy-eight times—and to the mother, the almost unknown Hagar—who is cited zero times.

Women's first 'mistake' in Islam goes back to Hagar. Perhaps Mr. Clean-Your-Hands should have talked about her when he explained the veil. But talking about her would have meant making her exist, and women only half-exist. Hagar's mistake was being a servant and being ordered by her mistress, Sara—who did not have an H yet—to bear a child by her master—Abram—who also had no H, like his wife. And very rapidly, things go wrong. Hagar is not content with just being a womb on legs, and does not want to serve Sara any more. The situation becomes so unbearable that Hagar gets kicked out. But the Angel of Yahweh appears to her and orders her to return to Sara, to serve her through gritted teeth, and he promises her a fine lineage. Hagar complies. However, Sarah—who has now gained an H—gives birth at over eighty years old, would you believe it, to a son. Another son for Abraham—who has gained his H as well—called Isaac. Sarah, who does not want to see Ishmael and Isaac grow up together, asks Abraham to cast Hagar out. Which he does, with the blessing of God who promises him land for Ishmael anyway. Abraham is made guilt-free by the divine, and Hagar and Ishmael are cast out into the wilderness, the Desert of Paran. That's when Hagar names God, *El Roi*, and does not die, but has an extraordinary vision that enables her to see the well that is hidden in the desert and to save her son. That is how Islam began.

Hagar: the only one who named God. Hagar: who does not appear in the texts. Hagar: who the ancient scriptures overlooked in favour of the official wife, Sarah. Perhaps as a way of erasing the dishonourable memory of that servant girl, the whore, who should have been nothing more than a womb. Hagar: the first rebel. Not describing her, not telling her story, means forgetting her. Forgetting who the mother of Ishmael was and why women have had to be covered up ever since. Hagar's mistake was communicating with God. She was able to name him—she named him without dying—and he was able to answer her—and she saw the well, even though it was invisible to the human eye. That was possible because of her third eye, which is inconveniently placed on a woman's forehead. Herein lies the woman's superpower: the third eye on her forehead. Paradoxically, it is this special relationship with God that transforms the woman into a danger for men. She has a power that she is not allowed to use. The woman in Islam is an eye that knows the path to God but has no right to take it.

There is yet another woman, a temptress: Ruqayyah. A Lilith, just as forgotten as the Lilith who wanted to be on top when she and Adam made love. Ruqayyah crosses paths with the father of Muhammad, on the day Muhammad is conceived, after an incredible sequence in which Muhammad's grandfather is about to sacrifice (murder) his son, but does not do it, sacrificing camels instead, for some Oedipal reason that is never really addressed. In exchange for his life, his son must go and live with the woman that his benevolent father has selected for him. On the way they meet Ruqayyah. She fancies Muhammad's father; she wants him right there and then. But Muhammad's father has no choice: he has just been saved by his father who wanted to kill him, so it is not exactly the moment to go against his wishes. He ditches Ruqayyah, promising her that he will return. Muhammad's father makes love to the woman his father has chosen for him. Then, clearly still obsessed with Ruqayyah, he makes his way back and finds her there. But she no longer wants him. The light on the forehead of Muhammad's father had disappeared. The seed of the prophet that Ruqayyah saw in him had inseminated another woman. He was no longer interesting to this woman, who had seen the mark of God on the forehead of the prophet's father. Another woman who *saw*. Another woman who knew the language of God.

Khadija, the prophet's first wife, also had something on her head. Before the revelation of the Angel Jibreel, Muhammad experienced visions. He heard the rocks and the hills talking, he saw a being whose head touched the sky and whose feet touched the ground, and who tried to carry him away. Worried he was going mad, he eventually confided in his wife Khadija. She didn't panic but told him to let her know if he ever saw anything like that again. One day, Muhammad had a vision in his house and he called for Khadija, who clutched him to her breast, took off her veil and showed her hair. Then she asked her husband if the vision was still there; Muhammad replied that it had gone. Khadija told him to rejoice, because 'It is not a demon, but an angel!' What would have happened if Muhammad hadn't confided in his wife and if she had not had her third eye to scare away the angel? Because the angel is modesty and does not benefit from the unveiling of women. Muhammad could be confident: he was ready to receive the revelation. It is therefore on the bosom of a woman that the revelation is revealed. Without Khadija unveiling herself there would have been no revelation and no prophet.

The women of the myths are strong and powerful. They see. They communicate. When Hagar, Ruqayyah and Khadija ask a question, God answers them. So why? Why has this privileged relationship with God been transformed into a danger to men? Why have men decided to cling on to this aspect alone: the denial of a woman's power? The woman is covered so she doesn't talk. She is covered so she cannot talk to God. She can talk only to her father, her brother, her husband. The path to God has been cut off by men, so jealous are they of her power.

As a child, face-to-face with my teacher Mr. Clean-Your-Hands, I could sense my power. His refusal to look me in the eye and his discomfort—so blatant, especially to a child—made me realize what a woman could do. Years later, when I discovered Hagar, Ruqayyah and Khadija, I was excited to discover the power I shared with other women throughout history and even angrier to see that at the beginning of time, woman was already a danger, and that the issue of her place in society was not even being raised. She had to be hidden. Already.

Years have passed since the veil of my childhood. Although I have read a lot, learned a lot, thought a lot, the sensation of a veil over my head always pains me. The idea of going back to Tehran and seeing the landscape of my childhood again is impossible for me: I would have to cover my head. Even if it was colourful, even untied or unfastened, I just don't know if I could play ball. Yet when I visit a church and my shoulders are bare, I don't mind covering them. I respect those who believe as long as they respect me as a non-believer. I play the game when both sides agree. But even today, in the streets of my childhood, I refuse to play the game. It is forced on me. I don't want to play any more.

Paris, 1990

I'm boooooooooored! The girls are boring and the boys are dumb. I am bored out of my brain. I turn thirteen, then fourteen, and frankly, it's not even funny. I am well aware that it was not just down to my friends. Or my lack of friends. My parents were trying to work out how to educate me in Paris and I still didn't know how to behave. I had a hard time understanding children my own age. I was on a totally different wavelength. The girls used to get together to watch endless Roch Voisine or Bruel concerts, telling each other their innermost secrets, which would be all over the school playground the following day. The boys were already interested in pretty girls, a category of teen I hardly fell into. I did have some friends, but I would always rock up to the 'girly afternoons' with a behind-the-scenes documentary on *Gone with the Wind* or *Amarcord*. In both cases, they were a resounding flop. I was just over fifteen years old before I was accepted into a group of boys and I could share in their penchant for the likes of Kubrick and Visconti, Coppola and *Star Wars*. But until that blessed day came, I had only girls to share with and we had nothing in common to share. What struck me in particular about that time were the different groups of girls and how impossible it was to fit in with any of them. There was the top-of-the-class group, all shy and lacking in repartee, who didn't smoke behind the bike sheds and who generally weren't allowed to go out; and then there was the group of pretty girls, who didn't give a fuck and wore make-up and went out with boys. The problem was that neither group had any particular interests, anything to talk about or any curiosity for anything. They barely knew what they wanted to do when they grew up; but they already knew the names of their future offspring. They were all obsessed with boys: the former group with their favourite singers and actors, and the latter with real, live boys. The only thing they talked about was boys, and the only books they read were the ones on the school curriculum. I remember how at fifteen, I took my 'top-of-the-class' school friends to the cinema to see Oliver Stone's *JFK*. They only agreed to go because Kevin Costner was 'sooo good-looking'. At the end of the film, my five friends were fast asleep, while I was absolutely blown away. I didn't understand them and they didn't understand me, and that was hard to accept, for a girl who wanted so desperately to be a girl. They also found me weird (and still do): *The Exorcist* was incomprehensible to young girls who loved Sunday school—because there were boys there—and who were used to seeing crucifixes on the walls at home; *A Clockwork Orange* was a disgusting film, *The Red and the Black* was just boring. Then there was my love of politics. I had very quickly come to understand the link between Khomeini and politics, and it was clear that to avoid another 'old man in black and white' scenario, I had to be interested in politics. There is nothing more off-putting than politics to teenage girls who are eagerly awaiting their first kiss with the impatience of virgins. And they were all shocked by my bedroom walls; my mother however had insisted that I cover up the nudes—for the first birthday party I had at home. The girls looked at me with their big girl-eyes before pouting in disgust, obviously beginning to think that I was into girls, not boys.

Today—with the famous hindsight that allows me to remember without burying my head under my pillow in shame—I know that the total lack of understanding surrounding me was also because of their habits, patterns and traditions. Their year was punctuated by visits to grandparents, family get-togethers at Easter and Christmas, the infamous Mothers' Day, summer holidays or visits 'back home'. We did not even have those visits back home. We had no home to go back to, we were political refugees; we were stateless. We didn't even have family any more, even though we lived in the same area. Although we celebrated Christmas and did an Easter egg hunt, we had no grandparents to visit, no family home where we could spend the holidays. I spent my summers in Paris with my books and I had nothing else to talk about when we went back to school. Meanwhile my classmates had all experienced their first loves, discovered their bodies, and come back beautifully tanned. We simply lived different lives and when they occasionally asked me why, they thought I was lying when I started telling them about Tehran. I had to dig out the photos of our house and my mother's designer dresses before they could accept the notion that once upon a time, my family had been (very) wealthy. I even showed them my school photos so they could see me wearing the headscarf. My family, the four of us, lived in a two-room apartment, yet my mother still served caviar toasts to my friends when they came round. She wore Lanvin tailored jackets while she wiped children's bottoms. I admit I would have found it hard to believe such a fall from grace and such odd vestiges of a former life, if I was not such an avid reader of novels.

There was not a lot I could do but wait: I had not lived in France long enough to bond with teens my own age. I didn't have a grandma who made a mean *tarte aux pommes*, was a downhill skiing champion or an ace at beach volleyball. And my life and my passions did not interest them, because they did not see the use in them. They were in their rightful place, in a world where they knew the rules, and were not thinking about how Balzac could save them from imminent danger. I needed to share my passions, and my friends got bored of me. It is funny that years later—I was thirty-one or thirty-two—a very funny, charming man who had tried his luck with me (in vain), saw me scare off a man I liked, following a conversation about libertine literature versus pornography. He called me up drunk in the middle of the night to tell me, 'If you want to get off with him, you need to learn to shut up!' I had the very unpleasant sensation of being thirteen again and my aunt telling me, 'If you want to make friends then stop banging on about Stendhal.' I have never known how to get off with guys. The good thing about your teenage years is that they eventually end, and from being a weirdo, I grew up into an eccentric. Which makes it a lot easier to make friends.

Paris, 1991–1992

Call it a burning need for independence, call it a need for a female role model or call it provocation, even. Provocation that was not too far off my childhood nudity and that went well beyond the nudes posted up on my bedroom walls. But whores, the famous whores of my childhood, were incarnated by the great courtesans and I cited them as examples whenever I could. At school they were the subject of my presentations and at the dinners my parents dragged me to, they were always on the tip of my tongue. Much to my poor mother's great dismay.

I might not have had real friends, but I invented them for myself. I might have had a body that embarrassed me above all else and that I still didn't know what to do with, but I imagined myself inside the bodies of my imaginary friends—not in the way you're thinking. I made them live inside my closed world and I talked to them when life got too tough. Before Thérèse and Madame de Saint-Ange, before Juliette and Fanny Hill, between the nudes in my bedroom and *Histoire de Dom Bougre, Portier des Char-treux [The Life and Adventures of Father Silas]* there were the great courtesans. Of course, hearing the word 'whore' at every turn, from every mouth, it was inevitable that I would develop a keen interest in them one day. I was fourteen and I had no friends. And the great courtesans took their place, and have never left me.

It began with La Belle Otero, in the memoirs of Colette. They are backstage at a music hall and waiting to go on stage, when Otero takes the opportunity to *educate* her younger companion, '*Don't forget that there is always a moment in a man's life, even if he's a miser, when he opens his hand wide ...*' Colette asks, '*The moment of passion?*' '*No,*' replies La Belle Otero, '*The moment when you twist his wrist.*'4 She had most probably just fleeced some duke or other, who was deemed to be unfleeceable. Was it just a witty remark? No, it was more than that: it was a warrior's confession. She had such an effect on me that I dreamed of meeting women like that and I wanted to know everything about the courtesans of the early twentieth century. La Belle Otero was born in Galicia, was raped at the age of ten or twelve, before being thrown out by her charming pious family; she then met a man who was essentially a pimp who eventually took her to Paris, where she decided to leave him to his seedy ways and went off to make her fortune completely independently. La Belle Otero was dependent on nobody and nothing, apart from her love of gambling. She ended up nearly a hundred years old and completely ruined, in Nice, a stone's throw from a casino that paid for her food and lodgings by way of thanks for all the money she and her wealthy lovers had brought them, the absolute fortune she had squandered there. There was no great love of her life, as far as we know. She is the antithesis of the Lady of the Camellias, and it is invigorating. She had a bank account in her own name—which was impossible for all other women at the time, whether aristocratic, bourgeois or working class—and she alone managed her purse strings, while infuriating all the crowned heads of Europe. She drove a number of her wealthy lovers to suicide. She could not care less. All she wanted was to never go hungry, and to be famous. Discovering La Belle Otero at the age of fourteen was ... wow! There is nothing shameful about La Belle Otero: she represented the female body really making its mark in style, right at the heart of the Second Empire. She was the first model to be dressed by Boucheron in undergarments embroidered with precious stones, which shows just how celebrated her body was. La Belle Otero was vulgar, flashy and erotic. She was not what you would call subtle: her rivalry with Liane de Pougy—which was talked about voraciously in the society news of the time—is a reflection of her fiery Spanish temperament. Picture it: one evening at the opera, everyone is eagerly awaiting the entrance of the two women. La Belle Otero, who has just unceremoniously dumped her famous lover, makes her entrance first: she arrives wearing literally ALL of her jewellery, covered head to toe with the rarest gemstones. The only sound that breaks the silence is the chink of pearls, diamonds and rubies moving against the body of La Belle Otero, who is very pleased with herself. Suddenly

Liane de Pougy steals the limelight by making her own extraordinary entrance: she is wearing only a minimalist diamond necklace. But she is followed in by her maid, carrying all of her mistress's jewellery on a red cushion. La Belle Otero was beaten that evening, but I prefer her crude frankness to Liane's bourgeois hypocrisy. Liane was more refined: raised in a convent, married at sixteen, she left her husband at nineteen and because of her slender physique, intelligence and upbringing, she soon became very rich. She wrote, and her writing showed her preference for women, whom she adored. Men were nothing but a source of money to her; a fact that in no way deterred them from pursuing this nymphet, at the cost of millions.

La Belle Otero was a courtesan who knew how to handle language and intellect. What she lacked in culture she made up for in witty remarks and pragmatism. She had known for a long time that in the end, men are always just men, and that a courtesan who falls in love is as good as ruined. Suffice to say, she abruptly stole my attention away from *Anna Karenina* or *La Cousine Bette*. I had never come across a woman like her. La Belle Otero would have scared the shit out of Khomeini! And she never sold her body for money; I mean, they say that she let herself be supported by men (as did married women), who had no more rights over her body than what she gave them (unlike married women). When she didn't feel like making love, her lovers just had to lump it. Which they did, fairly often: she was pretty sparing with her body. These days she would be a multi-divorcée billionaire who makes her fortune by bedding wealthy men.

There would be nothing revolutionary about her. But in the old days when women had not yet moved into the public arena, La Belle Otero and her fellow courtesans were the only truly free women. La Belle Otero was not a sell-out; she lived in a partnership, until the partner's bank account was empty. I don't think she could have been unhappy: she made a choice and she stuck with it. Although gambling was her downfall, she was nobody's victim but her own.

La Belle Otero, with her verbal witticisms, her high-flown attitude, her gambling vice, her financial independence and her unusually free spirit, could have scared away an army of Beards and Crows with a flutter of an eyelash! Not to mention her body. She had such an affinity with her own body, was so at ease with it that she made me feel okay about being a woman again. She had chosen and accepted that she would never be anyone's victim. She therefore became my best friend. And as for my mother, my aunts, and my female 'friends', she was the best comeback I could hurl at them.

Paris, 2013

One afternoon as I was trying to gather my thoughts before writing, I was walking along the edge of the Bassin de l'Arsenal, in the Bastille area. I saw a group of teenage girls there who couldn't have been more than fourteen years old. I slowed down my pace so I could eavesdrop a bit. A word jumped out at me. *Whore.* Still the same old subject of whores, then. The girls were talking loudly, brashly. Just your average teenagers, having to be loud to get themselves heard. They were talking about a whore, who was a really dirty whore, who had dared, the whore, to buy the skirt that one of the girls wanted and that she had to save up for because, 'my mum's not a bourgeois bitch like hers,' and so on. Whore, whore, whore. Naturally, I started to think about everything that the word 'whore' encompassed. In the mouths of the women of my childhood, as well as those teenagers. The whore is essentially everything they are not, so she is naturally the enemy. She is a traitor, of course. And often, very often, she is sensual. Treacherous and sensual go well together; it's the pairing that steals husbands away, destroys marriages and buys herself the coveted skirt. The whore often has no female friends and she is perhaps just as lost as those girls, and there is probably someone that she calls a whore too. I sighed all the way home, wondering if all women are condemned to be one another's whores.

I thought about my childhood and all the women who sought out the whore in all the others and suddenly, I thought I heard Hagar in their voices. What if Hagar was the 'mould' for all women who so quickly become whores? Hagar was only a slave girl who had to obey her mistress and give herself to her master. She had been nothing more than a womb for Sara and Abram before they both got their *h*. Hagar was nothing more than a piece of flesh before she was cast out. Even though some think that the concubine Abraham married after Sarah's death was Hagar returning. Hagar saved Ishmael from death by seeing the well that God had shown her, yet she is only remembered for being a whore. Not a mother, not the founding woman of Islam.

In the mouths of women during my childhood, there was, perhaps, an insult to that first woman: the one who dared to name God and the reason why all women have been punished ever since. Maybe without even knowing it, it is Hagar they insult and avidly search out—perhaps through fascination—in every other woman. Maybe the woman whose attitude seems too liberal, who has decided to free herself of her veil and walk under the heavens with her third eye, who has chosen her life and tells it like it is—without shame—maybe this is the woman who has a little of Hagar about her. And she is so reviled, so erased, that the only thing we remember about her is that she was a whore.

Although teenage girls looked at me with vague disgust when I sang the praises of the courtesans, it never bothered me. Although my mother might have shuddered when I regaled her, half in Persian, half in French, with the life stories of my favourite courtesans, I never cared. I knew more about whores than they did and it made me sad that they could not grasp the immense power that the courtesans held in their hands. The boudoirs or dining rooms of the courtesans—from ancient times up to the Belle Époque—hosted the most influential politicians and the most prominent (or obscure) artists. Just by being there, they made speech free. They set the tone; they summoned the world to their tables. The reason they were so sought after, why important men—and some important women—were so keen to sit at their sides, is that they did not abstain from anything, they allowed themselves everything; because their bodies were so free, the spirit followed suit. And culture, too. They must have known how to converse, how to spark a debate or revive a scandal. The courtesans are the descendants of the *hetaerae* of ancient Greece, such as Aspasia—the famous companion of Pericles, who used to entertain Sophocles and Socrates—or Leontion, the companion of Epicurus, and a philosopher herself. They were the only women in ancient times that had permission to manage their own property. Just like Émilienne d'Alençon and Sarah Bernhardt, centuries later. You were certainly not slumming it with the courtesans. You were putting the world to rights, exchanging banned books; you were meeting fellow free thinkers. The salons of the courtesans were like a free zone where everything was permitted.

The courtesans did more for the dissemination of ideas than the ministry lobbies did. From Phryne, who won over her judges by revealing her magnificent naked body—being tried for introducing a new religion to Athens which perverted young girls, Praxiteles' model was defended by her lover, the famous Hypereides, and escaped the death penalty thanks to her womanly *ass*ets—to Madame Pompadour who left her mark on French history and history of art, to Coco Chanel, who liberated women's bodies from their corsets and helped to bring them into the public arena, helping women assert themselves first and foremost through their bodies. But this body has no influence unless it is accompanied by education and independence. These women are not vulgar whores. It is not even their legendary beauty that makes them interesting. They have survived against the odds, over time, because they are the essential steps toward the independence of women. Nudity alone is not enough. If Phryne was just a body, no matter how perfect it was, she certainly would not have been saved by it. She had something else: culture, intelligence, and the certainty of being as guiltless as a man could be, and it is this that saved her from death. Phryne considered herself equal to a man. She earned her living by posing as a model and she made money from her presence, both intellectual and sexual. Let's not take men—even great men—for fools: they would not spend that much money just to get their leg over. These women are not one-night-stand women. They are the opposite of those who sleep with someone the first night, after randomly meeting them on a dating website. The courtesans were the pioneers of women's liberation and they certainly would not give their body to just anyone. Today, women's bodies are on sale every day. And we think of all this as progress! No, sorry, it's just that now women have a fulfilling sex life. So you say. You say it loud and proud, and immediately afterwards, you are crying on your best friend's shoulder because *he* hasn't called. Fulfilling, yes. For two hours. And then it's all, 'Whhhhyyyyyyyy?' But at least they earn their own livings, and that's the main thing. The great courtesans said this to themselves every day.

Some might think that this ancestry seems rather dishonourable. But they are wrong: the courtesans were clearly much freer than the 'respectable' women—who were still involved in the same financial exchanges through marriage, when all they did was be looked after by men their whole lives. They didn't even have power over their dowry! The only difference was the official nature of marriage and the unofficial nature of concubinage. Respectable women had been sold according to the rule of law, while the others were clandestine. I have always preferred the margins of society; they tend to hold much more promise than the mainstream.

The courtesans were single women and they were by no means fools. Many—if not all—tried to buy back a reputation for themselves by winning a husband whose name and rank would conveniently mask her past: a past deemed unsuitable in society's eyes. Thus, Liane de Pougy married Prince Ghika, before becoming a nun in a convent, to which she bequeathed her enormous fortune. La Païva never stopped rewriting her own story, multiplying variations as she aged, inventing and forgetting, a wonderful storyteller of herself. La Païva, who—living in luxury in her mansion on the Champs-Élysées, married to a real duke, who really loved her—entertained high society, dining and philosophizing beneath a ceiling where the splendid naked body of their hostess was ironically displayed ... They always ended up dreaming of being in high society and being accepted everywhere. There is always a moment where the courtesan begins to dream of respectability and that is precisely when I get bored of them. That's why I prefer La Belle Otero to all the others. She was less foolish than the others, and even prouder.

Ninon de Lenclos had this superior quality. Like Colette, the only female writer who was honoured with a state funeral (along with Victor Hugo, Maurice Barres, Paul Valéry and Aimé Césaire). Colette defined herself as a 'mental hermaphrodite'. In other words, she was able to rid herself of the gender norms as a point of reference. She considered her state of mind as mixed. And it is this quality that enabled her to start out as a ghostwriter for her lover, then become a music-hall star and finally, end up a renowned and respected woman of letters. Fame certainly erases everything, but with Colette, there is a genuine link between her respectable achievement—she never denied her youth—and her ability to think beyond the male-female. Whatever was lawful for a man, she saw no reason not to apply to a woman. She forged ahead with this certainty even in her private life, when—just as men who have everything soon get bored—she took a man twenty years her junior for a lover. He was also the son of her second husband, Henry de Jouvenel. A century later, Woody Allen did the same thing when he married his adopted daughter. I hear people still griping about Colette's escapades with her step-son, yet nobody seems to find it strange for a man to marry a woman that he potentially groomed from a young age to become his ideal future bride.

Needless to say, everything began for Colette—without Willy—on a theatre stage. Liberated from Willy, she bared her breasts and kissed her partner Missy, who was also her mistress. Colette, as if to resoundingly affirm her newfound independence, began by unveiling herself. Asserting herself, in total freedom and without any regard for what was or wasn't 'the done thing'. It was reassuring for me, as an angry teenager: there were many intelligent women who had gone through an unveiling.

Later, when I discovered the work and personality of Élisabeth Badinter, I had the same feeling toward her book. *L'Amour en plus: histoire de l'amour maternel (XVIIe-XXe siècle)* demonstrates that the maternal instinct does not exist. It is just a political, economic and cultural construction. Women are not *naturally* inclined to love their children. Élisabeth Badinter showed the absurdity of believing that women are born to have children, to love them and to create men who will give children to other women, who will in turn love their offspring, all because it is in their *true* nature. Badinter unveils women by freeing them of the prejudice that dictates that a feminine nature exists separately from a masculine nature. The only things that exist are education and culture, and in these areas women can be completely equal to men.

It is all about placing the woman at the centre of the political debate and not in a naturalistic perspective, which is her eternal purgatory. I never wanted to make a distinction between courtesans and intellectuals.

Paris, 1993

On the first day of the summer holidays, my father and I would take the bus to Saint-Michel, and the large second-hand bookshop there. In the paperback section I was allowed to choose what I wanted, as long as it fitted in the shopping basket provided. With more than two months in Paris stretching ahead of me, I had to keep myself occupied. So without any method at all, unlike my father, I would choose novels (which had to have the black or red sticker on the back indicating they were in the sale), just by the title, or the author. There was *The Grapes of Wrath* and *The Women's Room, Behind the Glass* or *Howards End, Clock without Hands, The Horsemen* or *Memoirs of a Dutiful Daughter*. There was the charm of a name like Carson McCullers that excited me, or a title that promised a thousand adventures, a thousand feelings, a thousand escapes, such as *The Diamond as Big as the Ritz*. On the first night of that long summer of 1993, my father showed me the film *Dark Eyes* by Nikita Mikhalkov. It was incredible. The impossible love, the beautiful sets, the pervasive melancholy; as a sixteen-year-old teen who had never been in love, I fell in love with that film. I was still under the spell of Marcello Mastroianni as I perused the multicoloured spines of the second-hand books. Suddenly, there it was: *Les Yeux Noirs*. I picked it up and read the back cover: '*Les Yeux Noirs' are three sisters, Hélène, Marie and Louise, the daughters of the poet José-Maria de Heredia. Of Cuban origin, promiscuous, brazen and voluptuous, they flaunt their charms in the late nineteenth and early twentieth century, amidst a remarkably brilliant society of writers and poets, from Marcel Proust to Pierre Louÿs, Henry de Régnier to Paul Valéry.* The only names I knew were Proust and Valéry. The author of the book, Dominique Bona, was completely unknown to me, and she was alive: apart from Rushdie I only liked dead writers. All of this had nothing to do with Marcello but I started reading the book anyway.

So I chose to start the summer with the Heredia sisters. I spent the night with them. That summer promised to be the most beautiful summer of my teenage years because I was drunk, not on words, but on love. I had just fallen in love with Pierre Louÿs. I wanted to read everything, know everything. He was romantic and iconoclastic, funny and adventurous, romantic and sensual. He was the perfect lover; the perfect man. But Pierre Louÿs was also the most prolific, fun and brilliant of the erotic authors. He wrote about the female body in all senses, in exquisite detail. He lived only for women—exclusively brunettes, whose pussy, in his words, became *that obscure object of desire*—old books, and literature. I was in love with him *and* I wanted to be him: tormented, temperamental, a free thinker who appreciated beautiful things and works of art. My father, who was at first frankly puzzled by my new passion, helped me to find the lost works, the out-of-print works, the erotic works of Pierre Louÿs. It was a treasure hunt, made even more enjoyable because I was sharing my first love with my father. This detail, which seemed pretty unbelievable to my friends at the time, did not even occur to me: the fact that my father helped me discover erotic literature (verging on pornography) when I was just over sixteen years old. My father, who I addressed with the formal *'vous'* until I was twenty. My father, who never found my interests weird. It never even occurred to my father to think that all the cocks and cunts, all the dildos and sodomy might be disturbing for a teenage virgin. And all that was apparently less offensive than the stripteases in the *Collaricocoshow*. It is because my father could not imagine that anything bad could happen in literature; because he firmly believed that there is no crime worse than censorship; because he believed, to quote Diderot, in the idea that *'it's a matter of getting some benefits out of bad company, just like out of being a libertine. You get compensation for the loss of innocence by also losing your prejudices,'*[5] that he naturally supported me when it came to reading, learning and inspiration. Even when it came to Pierre Louÿs and his sensual writing, his casual attitude to morality, his obsession with pure beauty, the bitterness of his novelistic style, my father was the same. The fact that my friends were sceptical, to say the least, about the freedom I had when it came to books, was further proof of the stupidity of educational methods that allow fifteen-year-old girls to wear the clothes and make-up of thirty-somethings, but punish them for reading a dirty book. If they were at least allowed to do both, they would not find reality so confusing.

Pierre Louÿs had taken me by the hand and not only taught me to love Love, but above all he taught me to be able to laugh about sex. About the body and all its romantic and sensual combinations. His descriptions of the female body—the hair, armpits, odours, anus, arms and buttocks—were filled with such lightness and such adoration, that you would have to be completely devoid of humour not to be touched by it. He made the body less daunting in such a stylish way that I learned to love my own. And that is how, as if by magic, I lost my excess weight, without even making an effort to diet. But Pierre Louÿs also had the dramatic thread that I needed for my anger: a refusal to combine eternity and love, to compromise, to give up on a piece of freedom, to accept prejudices that imprison the body, to play by society's rules. However, Pierre Louÿs ended up disappointing me, as a lover might disappoint you after a few months, when flesh is no longer enough to maintain the bond and you actually have to talk about your core beliefs. Pierre Louÿs was anti-Semitic, and he also despised Protestants who despised the body. He was homophobic but he loved Oscar Wilde—even though he abandoned him during his trial. He had crippling weaknesses. He hated Zola because he had brought politics into art—which was unacceptable for a follower of Mallarmé. Super Tolerance Man had educated me, however, and although I found out that a lot of the authors I worshipped were anti-Semitic—including Voltaire who combined anti-Semitism, Islamophobia, homophobia, racism and slavery—I like to think that, if I had been born in the same era, I wouldn't have been on the same side. I had spent four years at the Collège Anne Frank, her *Diary of a Young Girl* was on our compulsory reading list. I had cried so much and so deeply loved that girl who was the same age as me and who wrote so beautifully, that I could not even comprehend the notion of anti-Semitism. The first families that had accepted us when we arrived in France were Jewish families who, unlike the Muslims in our neighbourhood, did not hold our atheism against us.

I had to face facts: Pierre Louÿs did not understand much about politics but he was still a great writer. And I could always cheat on him with Zola. My romantic encounter with Pierre Louÿs was accompanied by the realization of another love. Because Pierre Louÿs was *my* discovery, and mine alone, because he seemed typically French to me—elegant, bohemian, alluring, erudite—by falling in love with Pierre Louÿs I married France. I appropriated the Belle Époque of Louÿs as if it were my own past. I walked around Paris, to the places where Pierre Louÿs had lived; I found out what he liked to eat, the cafes he frequented, his favourite tailors, the fashions that thrilled him, the newspapers he read, and so French culture descended from its literary pedestal and landed on my plate. I can talk about that era as if I actually lived through it. Later, I dug into the French Revolution and the Second World War with the same appetite, and my inconvenient wandering into the past always led to teasing from my friends. I knew the past of their great-grandparents better than they did, and it was another way of creating a shared past with them. However illusory it might be. The exile clings to any available branch.

I was in love with Louÿs like my friends were in love with gorgeous pop stars. It was all in the realm of the imagination; the stuff of daydreams. In short, it was all very chaste and it never occurred to me to put into practice the erotic teachings of Pierre Louÿs—at least not before I was the right age. Paradoxically, reading mostly salacious descriptions of sex, laughing at the plays on words and the slapstick situations that arise from human desire, only made me respect my body more. I didn't just want to *have sex*—no girl wants to just have sex, even though most of them end up doing so. I wanted to discover everything, go deeper into everything; I wanted to share that with someone who was as curious as me, as non-judgemental as me. I wanted to be in love and make love, but tastefully. I didn't know exactly what I meant by that, but I wanted the notorious 'first time' that all girls are obsessed with to happen with all the possible respect my body deserved. My body had cost me too much up to that point, there was no way I would forget all that under the pretext of hormones or peer pressure. So as my friends were losing their virginities, amidst the tears and confusion, I waited patiently for a man smarter than the others to snap me up. And that is what happened. I have always made love very tastefully, ever since the first time. It was out of the question for me to sell off that body cheaply: that body was my entire history, it was mine, and had been the subject of so much discussion by everyone including Khomeini and my friends, my mother and my aunts. The erotic literature of Pierre Louÿs had not turned me into a depraved, shameless woman, but one who was extremely sensitive to the importance of sexual pleasure in love. The body was no longer that of the *Ta'ziyeh*, it was no longer a landscape of suffering and bad memories. It became a vibrant and irreverent instrument in the service of intellectual and moral freedom. And without my first love and his erotic poetry, I would never have worked this out.

I still collect illustrated and first editions of the works of Pierre Louÿs, but also of Marie de Régnier, Henri de Régnier, early Gide, Jean de Tinan and José-Maria de Heredia. My heart still beats faster when, perusing a bookstall, I happen to see the name Pierre Louÿs awaiting my avid collector's fetish. One day, when I was completely broke, I was strolling through the antique and second-hand book market in the Parc Georges Brassens. I was looking for the cheapest second-hand books I could find, when a first edition of *Aphrodite* and *The Trophies* by Jose Maria Heredia, in a white leather-bound cover, made me instantly blind to the fact that there were still two weeks until the end of the month. I bartered, which I can never normally bring myself to do, and I got the two books for ninety-five euros. Needless to say, I ended the month practically dying of starvation.

Ashamed, and with a touch of guilt—as my parents were struggling to make ends meet—in the end I told my father the story. I was expecting him to yell at me, to try and drill some sense into me, but instead he just smiled. He was smiling because his daughter, without realizing it, was behaving like Pierre Louÿs, choosing antique books over a piece of meat. He was smiling because he had a daughter who loved literature above all else. He was smiling because we didn't have much, but we did have that. We still had Louÿs and all the others, who we were lucky enough to take refuge with, to forget that we had never travelled, never been carefree, never had a bit of peace and quiet.

Paris, 2013

The education I received was far from perfect, and my suffering at not being able to talk to my father except through books remains to this day one of my most painful memories. However, I would not swap my education for any other. Nowadays, when I see friends becoming parents themselves, it is rare for me not to get the urge to put Pierre Louÿs books in the cradles of their offspring. Especially if they are girls.

Let's not even talk about the disturbing need that mothers seem to have to transform their daughters into unbearable princesses (who will only end up realizing that in fact they aren't and will suffer for it the rest of their lives). And let's focus on the fathers—again. Men my age, men who—while they describe all the women they have slept with and never called as free and consenting—when it comes to the free and consenting bodies of their daughters, frown and make speeches worthy of the most talented Beards. Suddenly, girls no longer have the right to be free, or don't have the right to go out with boys, or can no longer laugh at dirty jokes. These are teachers, senior execs or actors, but when they become fathers, they are all limited men. Limited by an ancestral fear: imagining their daughters having a sex life. It is this possessiveness that is so unhealthy. As for the little girl, who, literally from the cradle, hears from her father's mouth, that he will kill the first boy she falls in love with? It's ... how can I put it? Paralysing? Destructive? Why should girls not have the right to have a body? I would love little girls to be congratulated like little boys, and loudly, for all the potential hearts they can break with their *derrière*.

There is always some lunch or other, where a dozen adults are cooing over a little boy with big green eyes and everyone applauds the future hearts he will break. There is always some lunch or other, where a dozen adults are cooing over a little girl with curly blonde hair and everyone laughs and applauds the father as he imitates the machine gun that will annihilate the first man who dares to come near his daughter. There is always some lunch or other where a dozen adults reproduce, without batting an eyelid, the ancestral reflexes that fundamentally distinguish girls from boys. There is always some lunch or other where a dozen adults make me want to throw my arms round my father.

I had never appreciated the true worth of my father's tolerance. He had to put up with condemnation from everyone for his choice of education. 'What education?' my father would reply. Yes. What education? An education that refuses to destroy—or to completely mark out—the path that children take to adulthood. The fact that he was a father who was authoritative without raising his voice, who was not very affectionate due to his crippling shyness, who was not very encouraging because he was so pragmatic, does not in any way diminish how good a father he was to me. He wanted me to be independent which meant aware. He refused to see me living in a bubble of innocence, being drip-fed absurd morality—which involved acting as if sex did not exist, or drugs or violence or emotional misery.

So when I was the right age—seventeen—to start going out with friends, my father and I had a little *tête-a-tête* with a bottle of whiskey. My mother and my little brother were spending the Saturday with friends; we were alone with our piles of books and three films to watch. My father opened the bottle and made me drink. It was the first time I had ever drunk heavily—although my father had let me taste wine from the age of thirteen, to *learn*. This memorable first piss-up was also my last. My father could let me go out with peace of mind: I would not throw myself at the first bottle I saw and I would never end any evening dead drunk. And he was right. I have never had to use the old bullshit excuse to justify my stupid behaviour, 'I was drunk.' What was true for alcohol was true for everything else. One shouldn't look for excuses.

Paris, 1994

Meeting in our local cafe. Drinking half pints of beer, paid for in centimes. Provoking without shocking. Confessing without being judged. Sharing literature and cinema. Laughing. Discussing. Being together—all the time, for any reason. Never being alone. It was great being almost seventeen. I was in college now, and far away from the hostile secondary school students of my early teens. It was liberating. I noticed in passing that the social change, from rue Trousseau to rue de Sévigné, was palpable. And although the inhabitants of the Marais were not exempt from prejudice or bullshit, I did feel more accepted. Let's be honest, the cultured daughter of a bourgeois Iranian couple who have become a childminder and a photo lab assistant, following a terrible Revolution and a terrifying war: it appealed to the more bourgeois neighbourhoods of Paris. It was a time when I had not yet realized that this was the position—Iranian political refugee, a victim of history, perfectly mastering French language and culture, with whom everyone always opens a conversation by announcing 'I have an Iranian friend who ... ' as if expecting me to clap my hands and jump for joy—the position that I should occupy if I wanted to carry on being accepted. So although I could see that everyone was talking to me about Iran, and I was answering with Pierre Louÿs, we all acted as if it was for the best. Even though I would never get back that absolute confidence that I had as a child, I was once again able to say what I thought. I had friends and they were interested in my interests. It was a victory over my isolation, my doubts and my fear. Khomeini was, for the first time, far, far away from me. He was confined to childhood and the early years of exile. From afar, I looked like your average Parisian.

It was a Saturday in May. We had a two-hour French class from 8 a.m. to 10 a.m. We had spent the Friday evening at the house of a friend; her parents were away and we had stayed up all night. We were a group of five girls still smelling slightly of booze, our eyes glistened from sleep deprivation, and the end of the school year was close. Everything was going well; we already thought we were big girls. It was the day when we got back our final essays on the subject of *Dangerous Liaisons*, by Choderlos de Laclos. There was a body of texts to study, and if I remember correctly, we had to demonstrate, through a series of letters, Merteuil's developing behaviour toward Valmont. I had not yet read the novel, but I already liked Merteuil. There was one letter where, already with a hint of bitterness, she describes the status of women. She said that she was born to dominate the male sex and avenge her own. She spoke to me; she was naturally kin to me. A heroine for sure! I was confident; I was sure that my essay was good. I was right, I got an excellent mark. But as I was reading through the teacher's comments, I noticed that she had crossed out in red every time I had applied the common noun 'heroine' to Merteuil. I put my hand up. I didn't understand. She told me that 'antihero' was acceptable but certainly not 'heroine'. Merteuil was not a heroine; she was a wicked woman who lived for evil. 'No, I don't agree.' I refused to let it drop, I had not read the novel, I lacked arguments, but I could not abandon Merteuil. Maybe it was tiredness, or hormones, or it was just that I was a bigmouth and wanted to impress my classmates. I carried on the debate, loudly, to mask the fact that I didn't have any concrete arguments. I asked my French teacher if she thought Rastignac was a hero, if Aurelian was a hero. Does the hero have to be a victim? In any case, by paying for her fate with death, Merteuil became a heroine. 'No, Abnousse, she isn't a positive character. She doesn't represent anything good. She has no morals. She does not evolve.' I couldn't believe my ears! 'Oh, really? And why is that? She defends herself as best she can, she is manipulative because she has no choice; she is a reflection of her times. And Madame de Tourvel, is she a heroine because she is a humanitarian? And Cécile de Volanges even more so, because she's an idiot? Shit, Madame, you can't say that!' I could not hold myself back. It came out of its own accord. The teacher did not answer right away, and I didn't hear the heavy silence. I kept thinking how I didn't want to reduce Merteuil to being an anti—just because she had a brain and ambition—and I went on out loud, 'And even if she chooses to use her ambition for evil, she is still a thousand times more romantic, a thousand times more alive than Tourvel or Volanges. She doesn't sit quietly like an idiot by the fireside, waiting for her destiny to come to her, she provokes the world, she plays, she is fucking active, shit!' Another heavy silence, but this time I heard it. I was the only one talking. A student had tried to intervene but I rudely interrupted, the teacher made me stop talking, I sat down, deflated. Then the bell rang. I was not punished; I didn't have any marks deducted from my essay. I might have gone too far, but it was for a good cause and perhaps the teacher might be reminded that I was a (poor) political refugee traumatized by the Revolution, the war, and exile: my own personal Holy Trinity, which can sometimes be used to hide behind without causing too much damage.

That very afternoon, I set about reading *Dangerous Liaisons* at great length. I had to prove to her that Merteuil was a heroine. Or perhaps I wanted to prove it to myself. That equality is when wicked women can be heroines just like wicked men, and especially that nobody should expect women to be victims, gentle, virginal and afraid. I was angry, but I didn't know exactly at whom or at what. When I sought out the heroine in Merteuil, the only expression that could cut it was: *it's not fair.* Merteuil admits her biggest flaw: she is a woman and women are not allowed to be out in the open like men. She is moving; she is angry. Angry because she is revolted at being *just* a woman. I knew how she felt. I understood why she had chosen to destroy reputations, to prove the stupidity of moral confines, to manipulate men and women, to turn everyone who reduced her to being just a woman, into her playthings. She was not just a heroine, she was powerful too. Powerful because she was aware of her status as a woman; powerful because she was intellectually superior to all the other characters; powerful because she was dominant. If all that didn't make her a heroine, then I was screwed. We were all screwed.

A few years later, I understood what I had so vehemently refused to accept in the face-off with my French teacher who had wanted to attach 'anti-' to my first female hero. I understood what I couldn't bear: the destinies of brave women who die so that truth wins out. I understood all of this when I watched the awful film by Lars von Trier, *Breaking the Waves*. The fact that he is a great director does not make any difference. As a woman and an atheist, this film is a declaration of war. The character of Bess, the vile, brainless victim, is the anti-Merteuil, but she has the honour of being a 'heroine'. I was disgusted. The fact that women cry and applaud Bess's absolute love for her husband made me even sicker. I am standing in front of my French teacher again, the Year 11 students of Victor-Hugo college are half asleep waiting for the bell to ring, and I am talking, defending myself, trying to defend single women, women who say 'No', women who don't need love to exist. Meanwhile, other women, other teenage girls dream of giving it all up just to be loved by some pig of a man. But it is art, and prostitution is acceptable when it comes to maintaining the sacred bonds of marriage. On the other hand, my magnificent whores who owed nothing to anyone except their arse and their culture, and who at one time held the most prominent position in Paris, were *real* whores who did not deserve to figure in the history of women. Except the Lady of the Camellias who dies saving a man; who had to die before she became acceptable. Marie Duplessis was definitely the most boring of whores, but under the pretext that she sacrificed herself in order for a man to live, she is still being endlessly played on all the world's stages. I wanted to puke. I got into fights with friends, I even lost friends, I was insulted, but I could never accept *Breaking the Waves* as a film about love. It is a film of religious propaganda; it is a film that demeans women—but also men—which reduces sex to suffering, marriage to purgatory, and death to a release. It is the Nordic version of the *Ta'ziyeh*. Bess, through the camera of Lars von Trier was proof that Merteuil was a heroine. But I never saw my French teacher again to prove it to her.

Merteuil might die alone of smallpox, her reputation forever tainted, society—which she despised and dominated—lost, and yet I hear her sniggering from beyond the grave. She had lost, but she had earned it. She was the author of her own fate and that was what I was trying to shout about on that Saturday morning in May, when suddenly Khomeini rose up in my throat. He wasn't gone. He wasn't even that far away. He reminded me that I was a woman. The battle was not yet won.

Paris, 2013

My mother is telling me about a whore who lived behind a flower shop not far from the big house in Tehran. She says that sometimes, when she was not with a customer in the back room, she would come out and hand out flowers to passers-by. She tells me how this woman thought I was so pretty that she would give me a flower every time we saw her. And each time, my mother would take the flower out of my hands and throw it away when we were out of sight of that florist whore. Then she would wash my hands several times. My mother remembers that this woman was murdered after the Revolution because she went on handing out flowers. I couldn't remember that woman, and my mother told me the story because I was asking her about memories from my childhood. I have tears in my eyes and my mother is shocked. 'Why are you crying? She was just a prostitute.' That was yesterday, my father's birthday, and despite everything (our history, my passions, the veil in France) she still didn't understand my tears. I shouted at her, she told me that prostitutes are sluts and my father calmed us both down, because he knows I am writing and even though he refuses to ask me any questions about it, he knows that *Khomeini, Sade and Me* lays into my family. We will have plenty of time to tear one another apart. Later.

The fact remains that I cry for all the whores of the world. Those who refuse forced marriage, those who want to go to school, those who want to have a career, those who don't want to wear the headscarf, those who don't believe in God. I cry for all those women and little girls who don't lower their gaze in front of men, all those women and girls who don't follow the norm, all those who are ostracized by society, all those who are forced onto the street against their will; all those who suffer because they are women. All of the women who are just different, who refuse to follow the moral diktat and who are therefore called whores. I cry for them, and the fact that my mother smiles about the murder of a woman who was a prostitute makes me cry even more. My mother has never understood anything about the body and has always been afraid of whores, but she is a lovely woman. I would like to make her understand that the body does not bite, that the body is not shameful, that the body is the key to liberation. But I cannot extract her education, her fear, her anxiety from her soul. And I can't keep fighting her. She fought so long and hard just to feed us. She is sixty-five and I can't keep on correcting her, explaining to her that prostitutes are women just like all the rest of us, and perhaps even more so than others. I can't keep telling my mother that the whores are the ones who saved me, while the prudes are the ones who demoted her, made her end up wiping children's arses for thirty years. I can't keep banging on about her education to rid her of her unhappy-little-girl reflexes. I love her too much. Or rather, no, I love her more since I started listening to her without interrupting. Perhaps it's my own madness that scares her. My constant provocation. But I cannot help it, I just can't. It's stronger than me, it's stronger than everything, and it's terribly repetitive for those around me. It's my own madness, it's my special hobby: women who are different, single women, women with a strong voice, naked women, tough women, women who aren't afraid to say 'cock', misunderstood women, disturbed women. I know that I will always shock my mother, just as I shocked my French teacher, my friends, and even my own father. But I would like once, just once, for my mother to remove the veils of her prejudices and take a good look at me. I would like her to cry for the whore who plied her wares in the back room of a flower shop in Tehran, a stone's throw from our big house, and for her to regret having thrown away her flowers and making me wash my hands to erase all contact with the woman she thought was the bad one. If that day came, I wouldn't love my mother more, but I would believe it is possible for things to really change.

Paris, 1995

When we arrived in France, we settled in the Bastille district. We had scarcely set foot on French soil when the history of France grabbed me by the hand. We were still in the taxi when I saw the golden statue of the Génie de la Liberté, on top of the July column in Place de la Bastille. My father very succinctly explained that there used to be a prison there before the French Revolution, but that the statue commemorated the days of July 1848, because several revolutions were always needed to make the Revolution. At first I was scared: Revolution to me meant the Beards, and here was my father, calmly telling me that it was the same in France. Seeing my eyes widen and flicker suspiciously toward the taxi driver, who was dying of curiosity to know what strange language we were talking, my father reassured me: not all revolutions had the same purpose or the same protagonists. In France, the French Revolution was 'something else'. This 'something else' fascinated me from my first day in Paris: what was there about this 'something else' that made it different from the Beards? What was the recipe for making revolutions without killing the woman?

In my childish imagination, I therefore thought that 85, rue de la Roquette—where we lived—was also built on the site of the prison. Especially because the remains of the entrance to the Roquette women's prison are in front of the Père-Lachaise Cemetery and opposite are the slabs where the guillotine would have stood. To me, the whole neighbourhood had sprung up on the site of the former prison. From the Place de la Bastille to Père-Lachaise, there was the victory of the Enlightenment, the trees and the laughter, the schools and the women running for the bus. There was also an evangelist church, furry-tongued tramps collaring passers-by, and a synagogue. There was a church that couldn't be any more Catholic if it tried, and the Théâtre de la Bastille and my father's bookshop—which rapidly transformed into a stationery shop to meet our requirements—and bars that I looked at longingly, dreaming of being a grown-up, sitting there alone with a book and a glass of white wine. And nobody would think anything of it. There was Fify's bar and Madame Renée and her cats, there was the passage Bullourde—nicknamed 'the shit passage' because the smell was so unbearable—there was rue de Lappe, which I was not allowed to go down on my own as it was in a rough area. There was, on every street, at every turn, newness, diversity, colours and voices. Don't laugh: as a child, this was freedom as I imagined it, because nobody seemed to give a damn about what other people thought. We lived between the Théâtre de la Bastille—where my father had an Algerian friend—and the synagogue, that one of my only female friends used to go to, opposite a cafe-restaurant we used to go to, run by a Kabyle family, and which was close to the church where our Portuguese friends used to go. It was already a victory for me. It was proof that people did not care about the others' beards, and that, for me, was wonderful.

I was enthralled to find out that in the streets I walked down, every wall, every paving slab, told the story of how men and women had liberated the prisoners and established Equality. I soon discovered that there were only seven prisoners at the Bastille, including two madmen and three crooks—and Sade until July 1789—but this didn't change the scale of the revolt. It was the prison of the king and his censorship, and it was the prison that had to be liberated before any others. I was still acting as if Napoleon and the Consulate, the Empire and the Restoration did not exist, as if the French Revolution arrived directly from the eighteenth century to me. There was something wildly romantic about it, to a child who did not yet know French. The proof that everything could change suddenly, as if just by not believing in a king's power, you could bring him down. As if all it took to topple Khomeini was to stop believing he was the Mahdi. His limbs came out of his coffin on the day of his funeral. The body fell, but the Beards clung fiercely to his corpse. I was glad to see that patience could catch a madman before it was too late. The first time I read the words French Revolution, I was captivated. It was as if I had discovered the name of my beloved. You have to fall in love to know real passion.

It was therefore by accident—but certainly not much of one—that I read an article on libertine literature. I didn't know any of the titles or any of the authors (pseudonyms, anonymous or unknown authors and Mirabeau) but my curiosity was definitely aroused: there were both women and Pierre Louÿs in libertine literature. I started with *Thérèse the Philosopher*, because it had a woman's first name in the title, and philosophy was more of a man's thing.

I started it one Saturday afternoon and I read it in one sitting. I was entranced. Not like with Maupassant or Kundera, and not exactly like with historical essays. I was entranced in a different way. I felt like I was reading Life, the Instruction Manual. There was such reasoning in the way Thérèse's adventures took place, which forced me, the reader, to throw myself into it completely. All readers of libertine literature know that state: the preliminaries are sexual and the whole body is tense, stimulated by the detailed descriptions of all the experiences the body is subjected to, but there is no downtime, and the story then leaves the senses, to tackle Reason. It is impossible to escape the thoroughness of the reasoning, the beauty of the ideas. I was captivated. Anyone who reads libertine literature is captivated. You cannot defend yourself: it is all designed to turn your brain on. Eroticism, in other words, acute sensory pleasure, also works with your mind. Eroticism and the art of conversation go hand in hand in libertine literature. They are equal, and that is liberating, because it is a complete and utter liberation.

It seems obvious to me that regularly reading libertine

literature has created a carnal relationship between me and books that has affected me so deeply that I cannot live without books, without the physical presence of books. I already loved them, but that love had been at first a way of imitating my father and then a weapon to defend myself in exile. But the book only became essential to my survival when it was made flesh. Living surrounded by books is essential for keeping my balance. Again, don't laugh: you have not read libertine literature; you still don't know what the revolutionaries of the Enlightenment are capable of when it comes to transmuting words into flesh and flesh into words.

Madame C, with her corset barely buttoned up, naturally asks Abbé T—as they have just said their 'Ahhhh Fathers'— to tell her his thoughts on religion. So we then have the licentious and brilliant Abbé T launching into a metaphysical demonstration that unveils the contradiction between the word of God and the laws that men ascribe to them to keep societies in place. He is fired up by the grace of Reason and covers everything from the origin of religions, the illogical nature of religious practice, the greatness of God and man's need for power. I had the impression I was reading a description of the Beards, who take the throne in the name of God. *'In the course of the centuries, and in various countries, many people decided to organize those beliefs and form religions. They invented the most fantastic and incredible gods. They organized themselves into orders and societies whose members had to be subdued and kept in fear. They became their leaders, political as well as religious.'*[6] In a language that fascinated me, the Abbé T and Thérèse taught me about life. A naked arse was just the beginning of political freedom. And it is because the protagonists of *Thérèse the Philosopher* are free from the shackles of the body that they are able to reason in that way. The body and the spirit are connected so as to tear apart the stupid prejudices that condemn men to obscurity, because it is clear that *'To be a perfect Christian, one has to be ignorant, capable of blind faith, disdain all pleasures, give up joy, honour, riches, leave friends and family, and maintain virginity. In short, one is supposed to do everything that is against so-called Nature, while this same Nature has been ordained by God, and surely is part of his unalterable will. These unbelievable contradictions are supposed to belong to a Being which is all-knowing, all-just and all-good!'* Replace 'Christian' with 'Beard', and fireworks went off in my head. There was also the certainty that my loneliness was altogether quite relative: other centuries had experienced and more importantly survived the Beards.

There is something key about the construction of the libertine novel that opens the door to the mind. Thérèse was not a distant heroine. This was a letter she had sent to us through time, telling us about and persuading us to accept her body as a celebration of Reason, the flesh and the spirit passing the buck from one encounter to another, from discovery to the metaphysics of life. And all of it is demonstrated in an enthusiastic tone that flatters the reader, invites them to share in the secret, introduces them into a sphere where anything can and should be thought, questioned, tested. *'How could people possibly start an idiotic belief which tells them that God is more happy and satisfied when they eat a herring instead of a chicken, onion soup instead of beef bouillon, filet of sole instead of a steak? And especially that this God would throw them in hell for all eternity if they happen to prefer a simple slice of bacon on a specific day rather than an expensive filleted fish? Oh, the stupid people who believe that they are capable of offending God.'*

And what does Thérèse do immediately after hearing this tirade—hidden behind the curtains to spy on the embraces of her mentors? She slips off to her room to reproduce the words of the Abbé T in writing. Libertine literature incites you to study! A glorification of the spoken word! Never had I so loved the pleasure of writing. I filled many pages after my encounter with Thérèse; it was as if I was paying tribute to all the revolutions that had succeeded in the end.

From the opening pages, Thérèse is sickened by the force of prejudice. And this prejudice is the one that denies the body. The body is dirty; the body is dangerous; the body is the enemy of true faith. Thérèse, under the combined influence of her mother and her confessor, suffers the dogmas of the Church; she has no weapon with which to defend herself. Thérèse does not wear the headscarf, but she is trapped by her mother in a convent—which is the same as wearing a scarf: each culture has its own women's prison. Thérèse becomes pale and loses her life force, because the body must be annihilated for the glory of God. She leaves the convent, convinced that her body is shameful and that only flagellation and suffering can bring her closer to God.

Then suddenly ... while hiding in a toilet, Thérèse discovers one of her friends—who is as penitent as she is—who she believes is being penetrated by the cord of St. Francis, when she is actually being penetrated by one of the most lecherous priests who has the reputation of a saint. Thérèse is shocked, confused, doubtful and ... excited, but she follows her instinct—for once—and confides in Madame C, who immediately grasps what is at stake and starts proceedings against the licentious priest ... However, we soon learn that Madame C is a great libertine. Thérèse finds this out by following her instruction, as well as that of the Abbé T, and by seeing the hypocrisy of power; of all powers. The colour returns to her cheeks. There is finally hope on the horizon for her. At every stage of her education, the duplicity of the men of the Church and the reality of pleasure seize her with the same force. Gradually, she realizes that the most virtuous women are the most salacious, and that men who preach penitence are nothing more than perverts. She learns that the body is the fruit of nature and that there is nothing wrong with following her instincts and it is impossible that the laws written by men can contradict her. Thérèse starts to take on the world, and every encounter unveils a truth. The veils of prejudice lift and Thérèse can stand up tall, say she is a philosopher and live with the man she has chosen, while deciding never to have children and never to get married.

If you replace the convent with the veil, the Abbé T with Pierre Louÿs, and sexual encounters with exile, then you have my life story. Right down to Thérèse's habit of hiding in cupboards, in dark corridors, or in toilets in order to find out the truth. I felt like I was seeing myself as a child again. And when an event was significant, she rushed to find her quill and write about it in her notebooks. More than a novel and more than a political essay, *Thérèse the Philosopher* is a survival guide addressed to all women— and all men—living under the yoke of absolutist power. The scenes of sexual instruction are interspersed with political discourse and the whole thing smacks of revolution. The Great Revolution, the only revolution: the inner revolution. It was also the first time that the truth was unveiled from a female perspective. Merteuil was not alone! There were numerous women who dared to say 'I' and who were not even victims, not bigots, or saints, or even animals! They were speaking out like men and were not to be outdone by them in their adventures.

I followed up with *Le portier des Chartreux (The Life and Adventures of Father Silas)* in which, from the very first page, the tone is set: *'I am the fruit of the incontinence of the reverend Celestine Fathers of the town of B--- I say of the reverend Fathers, because all of them boasted of having contributed a share in the formation of my individual person. (...) Alas! I must overcome this compunction. Who does not know that all men are men, and especially the monks? They certainly have the faculty of cooperating in the propagation of the species; and why should we hinder them, when they acquit themselves so well in that particular?'*[7] So begin the memoirs of Saturnin, who is constantly concerned with desire from a young age and who sets his sights on his sister Suzon (who is not his sister). What a surprise then to discover that Suzon—fresh from the convent—is much more knowledgeable and takes responsibility for his sexual apprenticeship ... The convent is definitely the school of pleasure ... And Saturnin pursues his emotional and sexual education, only to discover that the women of the world are bored and yearn for well-hung men, that the religious way is the best for those who want to shag most devoutly *(To correctly judge these different species of animals that creep contemptuously over the surface of the earth and who go by the general moniker of 'monks', one must regard them as the enemies of Society. Incapable of fulfilling the duties required of them to be honest people, they are removed from its tyranny and have had to resort to monasteries as the only sanctuary for their depravity)*[8] and that prejudice is man's worst enemy *(Prejudice is an animal that should be sent out to pasture).* It was a pleasure to read, as fanciful as it was intelligent. It was amazing how the act of laughing at men of God made them inoffensive! There were also all those enlightening conversations like the one between Angélique and Agnès (*Venus in the Cloister* by Abbé du Prat) which were such quick reads and always put a smile on my face, and in which the anecdotes from life in the cloisters are just a metaphor for the hypocrisy of society and in which it's always about handing down ideas, about books, about education or about overturning prejudices ('*You will be amazed to hear a girl of nineteen or twenty passing herself off as knowledgeable, and able to penetrate into the most hidden secrets of religious politics. (...) I am aware that I was even less enlightened than you at your age, and that everything I have learned came after a period of extreme ignorance; but I also have to admit that I could rightfully be accused of stupidity, if the care that several great men have taken in educating me had not borne any fruit'),* and further on: *'since we are not born of a sex able to pass any laws, we must obey these laws which we have found in place, and follow as known truths, many things which of themselves frequently pass as mere opinions (...) I will teach you in a few words what a Reverend Jesuit Father (...) told me when he was trying to broaden my mind and make it capable of these speculations.'*[9]

An education. Critical thinking. Learning to speculate. Opening your mind. Questioning. Doubting. All the time. Libertine literature is an education that leads to freedom; it is a transgression that gives wings to thought. Like the letters of Érosie to Juliette who remained in the convent while her friend learns to cure her hatred for men and enjoy life (*Le Doctorat Impromptu*, by Andréa de Nerciat), or even Mirabeau's *The Lifted Curtain & My Conversion* (one of my favourite bedside libertine novels, along with *Thérèse the Philosopher*) in which all prejudices, all taboos are passed through the mill of reflection to give Laure the chance to go beyond her destiny as a woman and to experience happiness in this world, and not wait for the hypothetical next one. (*'Have you taken leave of your senses, my dear child? Do you think I allow my esteem and my friendship to be swayed by prejudices? What does it matter if a woman has lain in the arms of another lover, if the qualities of her heart, the evenness of her temperament, the gentleness of her character, the*

charms of her mind and the gracefulness of her person are
not altered, and if she is still capable of a tender attachment?
Do you think she has less value than a widow, of equal vir-
tue, who has had a few mumbled words and drops of water
cast over her to allow her to openly sleep with a man, and
to ostentatiously parade the fruits of their union? (...) Are
women therefore like horses, whose worth is judged by how
little they have been used?')[10]

That was an incredible time for me and reading. I discovered a unique world where men and women were equal, and
even if only when hidden away, in private, in the protected
circles of the libertines, it was already the beginning of
something bigger that could influence the whole of society.
All the characters were born ignorant, and it was through
the power of reading, of debates, scepticism, experiences,
that stupidity was driven away and the heroines could live
life as it should be, free from the unfounded prejudices that
have done nothing but fill them with venom.

Sex was only there to overthrow the Church's omnipo-
tence—having it off without procreating is the perfect way
of sticking two fingers up at Christian dogmas—sex was
just a weapon against the extremism of power, sex was just
the noblest way of overturning prejudice. And I understood
that the body—especially the female body—has always
been at the centre of power, whether it is made invisible, or
rented out. The combined and absolute power of the monarchy and the church only tended toward a single aim: to
keep issues frozen through a series of prohibitions. It was
the Monarchy of the Beards and was no different from

the Republic of the Beards. They are still just men keeping other men in a prison of fear, in a false cage of security and who end up always taking things too far against nature. It all starts with a food riot, which is the first cry of the body. Then there is a total and absolute liberation. But the new power always gets scared. It trembles at the sight of the body in motion. And systematically, the freedom of the body is hampered by careful regulation. As if the absolute survival of the political body depends on its domination of the physical body. The woman is often erased from the picture. The French Revolution blithely erased the female body from the body of citizens. Plus, it prohibited women from wearing trousers. I mean, come on. They were so afraid of seeing women—if only physically—looking like men, that the revolutionaries prohibited cross-dressing. Tell me what you do with your body and I'll tell you what you're afraid of. But it's always the same old story. The Beards inevitably fall: they put so much pressure on the body that in the end it blows up in their faces. It's long, it's painful, but it can happen. We must arm ourselves. And there's nothing better than the libertine novel for laughing in their faces while lifting up their skirts.

Above all with Thérèse, I realized that I had not yet burned my headscarf, I had merely taken it off. For it is not enough to just bare your arse and to say 'No'; you also have to topple a whole series of convictions. And argue. And in order to argue, just having culture is not enough. No. We must learn to reason, we must learn to connect things that are not connected, we must reflect on the scope of a piece of fabric, exactly as during the Age of Enlightenment, something had to be found to overthrow the king, the priest and the courtiers. From inside. Find something to highlight their contradictions, their futile fears and their pettiness. And it is only then ...

Thérèse and her contemporaries did the work for me: all I had to do was read. Thérèse had managed to give my past, my naked bottom and my need to tell the truth, a sense of prestige. She opened the doors to Reason and gave me the ingredients with which to defend myself: curiosity, patience, and doubt. We must question, discover the hidden nature behind all preconceptions, transform them through unhampered thought, and finally—perhaps—at the end of the road, discover the light. A light that shows the universality of human rights, that transforms the French Revolution into a way of thinking, makes the possibilities for change immortal and infinite. Thérèse, or the possibility of happiness.

Paris, 2013

Libertine literature is movement. Movement that sweeps away, that liberates, that destroys the old kings and the dusty old bishops. That movement is the heavy breathing of a people that refuses—finally—to be told what to do by the representatives of the power, whether secular or divine; the power that crushes them. The movement, the breath of life into death, the refusal to accept, the inability to keep quiet. I had to accept and listen to this movement. But it didn't come easily. Because it also meant accepting that the Revolution of the Beards had also been a resounding and uncontrollable 'No' against the Shah and against poverty, against the West which fed itself on oil and hunger, against what they thought was a decline of Iranian culture. Accepting that the 'No' of the Beards and Crows had the same power and almost the same origin as the French Revolution, and lamenting not the Revolution but the absurd and suicidal choices of the aftermath. My Beards and Crows were not wrong to want everything to change; they simply ruined the possibility of democracy by taking refuge in the beard of the 'old man in black and white'. They were still too hungry and afraid of what they did not know. So they hid behind what seemed most familiar to them: the religion of their fathers. If libertine literature had flourished on the streets of Tehran, then perhaps they would have had another choice. Perhaps they would have been less afraid and would have taken a risk. A risk on the unknown, on atheism, on freedom. Add to that the profound mysticism of Persian culture and you have the Revolution of the Beards and Crows. It was not much, perhaps, but it at least helped me to understand—and to forgive. The question did not arise of whether it was my place to forgive or not, I really thought of myself as a child of history and felt I had the right to take stock. I didn't want to be just a silent victim of the Revolution, of the war and of exile. I wanted to be active, involved, a judge.

I would like to bombard the country of the Beards with libertine books instead of bombs. I would like to give everyone those forbidden books that were filed under philosophy on bookstore shelves. I wish they could learn to be less afraid of their bodies and stop imagining that women's bodies are just waiting for the freedom to leave them. In the course of my reading, through my desire to understand why women wore headscarves in Paris, I found some analyses that blamed colonization. It is because colonized men had been dispossessed from their land, their freedom, that they took it out on women by transforming their bodies into an ultra-private zone. As if the possession of women was the only form of honour they had left. And it is not hard to imagine the fear of dispossession for a colonized person. But the woman shut away in the house and imprisoned inside her hijab is a walled-in woman. She no longer exists apart from within the bounds of privacy. Extinct. Vanished. And when men were liberated through decolonization, they continued to confine their women. As if they had ended up enjoying it. As if it was a cultural problem, as well as a political one. As if men could not get it up unless a woman is covered, pure, modest. Even if it was fake, even if behind the walls and veils women were neither modest, nor pure. As if what mattered above all is that they appeared to others. Women remained enclosed within. In their houses and their veils. And the hammam.

Women's films that take place in the hammam where, in filthy language, they tell one another their private gossip and their woes, really irritate me. I couldn't care less that they are talking to one another, or that they are being open and vulgar inside the hammam or the beauty salon! I want to see them using that language in the street, in front of men. I am sick and tired of these scenes designed to reassure Westerners and the Beards. As long as the women remain enclosed in the hammam, everything's okay. The hammam is fairly exotic and allows them to strip off, yay! But when the camera is no longer filming, when ideas of Eastern sensuality are shattered by the veil of male domination, women remain alone, strangely alone, strangely silent. They are nothing more than women beaten by men. Women who have lost; women who have not even been allowed to play. Hang on, sorry, I forgot that there is always one of them who is different; one daring woman who acts the same way outside the hammam. She is often the one who makes you cry, often the one who meets a bad ending, the realist warning of these hammam films. The whole reality is based on her fate as a fallen woman, so that the others carry on laughing about other people's lives in the steamy hammam. But no! That's just not okay! 'Feminine' places of speech should no longer exist. The woman has become—and remains—the zone that demarcates men's honour. Decolonization did not free the woman's body; it has remained on probation until today.

Nothing will change if the mentalities born out of this cultural prison do not evolve. The odd woman might have enough power to move forward without fearing for her reputation, without fear of insults, certain about her future. But what about all the others? What will they do in the meantime? Apart from wait for a little ten-year-old girl to run away to avoid a forced marriage; for a group of schoolgirls to escape death in a school that has already been bombed twice; for a woman to be hanged because she was raped by savages who she no doubt provoked, inevitably provoked, because she is a woman and she lost her honour—and that of all her family, from her great grandfather to her distant uncle—by being raped? They wait. And while they are waiting, they should take the opportunity to read. They should take the opportunity to arm themselves with book-weapons and wait for the right time to end the prejudices that have made them wait for so long, since the beginning of time, when men could only exercise their power over women. They should, all these women, take the power of books and educate their daughters and sons about the power of Reason. And wait for the day when those children, as adults, will judge that time has come to destroy centuries of obscurantism and turn this power into a place of debate, of Equality and Reason. There will no longer be women walled up inside the prison of men who are so afraid of losing them.

I often think about the Philip Kaufman film with the symbolic title, *Quills*. The film tells the story of Sade when he was incarcerated in the insane asylum at Charenton. It's not a very good film. It is not a historical film; it is a symbolic film, a vindication of Sade who was driven mad by writing, incapable of living without the pen. There is a laundry maid, a fresh-faced beauty, not even a whore, who loves words and is convinced that Sade's words can do a lot for women and for freedom. So she helps him by concealing Sade's illegal pages among the priests and nuns' laundry, and smuggling them out to his publisher. There are lunatics and there is a bishop, completely ensconced in the veils of prejudice, who hates Sade and who marries a young virgin, fresh out of the convent. What shocks Sade more than anything: that a young girl should find herself in the clutches of a false puritan who makes her endure everything he condemns from his pulpit. However, the girl married to the bishop is blessed with a brain, and she knows how to read. She gets her hands on one of Sade's books. She changes the cover to make people think she is reading something acceptable. And she reads. And because she reads, and the clouds of her education evaporate, she notices the young handsome architect who is covering in marble the nouveau riche mansion that her lecherous husband is having built to keep his beautiful bride inside. But it is too late: the little convent girl has read. She has read and she knows that evil is not between her legs or flowing from the quill of the Marquis, but in her husband's hands. She runs away with the young architect, making sure she leaves behind, as a farewell letter to her enraged husband, the book that set her free. There you have it. It's that simple. It's that beautiful: a young girl destined to be the plaything of a Beard's unhealthy desires frees herself from her matrimonial chains by reading the uncompromising words of Sade. That is how women become free.

It's like that, and only like that, in the intimacy of reading, in the irreversible process of intellectual learning, that women will no longer be afraid of their bodies, of men, of their mothers, of their fathers, of power. Do not look any further, do not look for better weapons, more experienced soldiers, more impactful slogans; bombard the countries of the Beards with French eighteenth-century libertine novels, give them something to read, give them something to think about. Give them something with which to break their chains, something to help them breathe fresh air, something to burn all the veils of the world. When that day comes, you will see a mother and father proudly taking their daughter to her first day of school. And the first Beard who wants to tell them 'No', who wants that little girl to be illiterate, who wants to see her married off to some bearded old man, that Beard will not have the right to exist. He will already be dead.

Paris, 1997

The divine Marquis came into my life in July 1997 with *Philosophy in the Boudoir*. After reading libertine novels that were more or less anonymous, Sade, who so boldly claimed paternity over his writing, made me really ... embarrassed. From the very first pages, I was surprised to find myself hiding the book from the eyes of fellow users of Parisian transport, passers-by or friends. I stopped carrying *Philosophy in the Boudoir* around with me. It was something I read in secret. I was ashamed of censoring my reading from the eyes of others, but I couldn't bring myself to do otherwise. I understood the terrible things contained in Sade's words and was completely unable to read passages of his books out loud. Even Louÿs' 'worst' pornographic novel, *Mother's Three Daughters* was less terrifying than the tamest of Sade's novels. The Marquis transfixed me. I read it in my room, with my back against the door, braced for an intrusion by my parents or my little brother. I hid his books in my underwear drawer—it was the only place where nobody would go snooping, and it seemed the most appropriate place to keep Sade. I was, in a word, uneasy. It was the first time that I had ever been ashamed of reading.

The libertine literature that I liked was steeped in philosophy, political discourse and the sexual exploits were on the whole good-natured, funny and improbable enough to be just ... fiction. It was clear, clean and unequivocal. The opposite of Sade's work: sinister, ambiguous and stained. It was also fiction but it was ... too much. Anything is possible with words, and Sade did not mince his. In *Philosophy in the Boudoir*, flesh is anatomical, dissected, tortured, the object of all imaginable pleasures (and even more) and all forms of pain inspired by desire and desire alone (nature). It is a description so detailed that it becomes unbearable. I struggled with the Marquis' words but it was impossible to put down. It was a lecture, it was cynical and it was cringe-worthy. But there was, three-quarters of the way through the piece, a prodigious text ('Frenchmen, some more effort if you wish to become Republicans') from which I copied out whole passages so I could stick them up on my bedroom walls—between the naked women and the Rougon-Macquart family tree carefully produced by yours truly. This declaration of the new rights of men and women contains and summarizes all of Sade's thinking. His entire body of fictional work is a perfect illustration of this political pamphlet. The Republic according to Sade does not prohibit anything that goes against nature, which is the only antidote to the unjust laws of men. The anger of Sade, who built his republic, lies in the question, '*Can you possibly be so barbaric as to condemn a miserable individual to death for the sole crime of not having the same leanings as you?'*

Sade had an axe to grind and if he did not back down, it is because the government never backed down. 'Frenchmen, some more effort ... ' is a very topical text. Not for what it defends but because it demonstrates the possibility for men to have total freedom, which is essential for ending ignorance. Sade's atheism is not just directed at God and religion but against everything: morality, propriety, the monarchy, the clergy and the king. He does not believe in anything. He strongly believes that laws cannot do anything for men and that the Republic can only exist by accepting man's multiple natures. Thus, incest is only a crime under a tyrannical regime because '*it loosens family ties and therefore strengthens the citizen's love for their country; indeed, incest is dictated for us by the supreme natural laws, we treat it cordially, and the enjoyment we gain from the people belonging to us always seems more delightful than any other pleasure*'; murder is no longer a crime but a natural inclination, '*We must deign for an instant to illuminate our souls with the sacred torch of philosophy. What other voice besides the voice of nature suggests personal hatred, vengeances, warfare—in short, all those motives for incessant murders? Now if nature advises us to perpetrate those misdeeds, it must need them*'; prostitution becomes nationalized in Sade's writings and brothels are no longer reserved for prostitutes and, '*Thus, some pleasure houses will be designed for female lechery, and, like those for male delights, they will be under government protection. Individuals of both sexes will be supplied with all the people they could desire, and the more these women visit these houses, the more they will be esteemed. There is nothing so barbarous and so ludicrous as making a woman's honour and virtue depend on her challenging desires that she has received from nature, and that also ceaselessly excite the people who are brutal enough to condemn them.*'[11]

Sade permits everything apart from God, who is built on ignorance, and is the cause of all the nation's misfortunes, because '*when you are terrified, you are no longer rational. Above all, they were told to distrust their reasoning; and when the brains are muddled, you believe everything and examine nothing. Fear and ignorance, you will continue, are the two mainstays of any and all religions.*' Sade patiently dismantles society and replaces law with nature, in which exists the most savage and the most euphoric. He is 'naturally' against the death penalty which '*has never prevented any crime, since it is committed daily at the foot of the scaffold. We must, in short, eliminate this punishment, because there is no worse calculation than killing a man for having killed another. The obvious result of this action is that instead of our having one less person we suddenly have two less people, a reckoning plausible only to executioners and imbeciles*'; and in favour of reducing the constraints of law to a minimum even though he agrees '*that we cannot pass as many laws as there are men, but laws may be so mild, so few in number, that all men, no matter what their characters, can easily comply*'; he precisely questions the egalitarian nature of the law: '*Now I ask you: Is there true justice in a law that commands a man who has nothing to respect a man who has everything?*';

and he gives *exactly* the same rights and the same duties to men and women because '*No act of possession can ever be perpetrated on a free being: it is as unjust to own a wife monogamously as it is to own slaves. All men are born free, all are equal before the law; we must never lose sight of these principles. Hence, no sex is granted the legitimate right to seize the other sex exclusively, and never can any sex or any class possess the other arbitrarily.*' 'Frenchmen, some more effort ... ' is a text that deserves to be read by politicians and by citizens.

Sade is a born storyteller and a radical thinker, which makes his writing strangely poetic, and therefore perfectly acceptable. Yet in this call to arms, the desire to raise the citizens up *en masse* against tyranny, there is also Sade's desire to be accepted. He does not have the same tastes as everyone, and narrowly escaped the guillotine, he loves sodomy and 'strange' sexual practices (let's say it once and for all: Sade was definitely a sexual deviant), but he desperately defends his nature and his preferences. Perhaps it was this confession, behind all the political rhetoric, weakness and pain that touched me, and urged me to continue such difficult reading.

The first time I opened a book by Sade, my very sheltered world exploded, my certainties melted away, I became a born again virgin of knowledge. It is perhaps Sade's greatest talent: he strips everything away. In his wake, the earth is burned, flowers are dead, good taste smashed to smithereens. But his humour and extremism prevented me from wanting to close the book: I had never read so many crude words. Ever. What made me go on reading, was curiosity ... blended with masochism. It was also because I was stubborn: Sade embodied the libertine century and I would have been ashamed to stop reading him. It was exactly like the feeling I had when I was on the metro and a tramp sat next to me who stank to high heaven. Most of the passengers got off at the next stop. I couldn't bring myself to: I stayed there with the tramp because I was too ashamed to show that his smell was bothering me. It was the same with Sade: I didn't dare to leave his writings when he had paid for them with a life in prison. Perhaps he scared me too. As if he was leaning over my shoulder to watch me reading and was just waiting for me to look away so he could laugh at me. Perhaps it was absolutely necessary to be ashamed. Perhaps it was because Sade went so far beyond everything, pushed the boundaries so much, took such delight in shocking, in describing the improbable, in describing the things that are not even whispered in the bedroom at night, that one simply had to read Sade with the lights off. Perhaps the first step is to feel shame, then to overcome your shame. Perhaps if his readers can go beyond disgust and shame, they will finally be ready for the Republic.

When I opened *The 120 Days of Sodom*, I found it hard to swallow. If *Philosophy in the Boudoir* had made me uncomfortable, then Sade's first novel absolutely floored me. It was staggering, not just for the level of violence, but for the justification of that violence. The four men, who lock themselves away in a château to explore the depths of their desires, represent a gateway to a world where there is no form of law, no morals, no respect, no possible escape. There are just passive bodies. Submissive bodies enjoyed by those who have power and who are so bored of everything they have already felt, already experienced—the masters of ceremony are a duke, a bishop, a judge and a banker. The body is reduced to one function only: pleasure. And because these men had tried everything, pleasure is difficult to achieve and orgasm becomes almost impossible. So they go even further, the magnitude of pleasure goes hand in hand with evil, and the reader, although it makes him sick, is nonetheless sensually excited—despite himself, and despite his disgust. There is no escape from the château de Silling, neither for the body, nor for the reader. The victims are not willing. There are the four dominant men and four old courtesans working their way through the six hundred existing perversions, and the bodies who are subjected to them. Words are assassins, orgasms consistently merge into murder, nobody emerges unscathed either from the isolated castle in the heart of the dark forest, or from the reading.

I am still convinced, just as I was when I finished *The 120 Days of Sodom,* that I had just shed my skin. I changed category. I was no longer innocent, I was sick. I was not a victim of the Beards, I was their worst nightmare. I knew terrible things about my peers. And strangely, all this debauchery assured me of one thing: I was a slave to freedom. I was a slave to the idea that it was impossible to condemn someone else for being different, as long as they are not dogmatic and do not force you to be the same as them. For example, although it was impossible for me to accept incest, paedophilia, murder and rape as a matter of course, I also knew that behind these horrors, there were men and that they of course needed to be treated, locked up definitely, but condemned to death? Never. Since reading Sade I have never been able to say, 'I am against the death penalty, however, when it comes to paedophilia, etc.' Never. I am against the death penalty, full stop. There are no half measures. Either I consider paedophilia as a disease and I refuse to kill sick people, or I think that it's a preference like any other and in that case I cannot even prohibit it. Sade forces you to make precise moral decisions and to comply with them. With Sade I knew that being against the death penalty meant being against all forms of capital punishment, even when it seems like the most fitting choice. Sade also gave me a key to try and solve the huge issue that had been nagging away at me since my childhood: the question of inside/outside, private/public. Sade wanted everything to be permissible, everything to be out in the open, because he detested hypocrisy. Social schizophrenia is an open door to madness. His attempt to combine the private man with the public man was an attempt to resolve the main problem with Eastern societies today. Sade was on the front line against the *awrah*.

I knew I couldn't go on pretending to be someone I was not. I knew it was too bad for those who were allergic to my frankness, I knew that the pursed lips of my mother and aunts when I allowed myself to say what shouldn't be said (in other words, practically everything) were not a good enough reason for me to keep quiet. I thought back to when I was twelve, and how I didn't speak out when they bad-mouthed Rushdie. And I was ashamed of keeping quiet for fear of being isolated. Nothing is worth keeping silent. Even isolation. So, that's what Sade can do for you: he can give you courage, where before there was only fear.

And I now know that the only viable system was the Republic and the only way, secularism. The only way to live together is through the destruction of the dogmas that pit one against the other; that create a hierarchy of harmful values. Sade is more than just reading: he is an experience. He is a secret passage to Reason, passing through the abysses of hell. You have to tackle Sade in order to grow up. My shame only lasted for a while, the time it took to read two of his novels. My shame was only a preliminary. After Sade, my brain would function differently. After Sade, everything I wrote, everything I wanted to convey would have to pass the Sade test. Is this going to change a belief? Does this destroy an ancestral prejudice? Is this worthy of the divine Marquis? Am I living up to words that change, words that hurt, truths that are unsaid? Am I making Khomeini turn in his grave? Are my words sharp enough weapons? Of course, nothing I've written can be compared to Sade. I am much more gentle; I have too much hope. I am free. But my desire is always the same: to stir up, to think outside the box, to turn things upside down.

If Pierre Louÿs was my first love, then Sade was like a second father to me. He was too harsh (and too dangerous) to be my lover. I had put him on a pedestal and I had no intention of bringing him down off it. I had the utmost respect for Sade and was proud of my proximity to the most effective, absolute and extreme craftsman of the French Revolution. Neither Robespierre, nor Danton, nor Camille Desmoulins, not even Mirabeau could compete with him. It is Sade who changed the mental state of the Revolution. He profoundly believed in the absolute need to disregard morality, decency, and social hierarchy to lay *bare* the truth of the world.

While imprisoned in the Bastille, Sade began writing *The 120 Days of Sodom*, a book born out of the Marquis' dream of avenging his stepmother, whom he imagined being forced to undergo a series of abuses, each one as painful as the last) and it is possible that he contributed to the storming of the prison. In fact, on 2 July 1789, in his cell, aware of what was happening on the streets of Paris—in the words of the governor of the Bastille, the Marquis de Launay: *'He stood (...) at his cell window, shouting at the top of his lungs that the prisoners were being assassinated, their throats cut, and that they must be rescued.'*[12] Launay manages to get Sade, *'this being that nothing can tame'*, transferred to the asylum of Charenton. I like to think that it was Sade who put the idea of storming the Bastille into the heads of the 'almost' citizens.

He was imprisoned under all the political regimes, the monarchy, the Republic, the Consulate and the Empire.

Few revolutionaries can claim to be such a threat to power. Sade's absolute atheism was a threat to many people; but there was more to it than that. He was, as Launay described him, untameable. And nothing makes those in power tremble more than a human being that no threat, no seduction, no bribery can bring to their knees. Sade never bowed down to any power, to any man. Never. In short, he was dangerous. Even today, he would not be imprisoned but he would be silenced ... The Marquis was a pariah. A thug. An elegant and sophisticated thug. A thug who has transcended the ages, and who was as contemporary in 1997 as he had been in 1793, or in the 1930s with the surrealists, and later, after the war, when the intellectuals and poets rediscovered him and he could at last be published, this time not clandestinely—in 1968, thanks to Jean-Jacques Pauvert!

After the shame, and overcoming the shame, came militancy. I no longer hid and I kept Sade's novels in my bag like talismans. I remember racing through my essays so I could take out my book and read quietly in the concentrated silence of the lecture halls. I had never worked as hard as I did at university, and the only reason was so that I could get back to reading Sade as quickly as possible. It had become like a drug. I had to have my daily dose of Sade—it felt like a long time ago that I used to hide myself away to read him. I read all available editions of *Justine*—if I remember correctly, in his lifetime, there were more than ten editions of it. The fact that his vindication of crime or the endless torture sequences (especially in *Juliette, or Vice Amply Rewarded*) eventually sickened me—even I who could be pretty bloodthirsty—does not detract from the quality of the style and the metaphysical demonstration. Freedom had to be earned. And Khomeini fought against his murderous words from the grave. I could see him writhing under the blows of the Marquis.

What is great about *Justine* is the point at which the reader realizes that Justine likes it. That Justine likes suffering; that she derives a certain pleasure from her terrible and humiliating exploits, that her tears are orgasmic. Her sister Juliette is the complete opposite of her. Whereas Justine is an absolute masochist, Juliette delights in sadism. Juliette manages to escape from her environment, to erase her poor background and she only succeeds in this by being smarter than the counts and the archbishops. Juliette is my favourite heroine. She is a heroine because she fights, because she pulls through, because she is a woman of the future. More realistic than the women in Aragon's writing, Sade's Juliette is a successful woman, a complete woman, a woman who has no reason to be envious of men. Juliette is the ultimate woman. Perhaps she is even the feminine side of Sade. His alter ego; the one that all women will be once they are free.

There isn't a shred of sentimentalism in Sade's writing. There is no prince on a white horse riding in to save the princesses held captive by their authoritarian fathers. If the princess doesn't have enough balls to escape from her tower then too bad for her! No one can save her except herself. Sade glorifies resourcefulness and a refusal to accept your fate. Sade does not seek excuses for his characters; he demonstrates that if men are stupid enough to believe what they are told by the powers that be and by the law, then they deserve a life of misery. He dreams up autonomous characters that know, through thought and reasoning, that power is fragile, that power lies in a handful of prejudices that other men follow to the letter. Breaking the chain of poverty, breaking the chain of stupid beliefs, means liberating all men. Breathe in, lift your shoulders, throw off your superstitions, look beyond yourself and ... you are already free!

Paris, 2013

The Marquis is a constant presence in my life. Sometimes when I have just finished a novel or when I don't know what to read next, or simply because I look at my bookshelf and Sade's books are there, I take one out, open it at random and read. Sometimes it's a passage of torture and I force myself to read it. I force myself so that I remember that no censorship is legitimate and no form of violence should make me look away. I confront Sade's imaginary violence so that I am able to stand up to all forms of real violence. You cannot stick your head in the sand when you read Sade. The truth is never easily accessible, and the fear of violence is a frontier that must be crossed. Reading Sade whenever it falls into my hands means I cannot close my eyes to the horror. All of the horror.

Sade is unbridled sex, to the point of death. If everything is in nature, then so are the worst vices and abuses. There is no compromise in Sade. The body is ravished, tortured, torn, lost, pleasure-seeking, impulsive, capricious, boundless. In Sade, the body represents society as a whole, its ambiguities and its injustices. The body takes up all the space, overflows, suffers, grows. The body is not as playful as in Pierre Louÿs. It is tragic and omnipresent. But—and as always, everything is in the 'but'—the body as a receptacle of the unbridled imagination of men AND women, can also be interpreted as Sade's long torturous existence. The years go by, revolutions make and break the powers that be, freedom rears its head, but Sade remains in prison. Released once, sent back to prison thirty times. And as the years pass, and Sade remains imprisoned, the more violent his writing becomes, the more the body disintegrates. In his final writings, there is no smell any more. Sade is locked up, his imagination exerted to the limits, and the body becomes impossible. So much for smells and feelings, so much for realism, all that remains is the imagination that overthrows kings and ruins virgins. The imagination that can still elicit a smile, from the depths of his prison cell. The imagination that is the only loyal companion of the true revolutionary. After Sade, if I bump into a Beard I just smile at him with contempt. I've read Sade, and he has nothing but his beard. I've read Sade and he has nothing but his rigid, stale beliefs. He thinks he will dominate his wife and his daughters to the end like his father and grandfather did before him, but I know that's not the case. I know it would not take much for his daughter to turn round and tug on his beloved beard. The body according to Sade is not just the body freed from forceps; it is the body taken to its limits, the revolutionary body. Maybe Sade affected me more than others, transported me more than anyone else because he spoke directly to my imprisoned body. He was what that girl under the veil needed, that girl who didn't have the right to talk. And later when it was the time of fear, when it was time to keep my mouth shut, to create a persona in order not to be too lonely, Sade was the one who offered me a refuge. I understood that solitude is nothing serious, that solitude can be an opportunity for creativity and that, in the end, one day, freedom of thought will reign. Some more effort if you wish to become Republicans.

When I wanted to pass it on, when I wanted to hand it to someone else, I saw only pouts of disgust and I heard only the sighs of nuns. It was only older men who were in tune with Sade; young women my age felt offended by *Philosophy in the Boudoir*. It was too raw, too violent, too sadist. And yet, it was there, it was behind their eyes, it was already inside them, the possibility of complete independence, which also means confronting the dirtiest words, the nastiest words, the bitterest words.

I remember at university I lent the film, *Salò, or the 120 Days of Sodom,* to a friend. I remember him coming up to me on the Monday morning; he looked like he was about to smack me one. I think that if I hadn't stood still, if I had flinched, he would have done it. He had vomited while watching the film and he hadn't managed to watch it to the end, he had dreamed about it, he couldn't forget the images, the scenarios, the words. He found the whole thing hard to stomach. He was angry with me and he was not the sort of person to get angry at anyone. Ever. He was in shock: he didn't understand the film and felt violated. All I could do was lend him my copies of Sade. He read them. He struggled but he stuck with it. And he never gave me back my books. He watched the Pasolini film again and no longer wanted to punch my lights out. He had understood the limits of human violence, he had tamed the horror, he had agreed to face the utter filth. He felt much more intelligent. I smiled. I don't know if he was more intelligent but he was armed. Against all forms of dictatorship and against all kinds of political manipulation. He was no longer afraid of wicked people. He had grown up.

I am twenty years old. I am twenty and I have already experienced love with Louÿs and have discovered how sex can be revolutionary with Sade. I am twenty and I know that I am living the best years of my life. I only have to think of Sade, I only have to think of the dialogue of Madame de Saint-Ange and Eugénie to know that all is not lost. I need only to think of Juliette to know that women have a standard that they proudly hold up high. One day, Sade will be the only weapon available to break through the darkness. The violence of Sade is not violent; it is born out of imagination and faith. His faith in man being the centre of thought and no longer being the puppet of those men who hide behind God.

Violence is the successive attacks against the female body worldwide. Violence is forbidding a little girl from learning to read and a young girl from choosing who she takes into her bed. Violence is what the Beards make spirits undergo by grinding them down. One day, just as the French Revolution threw its Beards out of the door, other revolutions will break out, reducing the Beards to silence and celebrating the words of Men.

Paris, 1997–2001

Four years without politics, without struggle, without the veil. Or almost. My passions were deep-rooted; the future existed only in the present. Four years when nothing was very serious, I was in love, I wanted to make cinema, write films, and university was my playground. I studied History and I debated as an equal with my lecturers who came for dinner at my house. One of them had known Che Guevara in Algeria, the other taught us the period of history known as Modern Times, and both of them were contagiously passionate. It was the first and only time in my life when I felt like I was in my place and when Khomeini was reduced to being merely a historical figure. Iran was still in the hands of the Beards, but Iran was far away. Nobody seemed to remember my Iranian origin and like all young people, we would talk until dawn about how we had to change the world so it would be in our image, later on.

It's a cliché, but it is so fitting that I cannot describe this time of my life any other way: we were young, naive and witty. We were all at the same starting point; all we had was our dreams to describe our present. We were not quite fully formed, and we had the feeling of being a generation. Absurd and false. But I needed, perhaps more than the others, to feel that I belonged to a group, to ideas, to Paris, which were not all related to my distant origins. I had a structured mind, solid arguments and raw convictions. A future existed, and that future was equality between men and women. Maybe not everywhere, maybe not for everyone, but there was a kind of push toward it. That's the problem with university: it reduces the world to your classes, your lecturers, to knowledge, freedom and the future. The world was served to us on a platter and even the extreme left militants of Jussieu were plotting revolutions every evening. We thought we were all intellectuals who were going to save the world. That was before careers replaced ambitions, before life was not just about succeeding in life, before everyone took it down a notch, before everyone cared about something other than themselves and the high rate of tax. It was a happy, rewarding time. The nostalgia of what might have been still remains, and it finds itself face-to-face with the monster of reality. Since childhood I had held a grudge against that nostalgia, and the end of my teenage years was the final nail in the coffin. The reality monster was not about to let go of me anytime soon, but I had not come that far to let myself be defeated by an empty bank account.

My brain was functioning at full capacity, and so my body was no longer hidden away behind sloppy jumpers and baggy trousers. Because we thought of ourselves as free, the body obviously had to follow suit. There was no such thing as a threatening body, or an imprisoned body. It was so easy to get naked! It wasn't a nudist camp every day or anything, but there was rarely anyone who refused to go for a midnight swim. What was great was that the body was detached from any sexual possibilities. It was easy to strip off and for it not to create general lechery. Our language was filthy, as if by naming things to do with sex it liberated us even more. Our need to be together as much as possible and to run into one another's arms to capture the moment by taking banal group photos, perhaps best illustrates the way we thought about our bodies at the age of twenty. It was also a time when everyone was working out more clearly what would happen to their physical body later on. The tastes and preferences of others fascinated me. It was libertine literature put into practice. Because everybody's nature projected the body into fantasies so different and diverse, that you would have to be an idiot to believe that only one form of enjoyment existed. Our friendships would survive the discovery of the individual sexuality of others, but for some, there would always be some uneasiness. I felt the knot in my stomach that I always used to feel whenever the body was disrespected, when desires and pleasures were confined, when people were convinced they were right when they were in fact against the body. It was reactivated when I saw the lifestyle choices of some being met with silence from others. That knot is my alarm bell. It wrenches my stomach and tears my heart open, it reminds me of the Crows and the Beards and the charred body of the prostitute of my childhood.

The acceptance of individual tastes and character traits is the essential condition for freedom. As long as these tastes and colours do not impede the tastes and colours of anyone else, they are essential to the advancement of society. If you deny me the right to read, I'll deny you the right to talk, and everyone loses. There are laws and there are limits, and freedom is not license, but if we had to give credit to everyone's fears, the world would be populated only by Beards and Crows. Our friendships survived individual tastes, but that was only possible because we were twenty years old and our intolerance had not yet cemented itself. A few more years, and the rigidity of our tastes would have shattered our friendship.

However, slap bang in the middle of all these joyful hopes, F's breakup happened. She was a young woman of Algerian origin, born in France, a beautiful young woman with big eyes as dark as raisins, brown hair in curly ringlets, bright, earnest and kind. I met her at university, where we both attended a lot of the same lectures: History of the Muslim World, Political Philosophy, Medieval History and History of Thought. She had been in a relationship for three or four years with a future engineer, and she was also enrolled on an Arabic course at Inalco, the National Institute for Oriental Languages and Civilizations. And in the middle of her fourth year, her future engineer dumped her. It was a shock. She was hopeless and vulnerable. Another student at Inalco took the opportunity to get close to her and, bit by bit, she persuaded her to come along to see a preacher who fascinated her. F had never practiced religion and she had never seen her parents practicing. She went with the student, who wore a veil, to the apartment of a bearded stranger. The living room was divided in half: on one side were the women, on the other, the men. A curtain separated them from each other. She sat down and listened. What she heard was that her lover had left her because he was a native Frenchman, and because she was, quite simply, a Muslim. What she heard, was that her tears were the consequence of her shamelessness and her sadness was only the result of her forgetting her faith. What reassured her was that nobody would ever do her any more harm if she accepted Islam above all else. Two weeks later, she came to lectures without make-up and with an African turban carefully arranged on her head. We all thought it was an original hairstyle. Another month later and she was wearing a headscarf, a real one, several layers thick, and she had become ugly.

I sought answers among our friends but nobody seemed to pay it much interest. She didn't smile any more, she didn't hug us any more after a few beers—it was haram, forbidden—she didn't come round for dinner any more—that was haram—she no longer looked male students in the eyes—that was haram—and gradually she stopped speaking to me—I was not halal at all. F's body was the first thing to withdraw into itself; it refused to be seen, and refused to look at our bodies. I can still see the panic in her eyes when I went into the toilets at Jussieu as she was arranging her headscarf. She squealed and rushed into a cubicle, slammed the door shut and actually *locked* it. I stood there in shock as she rushed to hide her hair from my eyes. Khomeini was still playing hide and seek with me. I was so shocked that I no longer even needed to pee. At that moment I remembered a story that my mother had told me about a very religious old woman who lived near them in Malayer. She was in her garden with her hair uncovered, doing the laundry. My mother had arrived with her father, and the pious lady, distraught at seeing my grandfather, pulled her skirt up over her head, baring her arse in the process. And so, like that, with her arse on display for all to see, she ran into the house to protect her virtue. The intellect cannot grasp the absurdity of the misunderstood body, the locked-up body, the body that has undergone such censorship that it forgets what can be shown and what can't.

F and her veil slammed the door shut on the future I had been hoping for, for women's bodies. She told me, while hiding herself from me, that women were going down the path of shame. That they continued to scorn their bodies in the hope of a hypothetical place in heaven. F and her conversion sounded the death knell for our university years. And there was more. Those of Muslim origin understood her, the guilty non-Muslims as well, and others not only did not understand her but didn't even have the right to. Everything was broken. Friends, who I thought were close, criticized me for my extremism. *My extremism.* F said aloud how we should accept the *fundamental* difference between men and women and subscribe to the notion that women cannot be like men, however much they want to be, that something was wrong with the world because women had forgotten that they were women, and I was the extremist. So I was the extremist, my provocations were met with silence, and I was isolated yet again. I stopped trying to argue with F, and all of my friends were better off for it. Even though I had become the intolerant one. Even though F shrugged her shoulders whenever I was around, whispering to those who listened to her that I had had a traumatic experience during my childhood—which had nothing to do with Islam but everything to do with the Shiites who were not *true* Muslims—which made me impervious to the mighty spirituality. It was then that I discovered that Sunnis thought I was a Shiite. No kidding. Travelling all those miles, ending up in Paris in a left-wing university, only to have my origins labelled as Shiite! I smiled. I smiled, and am still smiling. I don't even have the right to be an atheist. A friend of mine, who remained dear to me for a long time but who I eventually lost—because she thought that France was racist, and the Beards were the victims—made me realize that I, as a 'Shiite', was not compatible with her as a Sunni. I am still smiling because, in the end, when they have used up all their weapons against the West and its decadence, the Sunnis and the Shiites will destroy one another over who is the most Muslim of the two: those who wear a black turban or those who wear a white turban; over whether the Mahdi is coming or not; over whether Ali is as respectable as his father-in-law, Muhammad. We are not done laughing yet. And I have still got more tears to cry.

Every time I think about F, I feel bad for my Republic. The fact that France has failed her, it's as if France has failed at everything. For if F never really found herself in the triptych 'Liberty, Equality, Fraternity', it's because she didn't believe in it enough, to be so easily won over by the first Beard she came across after a normal first heartbreak. It just goes to show that nothing can ever be taken for granted. It was depressing: all that, and for what? The reason modern art was born in France was not just because of Père Libion's *café au lait* and the lilac days of 'la bohème', it was because Paris drew the godless to it like moths to a flame. You might die of cold and hunger, but you were freed from the gods. And every time I think of F, it's the figure of Chaïm Soutine that comes to mind. Soutine who was locked up by his father and the butcher in the refrigerated cellar of the village butchers for having drawn human figures. Soutine who would never recover from the prohibition that weighed on his paintbrushes. Soutine who came to Paris to paint—and to flee the Beards who prohibited him from painting. To live.

Paris, June–July 1998 – June–July 2010

It was just a group of guys chasing a ball around. It was nothing; it was just sport. But it was France. It was Paris, it was all ages and all social classes united under the same flag. We had stormed the Bastille and we had marched on the Champs-Élysées. With a ridiculous pride and a sense of 'History for Dummies'. But the intellectuals wrote articles about metaphors, sports commentators lost their voices, the streets of Paris were like never before. You only had to step outside to be swept up in it, in the enthusiasm and the solidarity with our national team. I remember how during France's matches, the Parisian streets were empty, cafes without TV screens were deserted, Parisians lived to the rhythm of Zidane's feet. Paris belonged to us; it belonged to those who believed that victory was possible; there was no place for scrooges and naysayers. Victory was within reach; the atmosphere was electric.

With the awareness of history in the making, France's victory during the 1998 World Cup seemed to be the peak of those years for me. And it was not just due to the diverse make-up of the team, it was mostly because we were ALL proud of being French. For as amazing as it might seem, I often felt alone in my adoration of France. Mind you, I was—and still am—a patriot, not a nationalist. Patriotism is about being *for*. Nationalism means being *against*. Suddenly, we were all patriots because France had managed to haul itself up onto the first place of the world podium by scoring goals. I was not a football fan—like a large majority of French people before we won—but the gradual steps toward victory made our French hearts beat as one. I think most French people felt, for the first time in a long time, how nice it was to feel a common pulse.

The night that France seized its place in the final, we were in a Scottish bar in the Saint Paul area. It was only natural that after we won, we headed to the Place de la Bastille where we joined in with the joyful cry of 'We're in the final! We're in the final!' It was the first time that I had climbed up on the base of the July Column. We stormed the Bastille with laughter and arrogance. An extraordinary thrill of excitement rushed through us, and being in our twenties was a big part of it. The collective body carried us, the collective body ravished us, the collective body was all of us, united under the victory of the Génie de la Bastille. I loved being there so much! I really thought that France had come to accept France as it was, with its colours and its differences, its miracles and its endless possibilities! It was our heyday! But we should have remembered that pride comes before a fall. We should have known that what France was celebrating that day was what it had forgotten to celebrate for too long, and even in everyone's comments—in the inevitable game of comparisons—the only parallel that was made was with the Liberation of 1944. It was not a demonstration in the defence of some profession, some social benefit, some progress or decline of morals. It was French people, all French people just celebrating the win. And the victory was down to men who didn't have the same birth, or the same experience, or the same body, or the same representations of France. They were men who resembled France and all French people could identify with them.

We should have known that something was lurking behind the victory. Something that would make us regret not having been more vigilant, more aware of our limits, less confident. We had all forgotten that it was hard work to get there, that we needed to harmonize all those differences to make a victory. We are hopelessly lazy. We sat on our victory and while our arses were still warm, we didn't expect what followed. The logical follow-up to the win of 1998 was 21 April 2002. Action. Reaction. Are we so fragile that we couldn't build on what the win gave us: a common ground, a shared point of reference, a French heart?

History was not over; it had not even paused. History had just hidden away in the recklessness of our twenties. My war, which F had brought back to life, should have given me a clue. I didn't want to lose what had been so hard to achieve: coming together under the same flag to advance toward a common future where being French was not about excluding, but bringing together. But before 21 April, before the French surrendered to their love of France, a new page of history was written. We are still on that page. It is being written every day, and its outcome still frightens me.

In July 2006, eight years after victory, France came up against Italy again in the final, but our hearts were no longer in it—I don't even want to talk about the World Cup in 2002 in South Korea when France lost pitifully in the qualifying matches. Had we lost our good spirit with age, or is it that nothing could restore what had already been decaying since 1998? Whatever the reason, I was much less happy. And I was hoping—as many were, without admitting it out loud—that France being in the final would restore morale. We gathered in front of the TV, we knew we could count on Zidane, on the newcomers, on a memory, on a trophy that would return to our hands. The match was almost over. It was a close match, but we had talent on our side. We were playing better; we were convinced of a win, body and soul. We were smiling, not daring to lift our arms in victory yet; we had a few more minutes to wait. And suddenly, everything went dark. Everything went dark because Zidane headbutted an Italian player who had insulted his mother or his sister. Everything went dark because of a head butt. And it was all over. At that exact moment, we all knew that when Zidane left the field without coming back, we were screwed.

It was not so much the violence that had marred the victory; it was the individualism that pulled the rug out from under our feet. Zidane had thought only of personal insult, he had not thought about his action for a second, he had lashed out and was sent off. Finishing like that, it was pathetic. Finishing a World Cup, a career, like that, was having nothing to do with us, France, the symbol. We lost. In 1998 we had won it all; in 2006 we lost everything, at once. France was no longer harmonious at all. France had just shown the world its inability to connect, to sing as one, to ensure victory. Zidane's head butt was nothing compared to what would happen four years later. It was just the introduction, the dress rehearsal before the complete disaster. It was just an alarm bell. But yet again, the analyses saw nothing but an individual act, a personal outburst. I didn't see anything else in it yet. There was nothing more to see than the sad end of a man who had been too proud.

June 2010. South Africa. More symbolic, impossible. A French team that held promise even if it worried. Would it live up to all its expectations? It was a disaster and a disgrace. But it was above all a reflection of what France had become. A country divided. A collective body that was nothing more than an airtight border. What happened in 2010 in South Africa was discrimination taken to the extreme. What happened was the dominance of kingpins and intolerance. The French team was no longer diverse; it was made up solely of Beards. Thug Beards, spoiled Beards, Beards even more dangerous than the others because they were just kids chasing after a football. The snippets of the insults we heard in the media were so embarrassing that we could no longer hide from hearing it. What we heard, was that some of them resented the others for not being Muslim enough, for not being black enough, for not being hetero enough, for having too wide a vocabulary, for being too good-looking. What we saw was that these kids could not even pass the ball to one another properly because they didn't like each other. And if they didn't like each other, it is because they rejected difference. They rejected the Other, forgetting that *they* were the Other. They played a contemptible match; they portrayed a disgusting image of France. They made me even more nostalgic for my twenties. The fact that France even slightly condoned an attitude that should have got them excluded permanently from any national selection is a perfect illustration of what it had become: an overcautious country that had entirely forgotten its values and, afraid of further accentuating the division, it cut corners. But this is not the way to put a broken body back together again, the way to bring people together, to define common ground among us all. That is not the way to enjoy playing for France.

The 2010 World Cup was an insult to the whole of France. The pride we felt in our twenties was long gone. France was in pieces. Between 1998 and 2010, history was put through the ringer. History was September 11, and 21 April, the war in Iraq and the kidnappings in Africa, the London bombings and the ones in Madrid. France just pulled its trousers down and let history give it a good spanking, right in front of the pampered children of a Republic that had neglected to teach them how to be polite.

Paris, September 2000

When the time came to choose the subject for my masters in History, I studied 'women, love and sex in Italian and French cinema between 1945 and 1958'. I chose the general title, 'How do women make love?' but my master's thesis advisor, a feminist specializing in the nineteenth century, rejected my idea. It was, 'You're not serious?', 'You can't reduce women to the way they make love', 'Uh ... even for you, Miss Shalmani, that's taking it too far.' What I meant was love in the sense of to love, but also, of course, in the sexual sense. How a woman's body is depicted between 1945 and 1958 depending on whether you situate it in the context of Italian Fascism or French collaboration. How the female body is affected by the traumas of men. What I meant was how filmmakers of the opposite sex in two European countries portrayed a woman in love, the sensual woman; in short, women after the Second World War. How politics overflows into the female body, how history takes the female body hostage. But it was clearly provocative. Put women and 'making love' in the same sentence, and it's provocative. What I wanted to show was how Italian women were synonymous with the future and with progress, and how the portrayal of French women was affected by the image of the humiliated, shaven-headed women after the Liberation. If Max Ophüls or Jean Renoir did try to make the female body something other than the sacrificial victim of the women who gave themselves to the enemy, the Duviviers and the Henri-Georges Clouzots exorcised the figure of the sensual and independent woman. They were scared of losing another battle, that of possession of the female body. Arletty's response to her judges during the *épuration legale,* or legal purge following the war, could have been used as a banner for all those women humiliated by the newfound virility of men who had lost the war before regaining victory: *'My heart is French, but my ass is international.'* Post-war France was a painful time of atonement for French women. I studied and wrote my thesis with a militancy I had never managed to put into politics. I had the feeling that what I was doing for women, by studying them historically, was much more worthwhile than the feminist slogans that I thought were backward. My studies brought me closer to libertine literature because I had to clear up the misunderstandings, flush out the unspoken, and restore the truth. And cinema is culture, and I had known for a long time that only culture is sturdy enough material for forging a weapon.

The day of my thesis defence, I arrived really late. I simply didn't wake up on time. I arrived with a bandana on my head like a pirate. When I think about it, I realize it was pretty ironic for me to be defending my master's thesis with my hair covered ... I have a sense of irony built into my DNA. I arrived late and out of breath from running, and my thesis advisor was waiting for me. She greeted me with 'You have a real problem with authority.' I know, Madame, just ask my first head teacher at school who wanted to have me exorcised. I sat down in front of her and the jury member who was a feminist and who had just had a baby. In other words, they were both slightly on edge. They were already pissed off, and I had barely got started when my beloved whores already had them up in arms. I opened my thesis with Robert Bresson's *The Ladies of the Bois de Boulogne.* I had analysed the film, taking into account the personality of the women and their will, without passing moral judgement on their means—one was an actress and mistress, the other a dancer who earned money by receiving male visitors. I noted the difference between novels (an extract from *Jacques the Fatalist* by Diderot) in which female characters were more cynical (libertine) and films, where they were lovers, first and foremost. Hélène the betrayed mistress and Agnès the young ambitious girl under the influence of her mother are strong figures who struggle, avenge, retaliate, rebel, and sacrifice. Hélène because she still loves Paul who doesn't love her any more, Agnès because she is a prisoner to her mother and the men who court her, including Paul who she is actually in love with. But the women created high drama, unlike the men, who were strangely bland, as if overpowered. Interruption from the jury: 'No, Miss

Shalmani.' Already? I had only been going for ten minutes. 'No, these women use their bodies; these women are reduced to their bodies. So?' So, because they are nothing but whores because they have a body, it is impossible to view it as anything other than being pimped out. So, it is impossible to see them as strong women, dominant women, or women with a personality. Seriously, will this never end?

It took a good half an hour before we could move on. I wondered if it would be the same for *Lola Montès* and *The Golden Coach*, but also *Bitter Rice*, and the femme fatale, Silvana Mangano. And sure enough, all the women that I used as examples—that I analysed from the point of view that I judged to be fair because it did not reduce them to the role of mere bodies—were whores. So they did not count. My wonderful, liberated whores! It was a real battle. All the same, I had worked hard and I deserved a good mark. But I was disappointed. And so were my jury and advisor. They were expecting something from this Iranian political refugee that was more akin to the classic feminist rant. They expected me to 'victimize' the body of women in cinema. As if it was enough for them to be a body, to be reduced to that body. As if women lost their value by revealing their bodies.

In July 2013, I met a young woman, a friend of a friend. We talked about films and TV series, and I confessed to having watched more series than films in the last three or four years. On my list was the epic, geopolitical fantasy series, *Game of Thrones:* an intelligent, bold series that emphasizes inspiring female characters. Mothers, daughters, orphans, queens, whores, prophets, warmongers and humanists. But all of them—apart from one—are independent, brilliant women. They go off to war with their son, support their father, weapon in hand, and seize power by themselves. They are true warriors. I thought that this genre sadly might not really appeal to women. Dragons, scenes of war and political manipulations; it was all too masculine. And yet. It is exactly the kind of genre that offered women real roles that viewers could identify with. But what do you know, the young woman I had recently met told me that she didn't like the series because the women were too often ... naked. I kid you not. This friend of a friend didn't seem to have any problem with the hundreds of series showing men's bodies that air before and after every commercial break, but a series showing female characters that are liberated and 'virile', this is what made her turn up her nose. And when I asked her what she thought about the series *Californication,* which is just the sickening succession of sexual encounters of a junkie novelist, she told me proudly that she loved it—she obviously didn't want to appear too uptight. Body equality was not going to be achieved overnight. Urgh ... I didn't care. I didn't care, but it was clear that I was alone again with my women and their bodies. With my body.

It was clear to me that by choosing that masters, and by choosing that rejected title, I came full circle in my desire to place women at the centre of reflection. Paradoxically, it was still a way of sidelining women, of placing the history of women parallel to that of men. It's so annoying! I feel that having given my voice to the forgotten women of the post-war period, before the New Wave and the sexual revolution should have redressed the balance between men and women—in the West at least. Those women, between two worlds—that of the pre-war which kept them firmly in the private domain, and that of the pretty widespread emancipation of the 60s—those hesitant, pioneering women sacrificed to the shackles of the household, were majorly overlooked by history. I was drawn to them for exactly that reason. I have never been able to cope with mess, with grey areas. I want to shed light on everything; I want to light up all women with the same spark.

A Franco-American journalist friend, who is just edgy enough to avoid blindly regurgitating the obvious clichés, has never understood how a 'smart girl like me' is interested in the 'dried cat shit' that is women's history. He couldn't give a fuck. He really wants to empathize with victims of female genital mutilation, with women who've been raped, with women who have no rights, but including them in analysis? No, no and no. We haven't finished talking and although I am giving him figures that illustrate better than long lectures that the economic success of a country goes hand in hand with the status of women, he is not having any of it. I throw studies at him like that of the UN showing that if young Indian mothers waited until their twentieth birthday before having children, the country's gross income would increase by almost eight billion dollars. I'll never understand it—he is not an idiot even though he displays some of the traits of one—but I have not had the last word on the matter. I will follow him to the grave with my arguments; in the end I will show him how failing to take women into account means not understanding a society and its faults, its organic functioning, its future. From as early as the eighteenth century, Choderlos de Laclos made the connection between the education of women, their place in society and a nation's progress.

I finished my university studies the same way I had started my schooling in France: with my 'Queens of France' that my first teacher had not wanted, by placing women at the centre of my studies. By seeing the forgotten woman, the rejected woman, the humiliated woman, but also the warrior, the dominatrix, the liberated woman, the lone wolf. I am aware how important it is to feed their memory; I realize how vulnerable women who do not know their histories can be, and how inspiring they could be.

Paris, 2013

This colossal memory of mine does not give me a choice. I don't have the right to forget the story—neither the big nor the small. The history of the world and my own, humble one. I cling to what has gone before, as if my mental stability depends on it. I feel like forgetting is erasing. And I don't want to miss anything. I don't want to be superficial and go through life as if yesterday was nothing but a mirage. That wouldn't be fair. Not just to my past, not just to my parents and my whole family, suffocating in the present. I know that behind these words and these great theories, there are the children of history. The truth of those who did not have a choice, and who suffered. Understanding the past, means mastering it. Slowing the course of time, means never forgetting. I forget nothing, I live with the past, I cherish the past that gives me the opportunity to be as French as any Frenchman.

In June 2013, the excellent chef at a bistro we always used to go to, and who had become a close acquaintance through seeing him every day, and because of his talent for delighting our taste buds, suddenly told me that he didn't see me as French. Because I don't have French parents, let alone grandparents. Even if I jump through all the hoops, can speak more than impeccable French, have a greater knowledge than he has of the history of France, its great men, its key dates, even if I am ready to give my life for the Republic to live, I will never be, in his eyes, French. I didn't just take it badly. I did not just mull it over in my head for days on end. I suffered deeply. Even though he had been drinking, and he kept on repeating that he really liked me, he had failed to recognize the part of me that acts as my shield. I am French by culture and language; I am French through my knowledge of the past that I share with all French citizens. But above all, I would be lost in Iran. I would be more of a foreigner there than I have ever been in France. By dismissing me from France, he made me stateless, alone, unhappy. By not allowing me to be French, he sent me back in to the shadows of the memoryless. That was what hurt me the most: he denied me my memory. Memory, which was the most obvious form of my love for France. So yes, I need to remember, I need to keep turning over what has been before, ten years ago, a hundred years ago, a thousand years ago. I cannot be simple and carefree. I am responsible for history.

Paris, 11 September 2001

I was at my parents' house. I was writing a documentary on Madeleine Pelletier. I had headphones on, and my mother was in the next room with the children she was looking after. I was in love again. This time it was with a tall blond man, and I was riding high, feeling as though I was on the verge of conquering Paris. My mother came into my room and cried, 'Something horrible is happening.' I sighed, sure that my mother was being typically Iranian, and that the VCR had stopped working again or something. I got to the TV just as the plane crashed into the second tower. It was spectacular, it was like something out of Hollywood, it was an accident or an attack, and above all, it was a fucking mess. Nobody seemed to know what was going on. My mother was in tears, the children who adored her were in tears, and I remained standing in front of the television screen while the phone rang and nobody thought to answer it. I came to my senses and called my father, as if he would be able to give me the answer. I was irritated when he told me that he didn't know what was going on. I was hysterical and my father reminded me that the Afghan commander Massoud had been killed the previous day. Great. Do you expect me to give a shit about that? I called my Franco-American journalist friend, who told me, before hastily hanging up, 'Saddam or Bin Laden.' I did not think Saddam Hussein was as powerful as that and I had never heard of Bin Laden. I stayed with my mother watching the TV, then my father came home and we all stayed in front of the images on a loop until bedtime. We were silent—except for my mother's occasional sobs—and faced with the panic-stricken crowd, the smoke filling the streets of New York, we couldn't help but be reminded of our own war. It was poignant. And information trickled through, amidst the far-fetched commentaries of the analysts who were as con-fused as we were. It was Bin Laden, it was the Islamists; it was war. I was devastated. It was too much to bear: as if eve-rything was starting over again, but this time it was for the whole world. But ... maybe there was hope, too. For us.

For the more than twenty years we had been living in France, we had passed for traumatized victims of the Beards. So our commentaries on the issue of the veil, on the Islamists, on the dangers of cultural relativism—which was nothing more than the hidden face of religious extrem-ism—and on the clear conscience of the Left, were just met with sympathetic smiles and disapproving nods. I remem-ber my father never took umbrage, while I was the one shouting that we were right, that my father knew what he was talking about, that we should not let it happen, that we had to defend secularism, the Republic, keep religion at home, and citizens on the streets. And it was always my father telling me to be quiet and me slamming the door, in tears, because Super Tolerance Man could never imagine shouting at others just because they didn't know what they were talking about. Forgive them; they know not what they do. Super Tolerance Man never wavered. My mother was fretting about whether the terrorist wave would hit Paris and my father turned to us and said, 'That would be the last straw, wouldn't it, fleeing from the Iranian Beards only to be blown up in Paris by a Saudi bomb.' We were so tense that we just burst out laughing. The Beards were certainly right on our arses.

September 11 was the day when the Beards—who in others' eyes seemed to belong to us alone—made their mark on the world. I was certain that now that more of us knew, things would work out. I was still a child. I could not imagine that people in the countries of the Beards would applaud the mass murder of September 11. I could not imagine that mothers and fathers of families, poverty-stricken people, would jump for joy at the murder of Sri Lankan or Mexican cleaning ladies. I could only imagine that things would get better, that the Beards would turn everyone against them. September 11 taught me that I knew nothing.

In the days that followed there was widespread confusion. I was seeing a young man from a good family nestled away in the 6th arrondissement: above-the-fray, conservative, high society snobs, perhaps, but I had also kept my friends from the middle or even working class who were above-the-fray, progressive, artist snobs. I would go from one world to the other, and it was hard to weave the two together. In the 6th, I couldn't have been more of a spare part if I'd tried. The Tall Blond's uncle had even nick-named me the 'commie foreigner'. I mean, really? Although they were surprised by my culture and my sassiness, and found my passion for libertine literature original and my love for France amazing, they never really accepted me. I don't think they could make the connection between my culture and my social status. I had bourgeois attitudes—I was born bourgeois—and the bank balance of a Chinese factory worker. Put more simply: my parent's financial situation made me seem suspicious. They would forget about it, but when they remembered, they would close ranks. The pauper in the midst of wealthy people always incites fear. He represents what they fear most and they worry that he will take what they have. I still remember, like a wound that never fully healed, when The Tall Blond said to me, 'You're only with me for my apartment.' An apartment that was just a room, 25m^2, more or less the size of my room at my par-ents'. It had never occurred to him that I was madly in love with him. I was in love and I thought that my culture was the only valid passport to get where I wanted to be. The Tall Blond's family quickly pushed me back beneath the poverty line where I had come from.

I was definitely the only representative of the Muslim world that they hung out with and my atheism evaporated into thin air after September 11. They forgot who I was, seeing only the Muslim girl they wanted to see. I heard awful sentences: 'Don't you feel slightly guilty?'—'Don't you think it would be a good time to convert?'—'It's now or never if you want to have French children, right?'—'You can't say, after everything that's happened, that Islam is like all other religions.' Well yes, I can. And I do. And I say out loud that all religions are monstrous when they march toward conquest in the name of faith, that all religions are the same when they think they are right, that all Beards are the same when they cause deaths. They crushed me, and my friends from the 11th arrondissement helped. Because people in the 11th were also sharpening their weapons to defend themselves against ... racists. For suddenly, there were racists everywhere. That's how I, as an Iranian political refugee, became a racist. You should have heard it, the clear conscience of the suburbanites taking it in turns to denounce the unjust treatment of Muslims. I would clarify: 'Islamists' and I was always within an inch of hearing, 'it's the same thing', before they carried on.

As I was stuck between two worlds—one that only saw the Muslim in me, the other that saw the French girl—I was incapable of holding a logical argument in the midst of the chaos. As if repeating the past, I was in the same position that my father was in during the Iranian Revolution: he was against the Shah and against the communists, against the religious men and against the monarchists. He refused to take part in demonstrations against the Shah with the communists, then with their new friends, the religious men. He advocated democracy and the communists heard

America, he advocated secularism and the religious men heard St. Bartholomew. He witnessed the Revolution that was going to screw up his life, alone at the window of his office, and he had to wonder if it had all started the day he had been beaten up on the campus of his university, when a communist had caught him reading Graham Greene. A few days later, he had been taken to task by the religious men, because he was reading Camus. I was reliving a post-September-11 version of my father's life.

There were those in the 11th who excused the indiscriminate murders, explaining it through terrible American imperialism, and those in the 6th who, trembling with fear, made xenophobic comments against all of Islam, including my grandfather. It is one thing to denounce murders that have only a political aim, and it's quite another to reproach believers for their faith. I can still picture my boyfriend's bright cousin, quoting passages from the Quran, to explain that the World Trade Center was nothing less than the towers of Babylon, whose fall is described in one of the suras. Too many people bought the Quran, looking for an explanation in it, and it was laughable to see them searching, exactly like the Beards, for something to feed their fantasies. The Beards decipher truths in the suras that science has demonstrated or history has validated (the moon voyage, the victory of the Byzantine Empire, modern means of transport, the conquest of Mecca, the transfer of smell (no joke) and even atomic energy and fission) and the xenophobes do the same thing. They are all the same; they all have the same simplistic approach. The way they think is wrong.

September 11 is a huge question mark. It certainly created a relational vacuum, an unhealthy doubt about the extremism of one another. September 11 created a deep rift that has swallowed up the most brutal, the most intolerant, the most dangerous. One person's pig has become an insult to another's lamb. Although speech has been liberated, it is a sad fact that it has been liberated for the worse. I was cursing the Beards and Crows even more viciously, because it was out of the question to give up on universality of rights. It was clear in my mind: they were not going to win again. They were not going to drag down with them, yet again, those that were born in the land of Islam. No way. But it was difficult to stand up to all the extremists at the same time. It was hard to respond to right-wingers that no, murder is not genetically built into Muslims, and to the left, no, colonization is not a passport to doing whatever you like. The military intervention in Afghanistan, then the war in Iraq, only exacerbated the misunderstandings. We insulted one another as we did at the height of the Cold War: you pro-American bastard, you leftist son of a bitch! The realism of some versus the naive optimism of others. I was firmly left wing until September 11. And then I became a fierce reformist. And then I could no longer bear to support those who genuinely thought that September 11 was a consequence of colonization. The Americans who had financed the wars of decolonization became the traumatized victims of colonization. It was depressing when I think that Bin Laden couldn't give a flying toss about colonization, that his hatred of America was born much later when, *at the request of the Saudi king himself,* thank you very much, the US military set up camp in the holy land of Mecca. That was all, and that was enough to turn the world upside down. He had opened Pandora's Box purely because he could no longer bear to see the infidels in his country. And all the others saw the opportunity to heap all their failures, all their disappointments and their inability to cope with modernity on the backs of the Americans and their friends. September 11 was a victory for stupidity coupled with a lack of culture. September 11 was the victory of fools over thinkers, of extremists over humanists. September 11 announced the defeat of the female body.

My relationship with The Tall Blond who voted left wing—when he bothered to vote—and who thought right wing, was starting to turn sour. But I clung to past experience so I stayed with him. I waited until another page of history would force us to drift apart for good. I stopped arguing just for the sake of it, and I hid myself away in the eighteenth century, while I waited for everyone to calm down a bit. I am still waiting.

Paris, 2013

Everyone remembers what they were doing, where they were, when September 11 fell on the world's head. That was the point. The Beard-Terrorists knew exactly what they were doing. It was not so much that they wanted a maximum number of deaths, but a maximum number of spectators. They got what they wanted. Everyone saw September 11 live and direct. It was the first terror attack-show in history. And it was the Islamists who refused the representation of the human face, who staged it. It was another Beard, in grey and brown, who had financed and prepared it. It was another Beard, worse because he knew no borders. The 'old man in black and white' was not an expansionist; he just wanted to fuck up Iran. But the new one was an internationalist, he was Saudi and he hid out in the caves of Afghanistan, he was an heir and he was the spokesman of the poor. He was also a murderer in a robe and turban. But they all wanted the same thing: they wanted to cover the world up in black and tears.

What do we do about September 11? What do we do about post-September 11? What do we do about those who think Israel had a hand in it? Those who saw a manipulation in it? A conspiracy? A just vengeance? What do we do with those who saw a well-deserved parallel with September 1973 when Allende was overthrown by Pinochet, helped by the Americans? What do we do with the extreme left that forgives the Beards? What do we do with those who are convinced that poverty and hunger are an excuse for murder? What do we do? I don't know how we can justify that. What I do know is the only thing that makes me smile: the 'conspiracy theorists' take the responsibility for the attacks away from the Beards. They must be fuming with rage, far away in their caves or wherever they are, where people believe in the Beards, to see that even after September 11, some people do not think they are capable of mounting such an attack. That it could only be the Americans or the Jews. That is laughable.

However, after September 11, when I was expecting a healthy reaction from the famous French Muslims—and I say French Muslims, not Muslims in France, because we are all French—they disappointed me just as the Iranians disappointed me after the Revolution of the Beards. Out came the veils, *halal* food was on every plate and the non-Beards started to look like the Beards. I was outraged. Rue de la Roquette sadly began to see more and more veils, more and more aggressiveness. I heard phrases like, 'If you come over for dinner, don't bring wine, you should leave it on the landing outside.' Sorry? We are in Paris, in 2001, and a French Muslim friend explains that his living space is so sacred that not a drop of alcohol shall enter. Is this a joke? No, it's serious. It's very serious. It's so serious that they all ended up taking themselves seriously. I thought back to my Sufi grandfather, I thought about his faith that never wavered, I thought of that exceptional man who opened a bottle of wine every day for a thirsty traveller who might end up staying at his home, I see him making up a bed, and putting grapes, bread, and cheese at the entrance to his house in case a homeless person might try and find shelter there. I remember him as someone who never drank a drop of wine, who believed in God with a force I have never seen in anyone else, and who never wondered whether his wine cellar was an insult to God.

What has become of true faith? A faith that doesn't impose anything on anyone else but the self; a faith that talks with God in a healthy and spiritual relationship? Who is this Frenchman who calls himself a practicing Muslim, and who thinks that a bottle of wine will *dirty* his apartment? Does he have so little faith that he needs so many pretences, so much proof to feel like a believer? What has got into these children born in France and raised at the teat of secularism? Who do they think they will convince of their faith if they don't even believe in it enough? As of September 11, that was the end of French Muslims. They became just Muslims. Not just in other people's eyes, but above all, in their own eyes. It was the time of mistrust and the time of settling accounts. The time of disappointment and the time of resistance.

Oh my friend, oh my beautiful friend, who adores red wine and who is in love with a 'true-born' Frenchman, who had brought into the world two wonderful little mixed-race girls, whose father was as secular as you can get, who is so intelligent, so sweet, so cultured. My friend with the dark eyes and soothing voice, whose arguments were always measured, who calmed my ardour and held my hand when I was so sad, so alone, so isolated. What happened to you, my dear friend? What happened to the France in you? Why do you see racists everywhere? Why do you think that criticizing political Islam is an insult to the religion of your fathers? What happened to your agnosticism? Why this absurd return to a religion that blew up your mother's pharmacy in Algeria, because she was a woman? How can you tell me about faith when you are actually just telling me about politics? How have you let yourself be taken in? What happened to you and me? Why I am so uncomfortable when we talk? How have we lost one another?

Above all, we were French. We were political refugees in Paris. We had so many laughs, so many debates, and so many things to tell each other. My friend was lost because of September 11. She was lost because I could no longer keep my mouth shut. Because I couldn't let people talk, let it slide. I lost you because you still thought about the trauma of my childhood when I was far away from Tehran. I was a young French woman who knew both her France and her Islam, and whom you denied the right to ask: why? Why are French Muslims so unfriendly? Why are women covering their heads post-September 11, if it isn't in support of the Beards who are their number one enemies? Why did you look at me with such mistrust when I tried to get you to admit that you didn't seriously believe that women in burkas were making a choice. I resorted to telling you that the Nazis had also made a choice. I resorted to using arguments that were below us. But nothing swayed you: there are only a handful of Nazis in France. How you could give me such an unhelpful argument? One is already one too many. One is already a failure. And how can you defend what is not even in the order of religion, but a local custom that has become a symbol of a political rallying? You ended up blurting out: attacking women in burkas is rejecting all Muslims outright. It is stigmatizing. There. You said it. The only word that I didn't want to hear you say, the only word that belonged to the Beards. Stigmatize. Well yeah, I stigmatize those who restrict access to their faces, I stigmatize those who are so ashamed to be seen by us that they hide their eyes. And that makes me—and just writing it makes me angry—Islamophobic? You, you used a word that is the prerogative of the Beards? You, you are taking the side of those who create borders, who sneak in the back door, who reduce a woman to her shadow?

Oh my friend, I miss you so much. Just like I miss our Parisian mixed-race-ness. I would have loved for you to read these lines and to correct me, to tell me that I'm confusing faith and practice, that I'm forgetting that I am not in Tehran any more. Is there nothing left of our friendship? Apart from the memories and chance encounters on the Parisian metro. All that remains is uneasiness. I am intolerant and you are Muslim. One day, one of the final days before it became too hard for us to see each other any more, you told me you were considering going back to live in Algeria. Because you couldn't bear the gaze of the French people any more. I was startled: which French? Who? How? But nobody has ever looked at you as anything other than French, of exotic origin. I know, it's not the nicest, but I'm also exotic and so what? A Breton who never left Saint-Malo is just as exotic as you and me. There is nothing wrong with being exotic, for that matter. But no. You told me that I was too white, I had adopted the French physique, that I couldn't possibly understand. I couldn't understand, said in the same tone as my parents when they told me I didn't understand Iran. You don't understand, and that explains all the silences. I was a convert, more radical than the others and you, you stayed perfectly Algerian? For what purpose? What if it was you who didn't feel like refusing to ignore your origins to talk to me as an equal? You put distance between us, and it was Khomeini who carried on undermining everything, who reminded me that identity is sometimes wrapped up in a turban. You know what hurt me the most about this whole mess, this whole misunderstanding? The fact that the shared culture that connected us no longer mattered. It no longer mattered that we had read the same books, studied the same thinkers, and spent our twenties together. None of that meant anything any more because suddenly religion took up all the space. Religion became identity, it became essential; it became more important than anything. More important than having the right to vote and to think freely without being beaten by truncheons. You thought I was too much, I didn't think you were enough. And our divisions have become widespread. Anything that even touched on the issue of Islam in France became problematic, dangerous to debate, a cause for disagreement. What is so horrific about being French? What is so awful about being French? It means being a citizen, letting your neighbour eat whatever he wants, sitting at the same table as anybody, not insulting anyone who believes, thinks or breathes differently. What is so degrading about assimilation that it makes you raise an eyebrow? How do I respect my parents, my history or my past any less by being French? Where I see richness, you see failure and problems. And when the *banlieues* go up in flames, it's never the fault of the kids who take a whole neighbourhood—a whole population—hostage; it's because of police racism. Nothing else. Excusing the violence of some under the pretext of poverty is an insult to all the poor. As if being poor means being an uneducated idiot. It's insulting to those who do not look for excuses, who know that education has nothing to do with material wealth. So no, my dear friend, I will not let you insult the people who live in the so-called 'rough' suburbs, who are trying to survive under the dictatorship of those little pricks who take them hostage, humiliate them, who use them to stop the bullets. And you, you no longer looked at me unless it was with utter disdain, you saw me only as your enemy. That was the end of us. We drowned in September 11. We drowned in the dislocated body of the country that had welcomed us, you and me. We were part of the same body and since September 11, we can only glare at each other. I miss your twenties. My twenties make me melancholy. The 'old man in grey and brown' took my best memories away from me. And my closest friend.

Paris, 21 April 2002

My relationship with The Tall Blond was on its last legs. It was approaching its end, and it was my mother's birthday. She had wanted to invite The Tall Blond and his sister, and a friend of his sister, nicknamed Captain Hook on account of how evil she was, how poisonous. It was a Sunday and it was Election Day. My mother had really outdone herself in the kitchen. It was divine. I tried to think only about my plate so I didn't have to take part in the boooorrrring conversation that was going on. So boring! It was my mother's birthday, the sun was shining, and everyone was waiting for Jospin and Chirac on the 8 o'clock news, but nobody had voted—except for my parents who were French citizens already. I was still a political refugee—don't get me wrong: I wanted to be French by law, but I hated admin and I was lazy—and I had already had an argument that morning with The Tall Blond who did not vote. I wondered how I was going to get out of that mess and my father was throwing me subtle looks that were full of hidden meaning. He was wondering what we were all doing there. I ate my lunch, while in my head I kept telling myself that I had never liked blonds.

Finally lunch was over and I left with The Tall Blond to go back to the 6th arrondissement. I am not exactly sure how we got onto it, but we picked up that morning's argument and this time, it was not about politics, but about ... housework. He called me a 'gypsy' because the floor hadn't been cleaned for a week. I couldn't care less because I was just waiting for election night. I had always loved election nights and their cohort of bad faith, great words, victory, and defeat. It was a Greek tragedy every time and I always had fun. The Tall Blond had done so much shouting and I was so sick of being called a gypsy that I picked up the floor cloth and started cleaning the floor, while he bellowed that it should be both of us, that we should do everything together, and that I was selfish. I wasn't listening to him any more; I was listening to the pre-election results commentary. Because I was so used to these commentaries, I realized that something was amiss. There was too much 'surprise' in the presenter's voice, he was too flustered, as if he could no longer follow his teleprompter. I was still on all fours, floor cloth in hand; The Tall Blond didn't hear anything and was still bawling when the 8 o'clock news started and the face of Jean-Marie Le Pen appeared on the screen. I didn't make a sound, but I heard a huge cry go up all around, resounding from one apartment to another. The 6th arrondissement had many flaws, but voting for the extreme right was not one of them. They had simply not voted that day because of sunny terraces and impromptu picnics. I was still on all fours, and The Tall Blond rushed out onto the balcony to talk to his sister, who was also his neighbour. The first thing I did was call my mother. As predicted, she had started packing and my father was not attempting to calm her down. He laughed. My father has his own sense of humour, but it's still the best way of protecting himself against the absurd. She was in tears, it was her birthday, they couldn't do *that* to her. She was happy in France, she didn't want to leave again, she would not go into exile again. I kept telling her it was nothing, that there was a second round, and if the French voted in the second round, Le Pen's face would no longer be on the screen. I hung up because The Tall Blond, his sister, and Captain Hook had decided to go out and protest. I refused: the day had not yet come when I would protest against the right to vote. But I was outnumbered three to one, and they wore me down with their childish arguments—I was selfish, I was a gypsy, I didn't even have the right to vote and therefore had no right to blame them for not voting, so there!

I must point out that this was a very dark period in my life, a period of family breakdown. I clung to The Tall Blond as if I was clinging to the branches of a rotting tree, on the verge of letting go, but just keeping my head above water. This unlikely succession of troubles and tragedies that had rained down and would continue to rain down on us even harder, gripped me by the shoulders and in the pit of my stomach, as I finally followed The Tall Blond, his sister, and the inimitable Captain Hook. I followed them out onto the streets of Paris and we headed toward the Bastille. There were lots of people, lots of young people and old people, lots of confused people and lots of high spirits. I don't think anybody expected so many people to gather spontaneously like that. Of course, there were the night-time protestors who saw an opportunity to party, others who felt guilty for not voting, or not voting for Jospin in the first round, and even some who were there out of a deep conviction against the extreme right.

I wanted to believe that 21 April would bring something for us, the French Muslims, French Africans, French Asians, and all the others who were offering up the most beautiful attestation of love. The whole of France standing on the pavements, marching against intolerance, against the extreme right, against all those who wanted to destroy the Republican foundation upon which we have built centuries of history: we, the children of exiles, we, the lovers of France. She overthrew September 11, she hit back, she showed Le Pen and company that all was not lost, that France was what it was. Even better than the 1998 World Cup, even better than a football team, it was politics that made the harmony of all French people shine. 'First, second, third generation! All of us are the children of immigrants!' I was definitely moved. For me it was personal, it was about defending myself and my mother who was already packing her bags; it was a declaration of brothers in arms against the extreme right. I saw millions of French people on the streets of France, families, groups of friends, all those people who gathered to say 'No'; I suddenly saw a future after the shock of September 11, I already saw the Crows burning their garments and the Beards shaving, to return the favour to France. I saw my mother, who was protesting for the first time since Tehran and who looked as if she thought all the placards and shouting were for her benefit. So, the French really did love us.

I remember, in the days that followed, throughout the course of two massive demonstrations, bumping into my baker and my gynaecologist, friends of the family and neighbours, the tobacconist and the postmistress, who had been so rude. It felt like everyone was there. Even The Tall Blond and his family who were usually above the fray, they were all there in a row. I told myself that I was right to still stay with him, that I had been right to fall in love. It was already too late, but it was a final ray of hope. But where were the people who had voted for Le Pen in the first round?

Paris, 2013

In time, 21 April no longer seemed traumatic, except for politicians. Especially for the socialists. They wake up in the middle of the night in a cold sweat over not being in the second round and having to go into coalition with the republicans. The French no longer remember 21 April, they have forgotten the cries and the shock, they have forgotten that they didn't want Le Pen just over ten years ago. They don't remember the bewildered face of Jean-Marie Le Pen when he saw the results, and how nervous he was, as if he was shocked at the prospect of potentially having to run the country.

Since 2002, the National Front has become the leading labour party in France and not an election goes by without Le Pen's daughter clawing more and more votes away from the socialists who have forgotten the poor, and the UMP who forgot them a long time ago. Caught up in Europe's debt, the poor and the European middle classes both suffer and, as in any failure, they blame the Other. Brussels and immigrants. Especially immigrants. Le Pen's daughter who has really understood everything, the heiress, who has brought a top-level graduate into the party, has Jauressian overtones while continuing to attack immigration. And many French people agree and spit on the elite and Roma, on the unemployed and the Arabs, and especially Muslims in France, and are following ... the heiress. This is not amnesia, it's not stupidity, it's not irreversible. It's a profound reaction of the disillusioned. Because they feel they can no longer control their tomorrows, because the future is decided by remote and abstract bodies, because the politicians are nothing more than bureaucrats, the French who vote for the far right are no longer to blame. Marine Le Pen and her supporters would be incapable of running France, they would be incapable of keeping their promises. But they make promises and it seems that they speak the 'truth'.

It's not that she doesn't mince her words, she spews them out, she restores France to its former glory by painting an idealized picture of it. A France that feeds itself and lives on its own. An impossible France that has never existed. What I believe is that your average French person—a Northern worker who hears Marine's egalitarian nationalist refrain to a Southern Poujadist humming the anti-Muslim and anti-unemployed tune—cannot find anyone else to vote for. He no longer wants to be cheated by the Left who have promised so much and taken so much back, or the Right who have never paid him any attention. He wants an end to unemployed people who could actually be working, and for Muslims to stop their squalling. Tension, fear, identity. Going back to the past, with immigrants rubbed out and the unemployed such a minority that they did not really exist. Going back to a time when only the Frenchman existed is impossible. But it's so reassuring. As if the 'true-born' Frenchman was incapable of snatching a bag, or raping a girl, stealing an apple or causing havoc on the metro.

The problem is that facing them, among those who no longer define themselves as French Muslims, but as Muslims in France, there is a plethora of rigid, backward-looking people, worthy of Marine Le Pen herself. They are as absurd as those who vote against them. They are just as fanatical about identity and monoculturalism. In my opinion, they are all as unpleasant as each other, they have the same intransigencies, and they imagine with the same madness, the same black-and-white future. The National Front supporters who take the middle classes hostage by making them imagine the future as a simplified past, and the Beards of France who take the Muslims hostage to make them believe that happiness is found beneath a veil. They are in agreement: neither of them wants the other. They are monotonous, they are mediocre and they are hateful. They are as unpleasant as each other, the fearful National Front supporters and the bad-tempered Beards. They are the same, and still nobody really seems to care about 21 April and the national cohesion that should have come out of it.

As if solidarity and good living would spontaneously be reborn out of the disappearance of immigration and the poor. And the Beards of France, do they sincerely think that they would be happier and better accepted if Eid was a French national holiday? I mean, what the hell are these delusions that always exclude the Other but never make steps toward the Other? We have to strengthen our Republican morale for it to guarantee the faith of the individual and the freedom of all. I am a citizen first and foremost, before religion comes into it; France is above all my beliefs. I live with my faith, my passions, my hobbies, as I like, without wanting to prevent my neighbour from doing the same, without judging him, without disturbing him—whatever our differences—on a common basis that rejects the Beards and Crows. Because the National Front supporters are Beards. They are the same and they promise nothing less than civil war. You might think I'm a pessimist, you might still see me as a political refugee who sees war at the bottom of every ballot box. Don't laugh; take note. Take note that there are neighbourhoods in France where neither the police nor the fire service dare to go, there are businesses where Arabs are not welcome, and there are invisible barriers so visible to some people that few dare to cross them. Civil war does not need weapons. It needs Beards. And they are increasingly active, increasingly present, increasingly popular, and increasingly extremist. From all sides. They rely on each other, bounce off each other's intransigencies; they need each other to give sense to their nonsense. Marine and the Beards are gaining ground, thanks to abstention. They each use the capitulation of the other. If citizens took their role more seriously again, if the French Muslims saw themselves more as the citizens they are, there would no longer be a threat from National Front supporters or staunch communitarianism. There would just be French citizens.

Paris, 1994–2013

At first it was just a teenage attitude, thinking that everything is rubbish, sulking because everyone is so stupid, looking for a way of creating a visible persona—a teenager needs to stand out to feel like they exist. They laugh loudly, talk loudly, they make a lot of noise in general. It was the continuation of being fifteen and refusing to wear anything other than black, or being sixteen and wanting African braids and ending up with platinum blonde highlights—looking ridiculous was a way of rebelling.

It was adolescence and it was all, 'Look at me! Love me! I'm different!' Style-wise, your teenage years are so cringe-worthy when you look back as a rational adult. But there are some teenage rebellions that linger. For me, they not only lingered but increased over the years. Maybe it was the inevitable sequel to my naked bottom as a child. Maybe it was my fascination with women that continued. Maybe it was just a matter of taste. Whatever it was, skirts came back into my life at sixteen—the same time as blonde highlights.

At first it was purely for aesthetic purposes: I didn't look good in trousers. I am too petite and trousers make me look even shorter. Also, I have always hated uniform. I have always hated seeing a person dressed the same as someone else. Jeans became a uniform and I didn't want to blend into the background. Finally, it's militant. I wear dresses and skirts because I am not ashamed of being a woman. And I want people to see that. I look like a woman because the Beards hate women. I look like a woman in case Khomeini ever looks in my direction.

The militant aspect of the skirt began when I was seventeen. My first love was involved with the Trotskyite youths, and I wanted to share everything with him that was close to his heart. He introduced me to his militant friends and I had long hair, red lipstick, long nails and a black dress, high heels and a straw bag. I thought I was fascinating. They thought I was just bourgeois. They refused to speak to me and advised me to cut my hair and stop wearing whale blubber on my lips. They kindly told me that I was inaudible because I was hidden behind my femininity, which was just a sign of my belonging to a bourgeoisie that starved the people while filling its own pockets. They referred to the greatest of my faults: being a woman. Once again. They literally shut me down. I had a lot to say, a lot to shout about, a lot to blame them for, but I was too taken aback by those guys, like mini-Khomeinis, fussing about in front of me, with their long hair and their baggy T-shirts, their dirty nails, and their hard, cold stares that cut through me.

They were against the whole world, but especially against

women who looked like women, and bourgeois women who smelled of perfume and of whom I had become the most perfect representative. They were not even capable of imagining that my parents were poor, that I was poor, that my life up until that point had been a series of more or less difficult struggles, that my childhood had been balanced between total happiness and sudden violence. They were the sons of doctors and philosophy professors at France's most prestigious universities, the sons of journalists and officials, they had travelled all over the world with their 'bastard parents', but apparently they knew what *real* life was about. They just had their heads up their own asses. They had never even read Stirner. What can you do? I wore too many of the external signs that offended their budding Beard convictions. They were seventeen, nineteen at most and they were so old, so jaded, so aggressive. They looked furtively around them, on the lookout for a new enemy, a well-dressed man, a woman in a suit, a child smiling too much. And they came back to me, then nodded toward my first love to really make him feel like he was a social traitor every time he penetrated me. I had already met this kind of mini-Khomeini, at school during the Rushdie affair and after Adjani's grand gesture. I had already seen the hard eyes of Crows in the street, but the Khomeinis of the extreme left—I had never seen one so close. I didn't think that the Parisian extreme left could be as narrow-minded, as radical, as stupid as the lowliest Beard. They quickly forgot me and I sat drinking my white wine—they only drank coffee and glasses of water—and I carried on watching them. I was getting more and more angry. But I said nothing. I had to think. I was thinking about how I would come across them again in my life. How I needed to sharpen my words. That I still had a lot to learn.

I can still hear the sound of my high heels on the pavement after the meeting of the Trotskyites in that squalid bar; I can still hear that feminine sound that was so shameful to the good proletarian conscience. I listened carefully to the sound of my heels, I listened to the sound that marked my belonging to the bourgeoisie and the female sex, and that made the left of the left so ashamed. I listened to it for a long time; I walked home, I wanted to be alone and above all I was furious with my first love. He had tried to defend me as an Iranian political refugee to explain why I was different, but my poor love, I was already French. I wondered if all my life I would have to bear the shame of being a woman; I wondered if I was making the right choice. I wondered if maybe my first love was right. If I was different because I came from the country of the Beards. If I was doing the right thing by wearing the outward symbols of my femininity. I had suffered so much from being subdued, because I was a woman-child, that my skirts and whale blubber were the absolute proof of my newfound freedom, my joy of being a woman. I listened to the sound of my high heels on the Parisian pavement and I wondered if I looked more like a whore than a woman. Just a woman. And so what if I did? Did I have to wear trousers, jeans, have short nails like the Crow supervisor at school wanted, in order to be heard? Did I have to wear the trappings of men for my ideas to hold any weight? Is it so shit being a woman that I have to hide it? I was getting increasingly angry. There was no way I could be just a whore, or just a bourgeois. There was no way I could be anything other than what I had chosen to be. The melody of my stilettos helped me to take notice of the backward ideas of the Trotskyites who had no idea what to fight against, so settled on women's hair. Like the Beards. All Beards always take it out on women's hair. So, no. I would not swap my classic black dress for unisex jeans, I would not swap my certainty of being worth as much as a man for pale lips, I would not swap my femininity, which is the most radical exterior symbol of my struggle against the Beards, just to please three arseholes who had never even read *Das Kapital for Dummies*. No. I am proud of being a woman and do not want to be ashamed to show it, to state it, to affirm it.

I met my first love the following day, I met my first love and he was embarrassed and he apologized for his political associates and he tried to explain to me why, in fact, they were great. They weren't. They were the living dead, they were living but they led lives like dead people, they wanted to paint Paris black, they didn't like to laugh (it was too futile), they didn't like to eat (too bourgeois), they didn't drink (too bourgeois), they didn't take drugs (too bourgeois), they didn't believe in love since it was, of course ... bourgeois. Don't even talk about flesh. It was borderline dirty, a bourgeois thing. The flesh, for Trotskyites, should be hygienic and nothing more. What use did they have for a body, when they believed only in ideas? They were waiting for the great day to come when they could cut women's hair and put everybody in uniform. They were stuck in a nightmarish future where the individual is sacrificed to the revolutionary ideal.

The sound of my high heels has always reassured me, ever since that evening in October 1994. Whenever I am walking alone, especially at night, I feel reassured to sound so feminine. I find it reassuring that I have always stood tall in my heels and have never been ashamed. There are always meetings, however, that do not bode well because of my skirts and heels, my lipstick and my multicoloured necklaces. There is always doubt in the eyes of my interviewers and I've worked out how to read it pretty quickly: I look like a bimbo. At best. A fucking moron, at worst. It is perhaps a very French thing: intellectual women look like men. They wear trousers and 'nude' make-up. There is always a moment of surprise on the face of new people I meet, when I open my mouth. It takes a while for them to make the connection between my skirt and my brain. And sometimes they even dare to say it out loud: 'I thought you were a bimbo and you're actually really bright!' Perhaps the worst thing about it is the arrogance that permeates their remarks. There is a real problem between the skirt and the brain. As if a skirt short-circuits the brain and prevents it from developing normally. I look too much like a woman to have a brain. These days, I am even more proud of my high heels and the jangling of my necklaces. Because these days, in the streets of France and elsewhere, wearing a skirt has become a provocation. In some rough suburbs, wearing a skirt means you're a whore. Girls hide their bodies well, they cover their legs; they no longer look like women. Being a woman is provocative.

It turns out that it's not just in the tougher suburbs of France that skirts have become an invitation to rape. In April 2011, in Toronto, a young woman was raped by some subhuman scumbags. When she reported it at the police station, the cop who dealt with her commented on her outfit. I'm sure he wanted to help her, to prevent this from happening again. She had been wearing a skirt. That young woman had been raped but she had kept her dignity and her brain. Her blood boiled in her veins. He triggered something inside her, something we all have inside us. She had just been raped and a man was accusing her of asking for it. She stood up for herself, and other women made a stand with her. Other women stood up and the Slut Walk was started. Around the world, in India, Germany, Australia, Brazil, Senegal, in over 250 cities worldwide, women marched in skirts and high heels. No skirt, no shoe, no nudity is an invitation to rape. There are no exceptions, no man can hide behind that pathetic excuse, 'She was asking for it, Mr. Police Officer. You should've seen how short her skirt was, and how nice her arse looked. She was asking for it, with her great legs and that red dress, she was asking for it with her shapely calves and her great tits.' There is no excuse for a man to rape a woman. None. Not a husband, or a brother, or a stranger. Nowhere. Not here or anywhere else. Sluts walked the world's pavements and it was once again a chance to be a woman, head held high and confident in my body. I opened my wardrobe and pulled out my shortest dress, I donned some ridiculously high heels, and joined my slut friends to walk the Parisian pavements. I adored that protest march, I loved all those women, so beautiful, so sexy, coming together to tell rapists and men who believed in the provocative nature of a piece of fabric that they were arseholes, and that skirts and heels had nothing to do with their animal instincts and their lack of education. I loved being among all those women, I loved being those women. I thought that we were really on the right track. And that 'slut' was going to become a compliment. I don't know what the Trotskyites of my teenage years thought about these Slut Walks. I hope they were ashamed. I hope that they felt a bit stupid. But I think they probably became high-flying senior execs who didn't believe in anything apart from their family or their genius offspring. I doubt they even had time to notice the Slut Walk.

The skirt, that piece of fabric, whether it is mini, midi or maxi, that piece of fabric that tells the evolution of fashion, is actually just the story of the evolution of the female body. This body, corseted according to the moral fashion, liberated sometimes, contained often, is a sign of the times, the most visible outward symbol of women's status. The skirt shows the level of education of men—and of women. And as if to remind me that everything happens for a reason, that nothing happens by chance, Isabelle Adjani took centre stage again. In a skirt. Isabelle Adjani who had moved me so many times, since that day in March 1989, now assumed a new role. In a skirt.

Skirt Day is definitely a film that owes more to its subject matter than it does to its production. The intelligent screenplay, the performance of the actors, the soundness of its claim, gives this film the feel of a masterpiece. A French teacher in a rough secondary school, hated by her colleagues who gave up long ago on the animals that they have to give lessons to, despised by her students who couldn't care less about Molière, and who mock her because she is a woman who wears a skirt, takes her class hostage after discovering a gun in the bag of one of her wild students. It's at gunpoint that she does her job as a teacher in a difficult school in a rough French neighbourhood. What does she ask for? The introduction of a national skirt day. So that never again is any man or woman allowed to insult a woman for wearing a skirt.

It is wonderful because the rough areas need to be taken hostage by the Republic. It's radical but it's essential. Isabelle Adjani brings to her character, brings to the film, all the melancholy of the refugee world in her eyes. She brings hope where there was only blindness and rejection. It is not a vindication of living in harmony; it is a radical affirmation of the values that alone can hold the pieces of the body of France together. The character played by Adjani was born somewhere else, but had put France above everything. She had never looked for excuses. She had never blamed her failures on France. She had climbed the ladder of French culture. And she had progressed. She is heartbreakingly moving with her madness, her faith and her contradictions. *Skirt Day* is definitely the first film to grab the Beards by their goatees.

Take a typically Parisian dinner party, just a dinner with some nice people, often left wing, often anti-racist, always full of good democratic will. Then all you have to do is steer the conversation toward some sensitive topics, just announce that you are not only against the burka which concerns about two and a half women in total, but that you are also against the headscarf. Then just sit back in silence and listen, to become aware of how disconnected people generally are with reality. These men and women, puffed up with good intentions, do not know what it's like to be a woman and to live between those towers that mark the boundaries of their freedoms. They cannot understand that accepting the veil means accepting that a woman who lives in a troubled neighbourhood does not have a choice: if she doesn't wear it, she is reduced to being an easy girl—in other words a woman cannot be respected and is nothing more than a body. Casually accepting women in burkas means giving free rein to a hierarchy of women that ranges from whores to good women. Those who wear the veil are less 'good' than those who wear the burka, who are obviously more respectable than those who wear a skirt. Those who wear a skirt are not even women any more, they are pieces of flesh. It is always surprising to note that good consciences never take into account the reality, it is shocking to note that open-mindedness is just a way of washing their hands of the matter. Those respectable people, who think they are so open-minded, are effectively abandoning girls and women to the law of the Beards. Those girls who cannot wear a skirt, for fear of being dragged off to some filthy cellar, are the first victims of the good conscience of residents of nice neighbourhoods, diverse neighbourhoods, neighbourhoods where they hold nice dinner parties where everyone can dress how they like, without risking going home in several pieces.

I will carry on walking with my legs out for all to see, as a provocation to some, as a free woman in my own eyes. It took me some time not to give a fuck about those who only see me as a woman and the presence of my legs as detrimental to my brain. If I happen to wear trousers I always feel like I am betraying the woman in me, I always worry about not being a complete woman. I need to assert my femininity and be respected for precisely that. It's about time we introduced a Skirt Day, about time we established a day of femininity. It's about time that we no longer have to endure stares laden with innuendo, looks that are not sensual, but which make you feel sullied. The kind of looks that say, 'Because you are uncovered, you are giving me permission to let my eyes wander all over you, without respect and without even desire.' I sometimes feel like I have got my legs wide open, without knickers on, topless. I am simply wearing a skirt.

Wear a skirt to support all those who have spurned them for fear of rape, for fear of their fathers, for fear of being reduced to just a body. Wear a skirt and be proud of being a woman. Wear a skirt and walk. Walk through the streets, stomp all over the frustration, the prohibitions, all those who want to take the skirt away from you just because you dared to wear it. Daring to wear a skirt is saying 'No'. It's often how revolutions begin.

Paris, 27 December 2007

I got up really early and got ready as if I was going on a date. I hesitated over cardinal red or jet black, I donned a pair of high-heeled boots; I hummed to myself. I was going to see not just the Marquis again, but also Louÿs. I wanted to live up to our meeting and I had to wear the flagrant signs of our complicity. I left early to be at the front of the queue. I wanted to be as alone as possible with them, to take my time, to be moved discreetly. I had not factored in the Christmas holidays and the curious crowd. There was a first disappointment when the towers of the Bibliothèque Nationale de France came into view. There was a pink X on one of the façades. Pink. Not red, not black, no: pink. I frowned and started to grumble to myself like an old lady who no longer recognizes the neighbourhood of her childhood, its smells, its soul. I carried on, only to come face-to-face with a packed crowd who all wanted to visit the Enfer (Hell) section of the BnF. In other words, banned books, controversial books, books censored by the government to protect the souls of its subjects, then citizens. L'Enfer was founded in 1830 then closed its doors in 1977, but it contains all the banned and censored books, including most of the libertine books of the eighteenth century. The BnF had the excellent idea of bringing Hell to the modern day, exhibiting censored works and celebrating the taboos that have done so much to advance history. I expected to reach the exhibition surrounded by a crowd of people already excited about the acrobatics, the extravagances and the pranks they would discover inside. I smiled because they were going to be disappointed: they didn't know they were going to come up against politics.

Finally, I reached the exhibition. It was PINK. Everything was pink, corny, faux raunchy. It was pink and you could hear squeals of embarrassment. It was pink and they had staged it so that you could see others blushing. Above the display cases that exhibited open books, including, among other things, original editions of Sade with the author's annotations—I cannot describe the emotion for me—there was a row of mirrors reflecting the smiles and blushes, the laughter and the obstinately lowered chins of the visitors. It was Disneyland for the divine Marquis, it was wrapped up in fun, it was everything apart from libertine literature. It was *Justine* right next to a comprehensive list of all the Parisian brothels, whips of all sizes, giant ears that you had to lean in to in order to hear readings of illicit books, satirical drawings of the libertine century, but also more light-hearted nineteenth-century ones, the catalogue of l'Enfer established by Apollinaire in 1913, illustrations of the novels of Pierre Louÿs and pornographic drawings, no less. Sex was everywhere, and the Revolution was nowhere to be seen. The fact that I couldn't touch the pages of *Juliette* where Sade had rested his hand, or that an original edition of *The Songs of Bilitis* was locked in its display case, all that was to be expected. But this! Reducing forbidden literature, censored literature, to a catalogue of brothels with prices and specialities, no, just no! I was disappointed. I was sad and the more I heard giggling, the more I saw people's faces set in false concentration on the cultural significance of the exhibition, the more I thought how stupid it was: all of that, for this? Offering the public an introduction to libertine literature by dressing it up as fun and games: it was such a shame. No visitor could have imagined—if they didn't know—that behind all those arses and cunts, behind all those tangled bodies, behind that devastating humour, there was the heart and soul of the Revolution. The exhibition was short, I went round it two or three times, lingering at the original editions, imagining myself as Sade, dreaming of Louÿs. Then I walked home in the rain—I needed to get over the experience—and I decided that to make up for it, I was going to cook myself a Thai green prawn curry. I was depressed and it's always at those times that you need to cheer yourself up by eating good food. I did some shopping then went back to my miniscule studio that would depress even the happiest of souls. I was listening to the radio when I heard the news of the assassination of Benazir Bhutto. She was campaigning for the third time, she had been the first woman to lead a Muslim nation, she was corrupt, ruthless, manipulative, but she was, above all, a female politician in a Muslim country. And not just any country. Pakistan. She was a modern-day Merteuil. She was as pitiless as any man and that was why I admired her. She made her mark, she played the game, she was bad, but who cares? In a country like Pakistan where the leaders end their mandate with a coup, where political assassination is commonplace, where being respectable is not enough to be revered, where every street corner is prey to an ambush, she had been leader of the country twice. The only thing that bothered me about her was not the fact that she had certainly let her brothers and cousins who were too fond of power get killed, it was not that she had used the same weapons as her enemies, but that she had married a notorious playboy—who hurried to fill the position left vacant by her death—an unscrupulous businessman, who would certainly have made her married life hell. Why do even the most powerful women always weaken when it comes to their personal life?

In Paris, I had just left an exhibition that valued what had once been censored. In Paris, I could even allow myself to criticize the exhibition because it didn't keep its promises. In Paris, I was wearing a skirt and was going to cook a Thai dish and nobody would reproach me for still being single at thirty years old, and for not having children. In Paris, I was on another planet.

Everything was swirling around my head; I was devastated. L'Enfer and the assassination of Benazir Bhutto mingled together; it was not time to give up yet. There were a thousand battles to fight and Hell could resurface anywhere. I took it as a personal affront, the assassination of a female politician—whose work I didn't even admire, but the woman, yes—and I remembered that Paris was a special place, that Paris was an opportunity, that Paris, despite everything—despite its failings, despite its social tensions, despites its hipsters, despite its soaring property prices, despite the immutable Île Saint-Louis, despite its neighbourhoods that are no-go areas for skirts, despite its ban on smoking in public places, despite the pink X on one of the BnF towers—keeps its promises. And Paris could shine on the rest of the world. It doesn't take much to ruin my happiness: a failed exhibition and a political assassination. The contrast between these two events reassured me and backed up my criticism of l'Enfer unveiled at the BnF.

What they needed in Pakistan was libertine literature. They needed to send in Sade as reinforcement. A way of thinking. That's what the French Revolution was. More than just a historical date, it was a way of seeing the world; it was a way of contemplating change, of overturning the circumstances, of seeing the impossible becoming reality. I didn't have time to cook my Thai green prawn curry. I wrote about the death of the first woman to lead a Muslim nation, I wrote about the coincidence of hearing of her death as I returned from an exhibition on Hell. I wrote all afternoon to get my head straight. I wrote. And as I wrote, I gave meaning to my freedom, I took charge of my spoiled-little-Parisian fit of depression, and I swore to myself that I would never let myself be overwhelmed by sadness again. Paris was an opportunity.

Paris, February 2009

The Islamic Republic of Iran was celebrating its thirtieth anniversary and the TV channel Arte had scheduled a special day on 11 February, the anniversary of the Revolution. From morning to night there were reports, interviews and documentaries. In Iran and elsewhere, portraits of exiles, homecomings, comedy sketches. Iran in its entirety, in less than twenty-four hours: its history, its reality, its people. I woke up really early and settled in front of the TV at a friend's house—I didn't have a TV, and still don't. Iran, which I hadn't set foot in for twenty-four years, was served up to me on a platter. The first story had hardly begun before I was in tears. It had always been like this since exile: as soon as I saw images of Iran, I cried. It was not so much that I missed Iran; it was the terrible mess that the Beards had made of the country that depressed me.

Iran was paraded before my eyes, and I was in a Parisian living room, and I had done nothing for my country of birth. I was so far away from it; I was far from being a freedom warrior. I cried for Iran before the Beards, and Iran after the Beards; I cried for my Sufi grandfather who I had never seen again and who died without ever seeing his son again; I cried for my France, which no longer lived up to my Republican ambitions. I cried all day and all night. After all the tears and all the questions, after the nostalgia that gripped my heart and opened my arms to the huge void of memories, I cheered up. I had cards in my hand that I hadn't played yet. But I knew I had them. I was alive and I had Sade. Nobody had ever promised me it would be easy, life was not a gift, but I was full of the future, full of convictions and all those weapons I hadn't used yet could be used tomorrow, or the day after. They could be used to redraw the world map. I was euphoric and imagined myself leading an army of democratic women and men who would trample over the heads of the Beards to free all those who suffered because they were not allowed to bare their bottoms.

Three days later I received a letter. The letter informed me that I was French, as of 11 February 2009: the day that I had cried for my lost country. I was legally French since that day, the 'celebration' of the Revolution that had cost me my country of birth. I stood speechless in front of my letterbox in the lobby of my apartment building, staring at the piece of paper that gave me the right to vote. It was 14 February 2009 and this was the concrete proof of my love affair with France. It was the proof of the deep bond that existed between me and France. It was symbolic that I found out on that day, and that I became French on the day that I had cried all the tears I had left, over how the country of my ancestors used to be, and what it had become. What the country could have been, if it had been populated with free men and women. What Iran could have been without the Beards. What I could have become. How my parents would have suffered less. How much less my family would have lost.

That evening I was invited to a party by some friends of friends. Nice people, lots of Brazilians, Argentineans, well-connected French kids, bohemians who owned their own houses, musicians, people open to meeting new people, always up for a party and always politicized—as you can afford to be when you are not poor, when you are not caught up in the routine of daily life—ready to stand up to all the injustices of this world. I put the letter confirming my newly acquired nationality in my bag and set off happily to the party, which promised to be memorable, armed with three bottles of champagne, seeing as I had something major to celebrate. I arrived smiling, skipping about telling anyone who would listen, and others who didn't even know me: I'm French! At last! I had managed to get all the documents together, I had managed to go through all the administration, and I was French. And in less than a month I would be going to sing 'La Marseillaise' to confirm it. And I was going to vote! Not just forcing everyone around me to go and vote because I didn't have the right to yet. I was met with sceptical looks. Then once, twice, three times, ten times, I got the same jokey reaction, it was as if they had learned their lines off by heart: 'That's way less sexy than being a political refugee!' and others: 'And you're *proud* of that?' Had I announced that I had joined the National Front, I would have got a similar reaction. All around me, I saw faces of astonishment, disgust and even hostility. How could anyone be proud to be French? What about you, you arsehole, can you even imagine what it feels like *not* to be? How can you belittle France, where you were born; where you have received a string of benefits that three-quarters of the world's population would kill to have; where you can vote for who you want (all of them are corrupt, I admit, but you also have the right to say that out loud without being hanged for it); where you can read the newspapers that speak your language, whether it's extremely right wing or left wing; where nobody can reproach you for your religion (well, not always and not all of the time); where you don't just fall by the wayside if you lose your job (much less than anywhere else, even though it is always shit when you lose your job); where you have easy access to so much culture (national libraries, the Louvre, I mean the fucking Louvre!, the Musée d'Orsay, the Pompidou Centre, everywhere the government has ever laid a finger); where, when you are sick, everything is taken care of and you don't have to watch your father or your children die because you don't have the basic financial means to save them; where you can study what you want without bankrupting your parents and without lining the bank's pockets (even though things are changing, even though studying costs more, it is still marvellous to have such access to education)—how can you belittle France like that, with that look of disgust? What is it with these arseholes? They behave like spoiled children who look at the outside world and spit on France. What has gone wrong? They all only have one thing to talk about: illegal immigrants and the Roma people. France was still collaborating; France was not the country of human rights it claimed to be. But who said that being a country of human rights means accepting all the illegal immigrants, welcoming all and sundry with open arms? Who said that you didn't have to work hard to be French? And why were none of these sensitive souls protesting outside the Romanian embassy? It wasn't France that established a totally discriminatory and racist system against the Roma and made them flee. It is Romania that is scandalous and not France. France does what it can, does what it can and no less, to prevent creating even more misunderstanding and ruptures in the country. Is it up to France to manage the Roma issue, to explain to the poor inhabitants of rundown neighbourhoods where the Romani are settled that it is temporary, that they are nice, because they only steal from those they don't know? What do we do? Which misery do we sacrifice? Which camp do we choose? How do we do it? Do we let the Roma and the poor kill one another because France is a country of human rights? It's madness. I am more than sympathetic to the terrible situation of the Roma, but it is not up to France to solve Romania's problems. It is not up to France to clean up after the racist state that is Romania.

I stowed my champagne bottles away and danced, so as

not to get lynched by an army of sceptics who bit the hand that enabled them to pay their substantial taxes without actually having to forgo their holidays. I danced on the head of anyone who did not know what it was like to be stateless, to have lost their country and to have fallen in love with a new country, a new language, with a rich culture capable of filling any voids, helping you to grow, to feel alive. I danced and I went home.

Did it matter that I was misunderstood; did it matter that I wanted to stick up for my country of refuge? Did it matter that I seemed like a hysterical nationalist in the eyes of those who didn't understand France at all, or refugees, or the pain of having lost your home country? It didn't matter, it didn't matter that I was alone with my love of my adopted country and my eternal nostalgia for the country where I was born. It didn't matter. I still had two bottles of champagne and plenty of love in me. I had a little piece of paper on that Valentine's Day, which allowed me to vote in the next elections. And then ... it was more material for me to write about, to think about, to speak out about, to observe. It didn't matter. I fell asleep thinking about the following day. I would go to my parents for lunch, and all our exile friends and even some French people who were less jaded than the rest would raise their glass of champagne to celebrate my French nationality. Luckily for France, it could still count on its exiles, its immigrants, its poor, its stateless, for a bit of love.

January 2011 – August 2013

Stéphane Hessel sold an impressive number of copies of *Time for Outrage,* to the great surprise of nearly everyone except those who had always thought the same way as him; in Egypt a deadly bomb exploded in front of a Coptic church, killing twenty people; Marine Le Pen was elected president of the National Front; two French hostages were executed in Niger; suicide attacks continued in Afghanistan; the terrible floods in Australia, in Sri Lanka and Brazil panicked environmentalists and increased poverty; my parents still pained my heart and soul just as much whenever I saw them; a new love brightened up my life, and although I knew that I wanted to tell the story of *Khomeini, Sade and Me,* I had mistakenly chosen the documentary format for it. I had been writing for twenty years and for the first time in my life I had lost my taste for literature.

As if someone had heard me, Tunisia began to stir. At first it was just an individual act: a street vendor— Mohamed Bouazizi, who could not take the suffering any more—set himself on fire in Sidi Bouzid. Even though I am not a big fan of sacrifice, the act had its symbolic significance and showed the poverty and leaden future of a sick country. Above all, the only person he killed was himself and that was reason enough to be applauded. There were demonstrations that were initially about hunger, but which transformed into general unrest. The streets were full of people: mothers, veiled and non-veiled girls, Beards, students with no future, poor workers, unemployed fathers, the destitute semi-unemployed, clean-cut liberals, idlers from the residential neighbourhoods. They were all there suddenly as if word had got around, without making a sound. There was something about it that went beyond a rally or an ideological protest. It was too diverse to be insignificant. It was too multicoloured, too disorganized. There was not just anger among the protestors who refused to back down. There was laughter. It was too spontaneous, too cheerful and even though there was violence, it felt like a liberation.

The citizens were out in force on the streets and Ben Ali seemed to have lost control. Nobody seemed to know who was in charge of what in Tunisia. But I thought to myself that this is what always happens when a family is in power, that the family is always a nest of vipers: selfish and stupid. We went out to dinner and when we came back, Ben Ali's Tunisia was falling. Ben Ali's Tunisia dropped from his hands like a ripe fruit. It had fallen and in the images that reached us, I searched for the women. There they were, in the streets, and they were equal to men. Together they had toppled Ben Ali and his wife, the family clan, the rapacious family that had eaten the heart of the country alive. It was historic. Everything came together and it made me jump for joy. I placed my hand on my heart, the history of Tunisia running through my head. This could only happen in Tunisia. Bourguiba was not a democrat—far from it—but he had attempted modernization, he had filled his pockets and imprisoned his opponents, but he had introduced a Family Code to the country that included women. Tunisia had a past into which you could neatly insert democracy and gender equality. And there was Manouba, the Faculty of Letters, Arts and Humanities which had long been training thinkers and intellectuals who were attempting to reflect on religion, democracy, history and the future. There was something happening in Tunisia that might have repercussions everywhere in what we call, for convenience, the Arab World. And why not? There were the streets of Tunis, Béja, Kasserine, El Hamma, Tataouine and Gafsa, there was the Ben Ali family tearing itself apart, walled up in their palaces, and there was a whiff of hope.

That evening, as Ben Ali's plane circled around and around the skies in search of a refuge, I was glued to the jubilant images of Tunisia. I was hooked on the women's faces and the men's tears. I was with them, there in those crowded streets from which a tomorrow could be born, without Beards and without absolute power. My desire to write returned, with the faces of those Tunisian women, with a movement against which no army, no absolute power could do anything. A powerful hunger, a powerful desire: not just for freedom but for change. A movement. Just like in the libertine century, a movement that drives away fear, that dethrones fools and sycophants.

And yet. There was something nagging away at me, something I couldn't quite put my finger on. It was Super Tolerance Man who managed to pinpoint the source of my unease. My unease was Iran. The thing that frustrated me, when I talked about the possible upheavals in Tunisia, was Iran. Iran had been a modern country, with its universities, its intellectuals, its oil, its chic monarchy, its Dior-clad lady Shah and its lavish celebrations. Before 1979 it had been a rich country. The Shah was a dictator and freedom was an illusion, the communists were the enemies and the political parties didn't have the right to exist unless they kept their mouths shut. But Iran was also a country of poetry—even in a remote little village with a high illiteracy rate, it was not unusual to find men and women who could recite pure Persian poetry off by heart in incredibly erudite language. It was a country that on 21 March still celebrated the most ancient celebration of *Nowruz,* or the New Year, with the same fervour as it had done for nearly 3000 years. It was a country that had been conquered but never occupied, a country that could not fall into the hands of the backward-thinking. And yet. Nothing should ever be taken for granted. Iran is a prime example. Iran had to take to the streets in order to get rid of the Shah or at least to force reforms that would become essential, but it went further ... into the past. What I still find so incredible, even today, is this return to the past. The willingness to brush modernity and the future aside to wallow instead in a savage, inhospitable world dictated by idiotic dogmas that ensure a lack of progress. Iran sank after its Revolution. Masochistic Iran had overthrown a tyrant only to bring others, just as dangerous, to the throne. Tyrants who were much less glamorous. My father was right. No matter how much I wanted to hope, Iran always stopped me dead in my tracks.

Very soon, Egypt began its metamorphosis. Very soon, Tahrir Square became the symbol of the awakening of the Arab peoples. And yet. An enormous creeping doubt was already starting to take hold of me. I don't know if I am naturally mistrusting, or if because of my childhood all revolutions seem suspicious to me. Tunisia had earned my support—with all the limitations stemming from my past—but that was because of its history, and Bourguiba. Egypt, on the other hand, was the birth place of the Muslim Brotherhood. I had always been interested in political Islam (it had cost me so much, after all), and I knew that the Muslim Brotherhood had no intention of letting go. They ruled the streets, they looked after the poor, they paid dowries, they sent some to Quranic school, others to work, they handed out bread. They had endured the violent repression of Mubarak, they had been tortured and exiled, they were martyrs—a profoundly Shiite concept that the Sunnis nicked to justify violent death—they had been patient for so long, they had awaited the Holy Grail under so many leaders that they were never going to let power slip through their hands. And the Brotherhood remained strangely silent. They were smarter than that, and it was this eerie silence at the beginning of the Revolution that made me prick up my ears. They knew what they were doing. They were waiting to see. They knew that they were the only ones with a large enough organization to expect a victory if there were elections. Too many citizens owed them for a loaf of bread, a married daughter, an employed son. They waited. And the waiting paid off. The army, which decides everything—the money comes from the Americans and that is the only absolutely guaranteed salary—dropped Mubarak and the position opened up. The Brotherhood started poking their noses in, announcing that they would not put a candidate forward—I don't really need to point out that this was a complete lie. They had held back for too long just to go charging into battle headfirst. I started to worry. I talked to my father about it; he was as dubious as I was. But Super Tolerance Man was waiting for the elections. As usual, Super Tolerance Man chose to give them the benefit of the doubt. No matter how much I argued, he shook his head, repeating that nothing was certain.

My entourage was enthusiastic. There was nobody I met who wasn't applauding the Arab Spring. Nobody. And just as I had about September 11, I voiced my doubts, I spread my fear of the Beards, my fear that they would end up silencing the crowds. I was met with the same look; I saw the same uneasiness. And once, someone dared to say it. It was a boozy evening, I was in top form, I needed to spread my usual doom and gloom. And out it came. I was a racist. My scepticism stemmed from my lack of regard for Muslims. I didn't believe that they were capable of carrying out a successful revolution. I cried. It was the alcohol. But I cried. I cried, not because a friend thought I was racist; I cried because there was no army of hearts and minds to defend the Egyptians against these ogres, not even the French who are always so ready to brandish the declaration of human rights. I cried for all the dashed hopes of revolutions. No revolution succeeds in two months; no revolution naturally transitions into democracy. Sweeping everything away means that everything needs to be rebuilt. And is there anything more difficult to accomplish than rebuilding everything, with the same vision, after having been through so much for such a long time? I knew that Egypt would be ruled by the Muslim Brotherhood and I knew that it would not be a success. I know that all those who wish to marry religion and politics all make the same mistake: they concern themselves with morality first, before dealing with hungry bellies. They concern themselves with women's bodies before attacking corruption. I could see them coming a mile off. But oh no, I had become a racist, because I was worried about an even darker future for women.

From that night on I kept quiet, I stopped wanting to start a debate, share ideas, reflect on things with my friends. I stopped because I couldn't make myself understood without being insulted. For someone who loves exchanging ideas so much, I made a tough decision. But it wasn't that tough. What I couldn't say, I could write. Yet again I thought of my father during the Rushdie affair, I saw how my father looked at his daughter, who was so lost in the realm of human rights and who discovered that tolerance was not contagious. He didn't say anything to me, but he gave me notebooks. My first notebooks. With no further comment. And little by little, when I wasn't able to talk, when the words stuck in my throat, I would take out a notebook and I would write. Thanks to my friend who called me a racist because I was dubious about the challenges facing the Egyptian Revolution, I stopped talking and started writing. I filled page after page with thoughts and as I reread them now for the purpose of writing my story, I realize how much the loneliness of the blank page has saved me from isolation. That is why I experienced the Arab Spring-Autumn alone. I have only feelings and comments to share in response to the images and testimonies, to the articles and documentaries. I was often asked about it—after all, I am Iranian and have experienced a Revolution that made me strong, well-placed to analyse Arab revolutions—and yes, I know it's stupid, I know that better than anyone, but I said nothing; I shared nothing. The people asking me must have thought I was detached from reality when I answered, 'I don't know. We'll have to wait and see.' I hated that phrase, which I was saying far too often, but it was a mask that covered me just enough to give me some time to think in peace. In peace ... Easier said than done.

The following months sent me back to my childhood, my teenage delusions, my atheist itch. A French journalist just doing her job was caught up in the mob of protestors and in a flash they had torn off her clothes, groped her, reduced her to a mere piece of flesh, before the cameraman, with the help of one or two protestors, managed to get her away from the potential rape she might have become the object of. *The object.* That is the most appropriate term. The woman's body as an object that can be touched, groped, hurt. The woman's body as an inanimate object, because it is impossible for these men to consider the issue of consent. It's a woman, it's a body, it's an object, she is there just a few centimetres away from my hands, she is there and whether it's broad daylight or the dead of night, hands grab that body which is only an object and before you know it, I'm fingering you, I'm squeezing your breasts until it hurts, your arse is reduced to an outlet for all the frustrations that have been accumulating for so long. Touching. Touching that body-object because it is there. And this is just one of millions of stories of women, of all ages, in Egypt, who are victims of groping in the street, on public transport, in supermarkets, everywhere. And there are intelligent beings who are shocked by it. There are beings endowed with reason who ask themselves why. Well I'll tell you why, I who am just a woman that comes off as a racist when she fears for the future of other women. I'll tell you that any little boy—whether he is French, German, Algerian, Swedish or Egyptian—take that little boy, and from childhood, immerse him in a bath of strict gender segregation. Worse: keep him among women until they cut his foreskin off, with all the neighbourhood watching, all the village, cut off his manhood in full view of everyone, even though up until that day he was nestled among the women's bodies at the hammam. Take him and chop it off, when he is eight, nine, ten, thirteen. And after that, he will only keep company with men, until he marries a woman. And even after that, he will only keep company with men. And above all, keep telling him that men and women have nothing to do with one another, keep on telling him that he is different to them, that most women are whores, and whores are bad news. Hammer it into his head, the shame and danger associated with women, and then wait a few more years. And the first woman who passes by, he won't be able to control himself, his hand will detach from the rest of his body and he will grope around for a piece of flesh for his fingers to feel, for the first time in his life. And he will touch it. And he will wash his hands—or not—because, if he was able to touch her, it's because she was there to be touched. If his fingers managed to grab that piece of skin, that piece of flesh, it's because she was there, for that reason. If not, she would be cozied up at home, and nobody would touch her except her husband. It is not even a question of whether she is veiled or not. Practically all Egyptian women have experienced groping at some point, of varying degrees of severity. And Egypt experienced a Revolution with men who think that a woman's body is an object as soon as she leaves the private sphere. As soon as her body enters a public space, she is an object that can be handled, weighed up, by anyone who so chooses. And I'm supposed to be optimistic? I'm meant to forget that Egyptian women exist? Is it racist to say that some (way too many, according to the statistics) Egyptians are perverted because of the strict gender segregation? Is it racist to take women into account? What the Arab Spring brought to light is the terrifying reality of Maghreb societies. The virginity tests, the hunt for immodesty—which is in fact just a woman hunt—the disgusting groping and subjugation of women. And I'm supposed to pretend not to know, not to see it? But I couldn't turn a blind eye to what was happening; I was obsessed with what was happening on the other side of the Mediterranean. Perhaps more than anyone, I was looking for proof that it was possible for Muslims to free themselves of backward dogmas, that it was possible to destroy centuries of intellectual enslavement and that the domino effect—which (luckily) had not worked with Shiite Iran—could change things in the majority of (Sunnite) Muslim countries. I was afraid of the Muslim Brotherhood, but I was full of hope for the people, standing proud.

Then election time came round. In Tunisia and in Egypt. The time came for ballot boxes, and the ballot papers brought power to the Beards. Without hesitation. All I could do was roll up my sleeves and reread the libertines; I needed to be drip-fed Sade in order to bear it. It was all I could do to keep from crying every morning as I listened to the news. Both Tunisia and Egypt. And there was worse to come—is it possible that in each bad scenario, there is always worse? This worse thing was the massive vote of Tunisians in France. They had voted for Ennahdha; they had given their votes to the Islamists. Those who lived safely in the reassuring bosom of the French Republic had opted for those backward-thinkers, the Beards. They had chosen to push themselves into the past. Some of them gave an explanation that made me want to scream: it was because Tunisians in France wanted to keep their country of origin as it was. Because they were reassured to know that when they went back to their country on holiday, it would still be the same. What a load of crap! The Tunisians in France who chose to support the Islamists were born under Bourguiba. They had not known the Beards. There was no reassuring return. They were sufficiently politicized and convinced by the Beards to give them their votes.

So Tunisia and Egypt were well on their way to becoming Islamic Republics. And just as expected, the first measures were to do with religion, decency and women's bodies. All too soon, there was talk of religious morality. Maybe there was hope among the people again. Would they tolerate their new shackles? Did they truly believe they could be happy with empty stomachs and anaesthetized brains, as long as their heads were covered? What was to become of Tunisia and Egypt? Why has the Muslim world proved incapable of matching their hopes with the democracy they clamour for? What the hell is going wrong? What were the Tunisian Beards thinking, with the Revolution barely over, when everything still needed to be done, to go and beat up the director of a TV channel because it broadcast Marjane Satrapi's film *Persepolis*? What goes through the head of a Beard when he sees his fellow countrymen starving and there is a whole new world to redefine, and he uses his energy against a cartoon, under the pretext that God is represented in it through the eyes of a child? I know, I know ...

I'm the first to preach about how culture can change everything, that culture can overthrow the worst tyrants, and that a cartoon can do as much—or even more—than even the most powerful weapon of mass destruction. I know. But I mean, really! With the Revolution barely over, and the Beards on the throne, is a picture really where the danger lies—even if it is one of God? Are you kidding me? And it is not a laughing matter. The list continues after the Jasmine Revolution.

The dean of the University of Manouba, Habib Kazdaghli, was summoned to appear in court on charges of violence. He supposedly hit young women wearing burkas. He supposedly pushed intolerance to violence. Refusing to let his university be invaded by the Beards and Crows, he found himself at the centre of a frenzied conspiracy that put him behind bars. All because he refused to let female students wear the burka. For such a simple reason: that it is impossible to verify the identity of a student whose face is completely covered. But for the ultra-Beards opposing him—the Salafists—it was nothing less than an insult to God. So they invaded the faculty. They ensconced themselves in the gardens and began their work of undermining the heart of knowledge. The ultra-Beards have a dream: a world without knowledge and without a face, a world without diversity and colour, a world where no public space exists except that of prayer, and there are a plethora of private spaces; ultra-private, locked up, closed to the world. But Habib Kazdaghli stood firm, the faculty stood firm and the students clung firmly to their knowledge. Once again, it was a young woman who dared to face the ultra-Beards with a small but highly symbolic act: the ultra-Beards had replaced the Tunisian flag on campus with the Salafist flag. And one student dared to say 'No' and had climbed up the flagpole to the ultra-Beards flag, with boos and threats being hurled at her by the Beards and Crows present, and threw it to the ground, to replace it with the national flag. Sometimes, the 'national' is a humanist revolt.

The dean of Manouba was released and it was proved that he had not laid a hand on the young women in burkas. It was just one battle won, but it wasn't half bad. It wasn't half bad when at the same time, a genuine guy like Chokri Belaïd was assassinated in front of his apartment by the Beards— nothing has been proved yet, but could it have been anyone other than the Beards?—and in the wake of that, crowds of protestors took to the streets once more. Against the Beards, against those who had assassinated someone just for speaking out against them, someone who celebrated the power of change in every individual, who advocated freedom above all else, who spurned the moral diktats. And once again, it was Chokri Belaïd's widow, Basma Khalfaoui, who became one of the most striking images of the Revolution. A woman standing, wonderfully dignified, walking with the Tunisians in memory of her murdered husband, but above all to continue the fight that her lawyer husband began. On the day of the funeral, there was also the couple's young daughter. A girl of ten or twelve who did not intend to show her tears, but instead raised her fist as the perfect tribute to her father who was taken from her too soon. As long as there are always women prepared to stand up for their rights, there is hope.

A young woman raped by policemen after she was arrested because she was with her boyfriend in a car at night in Tunis. If she could do that with him, then she must be open to doing it with everyone; if she was out so late, and with a boy as well, then she must have been a bourgeois and it was a neat opportunity to take a few banknotes off her in the process. The young woman decided to lodge a complaint; she decided to stick up for herself to avoid going mad. She will certainly be forced to leave her country.

There were also other political crimes: the opposition leader Mohammed Brahmi was shot dead outside his apartment just like Chokri Belaïd was, and so many violations of the female body and liberty—have you noticed how that is often one and the same? The country is in economic collapse and the Beards are clinging firmly to the veil and respecting Ramadan. Do they really not have anything else to care about?

As for Egypt, after two years of constitutional failure with the Beards in power, they were overthrown by the army. The mob of protestors took to the streets again, occupied public spaces again, signed a petition in favour of ousting the democratically-elected government, and the army led a coup, something they are no strangers to doing. It was a coup, not a people's call for freedom. And since July 2013, they have been chasing, imprisoning and assassinating the Beards: the Beards who had chased out Mubarak. I could not even be pleased about the departure of the Muslim Brotherhood; I am an incorrigible democrat. It was not an election that deprived them of power, but a military coup. Wherever I turned my head, all I saw was shit. And as the military was getting ready to take back the reins of power, the mob of protestors was occupying the street and women were getting raped. One man, the president of a woman's advocacy group, reacted on French radio, blaming these women's rapes on the crowd who had turned out to support freedom. Men were taking advantage of the opportunity to rape women who dared to cross the barrier into the public arena. Raped. During a demonstration demanding more rights, more bread, more political pragmatism. Raped.

It was at that moment that my friends decided to make the remark, 'You must be happy, the Beards have been thrown out by the army!' Months of keeping my mouth shut, only to hear that? Well, no, I'm not happy, I am an unapologetic democrat and although the Beards aren't, they had nevertheless been elected *democratically* and overthrown *illegitimately* by the military. Even my silence allowed others to embellish my thinking. My friends and those around me had never understood my fight at all. The word 'fight' was too forceful for them. My fight was silent; it was written only on paper and nobody knew about it. I fanned the flames of my Revolution with words. Nobody could imagine how much the Springs that turned into Autumns fed the mill of my thoughts with arguments.

Paris, 2013

About ten years ago, I was working part time in a shop selling rare books on the Boulevard Montparnasse. One Monday morning, the bookseller asked me to gather together a large number of books for a client. The books, which I lovingly wrapped up in tissue paper, were a selection of the finest works of erotic literature. Regretfully, I watched the magnificent books leave. Three, four, six, a dozen boxes were needed. It was a really good sale and I was dying with curiosity to know who the buyer was. Who knows? Perhaps it was some amazing collector, and we would get on, and he would invite me to visit his library, which promised to be one of the most beautiful in the world. But the bookseller had other ideas, and when the eagerly awaited day came he wanted to send me off to lunch far too early. I loitered, I made fake phone calls, I was hanging around so I could meet the collector. The bookseller shot me sideways glances, and I carried on doing my work of stacking boxes. Finally, two cars with tinted windows pulled up outside the bookshop and some bodyguards got out. I started to doubt the amazingness of the collector when I saw a little flag fluttering on the rear-view mirror of one of the cars. The bookseller rushed over. He told me not to look at them, told me to act as if I wasn't there, he asked me to hide in his office. I didn't move, I didn't look away. The bookseller was in a cold sweat. Two bodyguards entered, and then the collector. I got up and before the bookseller could silence me, I proffered a loud 'Hello,' and held out my hand. The bookseller gulped audibly, the collector did not hear me, did not shake my hand. He could not see me. I was just a woman. The bodyguards stood closer to their master, as if to protect him, to hide me from his gaze while a dozen boxes of erotic books were laid out at our feet. The collector needed to be shielded from my eyes, my presence, my voice, even. I am just a woman and that is exactly why I am dangerous. The collector was some Saudi minister. The collector who did not glance at me, who did not return my greeting that sent his henchmen into a panic, who left with the pearls of erotic literature, was a Beard. A real one. A pure one. One who refuses to let other people get their kicks, and then locks himself in his library to get himself off in private. A character from libertine literature. A real phoney. And off he went with my boxes and my books wrapped in tissue paper. Off he went to the graveyard of books. Because who else apart from him and perhaps other Beards of his calibre would ever again look at these masterpieces? He went off with all those books that would be hidden from the eyes of others. He was going to bury my books. The collector was soon gone and the bookseller mopped his brow. 'That didn't go too badly.' Seeing the black look I gave him, my eyes telling him clearly what a total coward he was, he hurried away into his office. It was clearly a good thing to be a woman, to be so dangerous.

The Beards are no different from the clergy of the Ancien Régime. They are just men who are eager to debase. I therefore 'entertained' myself watching each event that came out of the Arab Autumns, by weaving them into the plot of a libertine novel that would unveil the truth behind the wall of secrecy. I 'entertained' myself with the policemen who carried out virginity tests for the sole purpose of sleeping with pretty girls, and the Beards who convinced their mistresses in burkas to attend universities so that they could influence other young women and other young men. Not toward religion, but toward gang bangs. The more an imam was listened to, the more hard-line he became and the more depraved he became, the greater his imagination for fucking in peace while others were whipped for godlessness. And after every call to prayer by the most extreme Beards, those who mistreat women who are not properly covered and young men for wearing jeans that are too tight, I could clearly imagine them squeezing up against them at the first backdoor. I saw a babe in the woods, who truly believed in religion, who really believed that paradise awaited her if she followed the path of piety and modesty, discovering behind the speeches that keep people in ignorance, discovering through meeting people, the reality of human impulses, the truth about men and women and the impossibility of drowning them in abstinence. Libertine literature goes so well with moral barriers! And the Beards happily maintained the illusion. The more they reacted to every little thing as an attack on God, they more they resembled the clergy of the Ancien Régime.

The various hoo-hahs that ensued over cartoons depicting the Beards were exactly the same as those of the Ancien Régime. Censorship, formerly under the leadership of the famous Monsieur de Sartine, was in charge of monitoring all the books and drawings published in the Netherlands or in England, and invading France more every day. Diderot had himself a little fun by offering Sartine this dedication: '*Line all your borders with soldiers, sir, arm them with bayonets to repel any dangerous book that may appear, and those books will—pardon the expression—pass between their legs or jump over their heads to reach us.*'[13] Dangerous books will always win; it is just the game that is more or less long, more or less fraught with pitfalls. There are a plethora of new Sartines. They are even more reactionary than the original one. They are even more alert. And their grievances have far-reaching consequences. Why do they all get so crazy when they see cartoons, both the clergy of yesterday and the Beards of today? Why is it such a threat to their faith to represent religious characteristics in the form of funny drawings?

It is because all upheavals are born out of laughter. It is because all revolutions succeed by thumbing their nose up at the serious, at drama, at tragedy. What Diderot knew, what amused him, was that nothing can halt the march of progress. And forgive me, but progress means laughing at God and especially at his soldiers. Forgive me, but laughing at those who hold the secular power or religious authority, those who have a stranglehold over the heads of those who fear that the sky will fall on them, those who hold all the balls in their iron fist. It means having a lot less fear, it means being in the midst of change. Forgive me, but there is no reason to apologize for laughing at religious figures, or at figures of power. None. And even if the premises of a certain satirical newspaper are bombed, even if the leaders of friendly—or unfriendly—countries complain, even if international deals are messed up, even if politicians don't know how to handle the situation diplomatically, we should carry on caricaturing the absurd, we should carry on being sacrilegious, we should carry on laughing. It is always the moment for caricature; it is always the time for laughter. It is always the good fight when it is the fight for freedom of the press. And that's all there is to it. No mega deals, no sensitivity toward the Beards, no limitation can obstruct freedom of expression. End of story. And so, with each laugh, with each Beard overthrown, today's Beards will no longer be heard by anyone; they will be left shouting into the wind.

By applying libertine literature to the Arab Autumns you are making sure that you remove yourself from the drama by putting religion back where it belongs, in the private sphere; that you never take any religious leader seriously if they want you to believe that the demonstration of his faith is worth more than belief in God; that you live in peace with a spirituality that cannot be offended by schoolboy jokes. For what is a religion if it sees a simple drawing as a full-frontal attack on its belief system? Why all this seriousness over a couple of pencil strokes? Why all the shouting and big words like 'respect', 'blasphemy', 'Islamophobia', 'discrimination'? How do these words hold up compared to hunger, rape, liberty, women's bodies? How can they say them? Libertine literature is all about poking fun at religious figures, taking the drama out of the female body, bringing smiles back into politics, sitting down together to write a future without segregation, without restricting freedom of expression or insult, without delineating knowledge, without pinning a religious tail on society's body. Just let them live! Let them breathe! Let them learn to take the piss out of each other!

Paris, March 2012

I only carry raffia bags, handmade in Madagascar and created by three beautiful, smiling sisters, full of talent. I hate shopping but I can spend hours with these designers who honour the art of conversation as much as the art of leatherworking. It was 20 March 2012, I was chatting with a friend of the designers about our exiles, hers from Algeria after independence, mine from Tehran after the Beards, and we were comparing our lives with those of the young immigrants of today who want everything, right now. We thought about our parents, who kept their heads down, because you have to keep a low profile when you come from elsewhere. The conversation naturally turned to recent events and the murders in the previous few days of three French Muslim soldiers and four French Jews, including three children. The murderer was on a motorbike, and had chased a six-year-old girl into the playground of her school to shoot her in the head. We were shocked, above all we were convinced that this could only be the work of a degenerate. A degenerate of the extreme right. It was not all that long ago that Anders Breivik, a Norwegian lunatic, drunk on Nazi theories, obsessed by the idea of purity, Western decay, and preserving white blood, Christianity, had murdered seventy-seven socialist teenagers in cold blood. Because they represented the future he did not want, the future that did not have his colour, pure white, the future that he wanted exclusively in his image. There was an obvious tension over identity between north and south, from Norway to Greece, the extreme right was advancing everywhere, and there was no reason why France should be safe from it. It was so obvious, so logical, as it was targeting Muslims and Jews. How crazy must you be to shoot a little girl of six in the head? How much of your humanity must you have renounced to follow her into the playground of her school and shoot her in the head? It was reminiscent of one of the worst pages of history. We were chilled by it, but we were on the same wavelength. We were convinced, as girls from diverse backgrounds, that only a Nazi could commit the irreparable. Convinced, as girls from diverse backgrounds, of our brilliant analysis of the socio-political situation of *our* France. Convinced, as girls from diverse backgrounds, that we were in the right. We said goodbye and hugged, because *Vive la France*! Long live the Republic and our parents who succeed in making us French.

Uniting against the murder of the French Muslim soldiers and the French Jews reassured us, strengthened our convictions. The non-practicing Jew and the atheist Muslim held hands and it was a nice end to the day for me, as someone who is always looking for symbols to remind me of why I love France so much.

I got off the metro and a Roma teenage girl, who looked like an old lady who had lived too much, seen too much, pushed past me, clutching a bag belonging to the woman behind me. The woman was shouting, but nobody stopped the teenager and the group of young girls who were watching her back. The battle was not yet won. As I went up the stairs, I wondered if the woman who had her bag stolen would tell the story, cursing the Roma instead of poverty—even though that should never be an excuse—and if the teenager with the look of an old woman would laugh at the woman's frightened cry and her frantic escape, or whether she would be silent and think about the damage she was doing to her community with her actions, reducing everyone in it to mere thieves. When I got home I felt sick.

When I got home, I thought about a young man who had asked me for a cigarette. I had given him one, with a smile. He had pounced on the chance to ask me for my number. And when I politely declined, still with a smile—I am polite and I hate conflicts—he abruptly grabbed my left hand and said to me, 'You're not even married; you're a racist whore.' He was of North African origin, I was of Iranian origin: so that's how you become a racist whore. Could this mundane episode have made me change the way I talk, just like that? Could it have made me spout forth arguments that all young men of North African origin are absolute pigs? Of course not. But what about a different woman? A woman who does not think all day long about collective living, the dangers of xenophobia, possible solutions, and who was doubly insulted after giving a cigarette to a young stranger, wouldn't she cross the road the next time she saw a North African face?

And what about the young man who thinks I am a racist whore, will he do the same with his mates? Will he tell this banal urban anecdote and will they all look at him, shaking their heads, muttering in agreement, 'all whores, all racists'? And will they not stop to think for a moment that they should honour their origins more, be more aware that they carry the responsibility for everyone? That it is shameful toward their fathers, their brothers, to behave that way and talk that way? That there is no justification for dishonouring your origins? But I didn't have to look further than my own personal experience to see the lack of trust these young French men of North African origins are treated with.

One night, I was making my way home at about 3 a.m. from a bar in the Bastille area. I was twenty-three and I was back living with my parents. I was alone on rue de la Roquette, my heeled boots click-clacking on the pavement, noisily announcing my presence. Just then, a group of guys, clearly from the *banlieues*, noticed me as they were getting into a car. The one furthest from me shouted out, 'Lookin' classy, girl! Real nice!' I was alone in the street, it was three in the morning, I had a good twenty minute walk ahead of me until I reached 85, rue de la Roquette, so I decided to be civilized and without stopping, I turned and shouted back, 'Thanks!' The boys then piled into the car and pulled away at breakneck speed to drive up alongside me. They found it amazing and even more 'classy' that I had replied to their 'compliment' and they wanted to accompany me home. I replied with a smile that I lived with my parents really close by, but that it was nice of them to offer. So then they decided to escort me. The car was crawling along at two miles an hour, with two other cars stuck behind it. One of the drivers made the mistake of honking his horn, and one of my bodyguards stuck his head out of the window to yell at him, 'Back off, you piece of shit! Can't you see we're escorting this young lady home? Keep your fucking hair on, asshole!' So that's how five young men, who would make any other woman alone at 3 a.m. cross to the other side of the road, accompanied me home as gallantly as possible. Is it because I politely answered their pathetic attempt to make contact that they showed themselves to be wiser than expected? Is it because there was no contempt in my attitude that they felt obliged to become more sensitive? It was a really strange day. It was a day that made me dizzy.

I remember my parents explaining to me that we are not quite at home yet in France. That it is something you earn; that it takes time. But that we shouldn't be ashamed of Iran. That the French think that all Iranians are terrorists and religious fanatics, and we have to be careful to honour our origins and show them that this is not true. But we also have to honour France, which welcomed us in after the Beards. I remember my parents trying to teach me about France, without letting me forget Iran. I remember their efforts, their humility, their difficulties. I remember hitting a pupil in my first year of secondary school because she had just read *Not Without My Daughter* and was insulting me, telling me that all Iranian men are pigs who lock up their wives and eat cockroaches, that they don't know what a fork is and that they're dirty. I remember my father's embarrassed face when he was called in to the school. I remember that I was puzzled—I wasn't sure if I should apologize to her or hit her again. I didn't know if I should react like a French person—calmly explain to her that not all Iranians are like that and that there are also bad husbands in France—or like an Iranian (like a foreigner), and hit her again so she took back her words, which, by insulting an Iranian, insulted me. My mother solved the problem by inviting my classmate, who had taken quite a beating, and her parents, round for dinner. They saw for themselves that Iranians know how to behave at the table, that Iranian cuisine is very fine, and that my father knew Kant and Sartre like the back of his hand. They left stunned, but we had won. My mother always has a culinary solution to all ills. And it's often the best solution.

As a child, I was always getting into scrapes. My grandfather often tried to calm my bullheadedness. One morning, while I was sulking—my father had hidden my books to punish me for hitting my cousin who refused to watch the film I had chosen—he led me into the courtyard of the house where there was a fountain. He told me a story. Four poor men, a Persian, an Arab, a Turk and a Greek, were travelling together. A man, seeing that they were poor, gave them a dirham to buy food. The Persian declared that they should buy *angur* (grapes), the Arab replied that they should buy *inab* (grapes), the Turk wanted *uzum* (grapes) and the Greek wanted *istafil* (grapes). As none of them spoke the others' language, they rapidly came to blows. Just then, a scholar who was passing by pulled them apart and demanded to know what they were fighting about. Each of them explained in their language that it was impossible to eat anything other than grapes, not in that kind of heat. The scholar smiled and offered to be their arbitrator. They agreed and gave him the dirham. The scholar came back with grapes. All four of them understood that their fight was a misunderstanding because of their ignorance.

The following day when I woke up, this forgotten story from my childhood came back to me. Ignorance was the cause of everything. It is ignorance that turns the heat up among the bad-tempered; it is ignorance that is the Beards' raw material. Ignorance is a loss of reference points; it is dangerous; it is a killer. Ignorance should never be an excuse for hitting harder, for turning your back on the Other, for remaining locked in easy convictions. My grandfather's story came back to me as a reminder that I was not immune. That everyone proclaims their truth while hiding behind their ignorance.

A few hours later, the friend of the raffia bag designers must have been as shocked as I was. The murderer was Mohammed Merah; the killer was a French Muslim. I could hardly breathe. This could not be happening. And yet. He killed French Muslim soldiers for treason—to which country?—and Jewish children just because they were Jewish—and also because of the Israeli-Palestinian conflict, but what do French Jews have to do with a conflict in the Middle East? And what does a French Muslim have to do with all of that? It was crazy, unbelievable. He was worse than a monster; he was a human being. My grandfather's story was still fresh in my mind. Merah was ignorant. It was the only possible reason for his madness.

I don't know whether all those of Muslim origin, all those who had a Muslim grandfather, felt it as I did, like a kick in the guts. He reduced us to worthless trash. He drove the final nail into the coffin of misunderstanding between French people. He was the most despicable incarnation of Khomeini and his murderous apartheid. That young man was a gravedigger of the Republic. I read all the newspapers, searching among all the controversies that were sparked, for a truth, a meaning, or a past that would justify this French Muslim's spiral of hatred. But how on earth could such an abomination of a plan develop in his mind, leaving out any possibility of going back? He had no guilt, no sense of shame; he would have carried on his killing spree. He was the monster incarnate of all my fears, the worst of the worst failures of integration.

I expected French Muslims to stand proud and march silently against this atrocity committed by one of their own. Although the humanist imams unambiguously denounced the carnage, French Muslims did not gather together in unity. What was needed was to demonstrate with strength and without any doubt that French Muslims were not

Merah, that they rejected him, that they did not want him. Nothing happened. I did not hear a strong protest coming from the heart of France, a protest that would have restored the status of French citizen to its former glory. French Muslims should have proved themselves with a gesture. A powerful gesture, a symbolic gesture that would have consolidated the diverse body of the Republic. Because French Muslims are not Merahs. They are not, but all we hear about is those who are. And by remaining silent they detached themselves even more from the body of society. Merah's killing spree and the silence that followed it reminded me of my childhood and the Iranians who bowed their heads before the inevitable, who accepted it and carried on living their lives as best they could. What should I do, and what should they do, all the others with Muslim origin, atheists or believers or practicing? How can we feel like full citizens without assuming responsibility for the rights and duties that come with citizenship? How can we demonstrate our commitment to the values of France? How else, other than shouting it from the rooftops? How will we deal with another Merah in the future? What did we do when faced with this one? Nothing. We did nothing. Ignorance had the final word. Words were taken hostage by Merah's sister, who after all that slaughter, dared to voice her pride and support for her brother. Words were left to the murderer's sister. She held forth on all the news channels, celebrating murder and hatred. How could we give the floor to *that*?

Paris, July 2013

Paris, which was still an island, which was still as beautiful to me through my exiled eyes, was living to the rhythm of Ramadan. It was deathly hot but nobody died. And yet. A friend was eating a croissant at the new Place de la République. *Place de la République*, it had to be there. She was eating a croissant because she had skipped breakfast. Not because of Ramadan, but because she was super busy. My lovely friend had several appointments back to back, and was looking at her phone. Suddenly, she heard a man's voice speaking—badly—in Arabic. She heard 'shame' and she heard 'parents'. She looked up and a man was standing in front of her, and it was her he was talking to. He carried on in French, his Arabic was too poor. It took her a while to realize that she was being insulted. She was pretty surprised to hear him talking about the shame of her parents for having a bad daughter like her, who was wearing a skirt that was too short and eating a croissant. It was a Parisian Beard, who recognized the North African girl behind her

French look, and who thought he had the right to demean and humiliate her. To stigmatize her. There is no other word for it.

My friend is beautiful; she stood up in all her womanly glory and refused to let herself be told what to do by a Beard. And the Beard, clearly shocked by this woman who said 'No' to him, called five or six other Beards to his rescue. Faced with a woman measuring 5'3", he called five or six Beards over. She had to get away; she had to leave the Place de la République to the Beards who lived in their imaginary country in Paris. A country where men give themselves the right to insult women who don't follow their rules for living. It is terrible, yet it is also full of hope. Because he could not defend himself alone against one woman's words. She may have had to leave the Place de la République to be safe, but she definitely put the fear in him. Even in this story, there is hope.

Schools are destroyed by the Beards because girls are studying in them (400 schools destroyed by the Taliban in Pakistan in 2008, 500 in Afghanistan in six years); a Pakistani teenage girl called Malala Yousafzaï is shot in the head by the Taliban but continues her fight, which was started by her father, a school principal; the Beards refuse immunizations because they are weapons of Western destruction; a young Moroccan woman is given a prison sentence for smoking in the streets of Rabat during Ramadan; a Norwegian, raped in Saudi Arabia by Beards who don't see any problem with it because not only is she a woman, but a blonde woman, is imprisoned for provocation. It will take several months before she is released from the Beards' prisons. In France, on the pretext that skinheads were supposedly ripping off veils and assaulting Muslim women—nothing has been proven yet, no trace of DNA was found on the women—the phoney imams *advise* their *sisters* not to leave their apartments unless absolutely necessary. The insidious confinement of women has begun. Advising women not to venture out in public is just a means of negating them. In Saudi Arabia, as women *should be* voting for the first time in their history, in 2015, they are fighting for the right ... to drive. To simply get in a car and drive from point A to point B. They do not have the right. How can we forbid a woman to drive? And yet. There is always hope. There is hope when a little Yemeni girl of ten runs away on her own in the middle of the night to escape a marriage arranged by her mother and father. She flees, helped by an uncle who is more compassionate than her own mother, so as not to be penetrated by some old Beard. And she speaks out a few days later in a child's voice with the maturity of an experienced woman, to say 'No'. To say that it was either running away, or death. Because she could not have endured a marriage that would have pushed her to her death. Like her cousin who preferred to throw herself into a well and who is dead. As long as there is a little Yemeni girl ready to say 'No', and to say it out loud, there will be hope.

There is hope because there is Nedjma. Because a woman of Muslim origin is writing libertine novels today, under a pseudonym. The only way she could write them is anonymously, just like during the Enlightenment. She is the first Muslim woman to write cock and cunt. The first to write a plot based in the Maghreb: even though the country is never mentioned, even though the names of the cities are imaginary, they narrate the Maghreb from past to present. *La traversée des sens [The Journey of the Senses]* is an eye-opening novel, a bildungsroman of sorts.

It is the story of a forty-year-old woman, Zobida, married too young to a man who is too old and whom she does not love, and who beats her. When she is widowed, life finally begins for her. A lifetime spent loving men in the utmost secrecy. In a small town where her reputation is spotless and her nights are full of orgasms, she takes a young woman under her wing who has been disowned by the husband who never managed to deflower her. The young Leila is still a virgin but her honour is tainted. Zobida and Leila set off in search of the witch who 'shielded' the young girl's vagina, in order to lift the curse that obstructs entry to her cunt. But above all, it is a chance for Leila to discover something else other than her village, sounds other than those of prayer, examples other than those of women's misfortune. There is irony at every turn, and the situations are timeless.

Leila's mother, who spent her whole life inside, is said to have died when she took three steps outside the house. She no longer knew how to put one foot in front of the other ... Leila needs to shatter the voice of her mother inside her, the voice that envelops her soul in a shroud, repeating, *'Her body? What is a body? Food for worms, plus a bed for men, a mattress, preferably well-stuffed, upon which the man can sleep or piss, it's up to him. Women's bodies, they are nothing to do with women, they are their husband's property.*[14] It is this unhealthy litany that Zobida tries to combat by showing the young girl the body's beauty and the importance of pleasure. It is exquisite and exciting.

As with any great libertine novel, their encounters provide an opportunity to discover a new 'secret' about reality. The women spend a night in the ruins of a village called *Ishq* (Love), which was destroyed because of impiety. Its inhabitants dared to write poetry and took blasphemy as far as pinning the most beautiful poems to the door of the mosque. In these ruins they find women dressed in black: '*these women, who seemingly hid away all day and came out at night, had found no other way of warding off evil than narrating it. Words were their big weekly wash, their way of scrubbing the filthy corners of their life, wringing out the darkest creases of their hearts.*' Words to save you from evil. Speech as the only escape.

There is another village that is inhabited only by women. The main village chased them out, deciding once and for all that women were far too dangerous, and the men travel to the women's village every month to shoot their loads. The girls who are born out of these assaults stay in the village to wait for other men to come and fuck them without any tenderness. The boys are raised by the old women, a bit further away, until they reach puberty, when they go to join the other men in the main village. Yet behind every door, behind every window, when you turn your back on the street, there is flesh, there is pleasure. But you have to be discreet; you must be on your guard. The walls have ears, and women's bodies are blamed for everything. Everything must be whispered; even the most depraved man in private might prove to be the most puritanical in the public arena. Like the merchant that Zobida meets on the road, because *'despite his adulterous behaviour, the old merchant belonged to that species of believer who can ignore behaviour when it suits them, but become supercilious when it comes to other people's lives. Although they sin, disregarding the verses of the Quran, they are determined to keep a lifeline, scrupulously observing two or three ritual practices, adding a few sayings of the prophet which they do not compromise on, in order to improve their chances of escaping hell.'*

Nedjma's talent lies in politicizing her subject without losing sight of her intimate story. While staying for a few days in a town known for the tyranny of its Emir, Zobida tells the virgin how the women there are even more abused than anywhere else in the country, because *'There was no alternative for these men than to shut themselves away in their houses and to let terror reign there, striving, in particular, to punish their women for all the mistakes they had not made. Ruling like kings in their homes because they were worthless outside of them, lording it over their womenfolk because they could not manage their city's affairs. This had become their strategy for survival.'*

The whole aim of the journey is to make Leila come to terms with *'a real night of love! Without fear, or hesitation, or blackmail, or considerations of honour or virtue.'* The beautiful Leila gets there in the end and it is touching to see her recoiling from her body, touching it with her finger-tips, taming it, loving it and finally letting herself be loved. The fact that it is a poet, who ravishes her virginity with his graceful words, is proof that the unveiling must be total. The body and the mind. Leila can call herself a philosopher the day she leaves home, the day when breathing the stale air of prejudice drives her mad, the day when she no longer fears her body, her father, her sisters, the ghost of her mother, or tradition. Zobida has passed on her knowledge, she has liberated a woman. And it is the greatest of victories. The final paragraph of this libertine novel could apply to the Arab Autumns: *'As for the rest, I shall enjoy watching the Zebibians seething and raging, not knowing, in these clearly divided times, what they should or shouldn't tackle, whether they should deal with the honour of their women, or with the arrival of the blue-eyed ones they say are at the gates of Zebib, and who might steal Leila's pussy or something even more precious!'*

I have hope because Nedjma is writing libertine novels today, for today's women, and because I hope she will destroy all the prejudices, all the mental prisons of women, with powerful words like *cock, phallus, shaft, sword, knob, drill, pounder, penetrator, trunk, prick, appendage, quivering, smooth, hairy, horny, licker, snooper* ... but also with the help of *vulva, vagina, slit, bush, splendid, shameless, tight-lipped, grinder, sprayer, guzzler, swallower, snatch, hungry, silent, mangler, inferno, open, accommodating, sucker, juicy, hot*. I want to believe it.

Paris, February 2012

My dear uncle is lying in a hospital bed; it is pretty dismal, like hospital rooms the world over. He is wiped out, he is tired and with him, I can see my childhood gradually slipping further away. My little brother is in the room. The next bed is empty. My great-aunt, his wife, has gone downstairs to have a coffee, to take a break, to cry alone. I take my uncle's hand. He asks me and my brother to recall what our life was like *before* the Revolution. My little brother cannot remember it, I was the only *child* who knew the reality of our bourgeois, carefree, optimistic lives. My little brother has only known this dislocated, envious family. A family on its last legs. Exiled. My dear uncle squeezes my hand and sits up a bit, his eyes look more alive, dark, belligerent. 'They took everything from us. They destroyed us.' I know, dear uncle, I know. He lies back down again and speaks, without looking at me, but I know what he is thinking, I know he is going to utter the name that stabbed our culture in the back. 'Khomeini took everything from us.' My little brother gives me that panicked look that he has had ever since childhood. He doesn't know. All this seems incongruous to him, excessive. As for me, the tears come. I have not finished with Khomeini yet. I will have my revenge! At that precise moment, the door opens and a patient is moved in to the room. He is Tunisian. He is young. His mother is wearing a headscarf. I see my uncle waver. He raises his eyes to heaven. He is really in the shit. My aunt chooses that moment to reappear. The circles under her eyes are verging on purple, her trousers hang loosely, playing down her tall stature; she slouches. But at the sight of the headscarf, she stands up straight, as if all of the Iran of her free youth and her place in Tehran's society suddenly straightened up her spine. She comes to life again at the sight of a headscarf. The woman in the headscarf is very sweet, touching. My heart has softened—I had only been in exile for eight years, and I had resolved a number of my nudity issues—so I speak to her. My uncle and aunt close ranks. They are hostile. The smiling Tunisian mother in the headscarf asks me in a sort of confidential tone: 'Are you Turks?'

'No, Iranian.'

'*Bismillah*. But you're Muslims?'

The great moment of shame. I want to say yes. Because in a few hours she will leave the hospital room where her son is waiting for his operation and she will feel more reassured if she knows my uncle shares her faith. I don't know what to do. I look at my aunt and my dying uncle. I glance at my little brother who understands the irony of the situation.

'We haven't been practicing for several generations now.'

'But you're Muslims?'

'Yes.' We will never rid ourselves of it. Iranian means nothing any more. Muslim. That's all there is.

'Is that your grandfather?'

'Yes.' And it's as if he really was my grandfather.

When I ask her about her son and am about to say that he will be fine, he is young, he has his life ahead of him, and so on, that whole difficult litany that you have to say in hospital rooms, she smiles at me and says, 'It is all in God's hands! *Inshallah!*' At that moment, I want to hit her. I want her to forget God and just cry for her son. I am also envious, because that conviction is something I have never had in tragic moments. I am envious and that envy scares me: such conviction can only be imposed on others. Behind her smile, there is a world where that conviction is the law. In her smile there is Khomeini.

A few days later, my dying uncle came out of hospital on his own two feet, in total remission. More than a year later, he is still with us, vilifying Khomeini. I am still convinced that without that charming veiled Tunisian woman, my dear uncle would never have made it through the winter.

It is because my beloved uncle was on the brink of death that I started to write *Khomeini, Sade and Me*. Without my uncle, I would never have found the courage, or the audacity, or the desire, or the need to write. Without that Tunisian mother and her headscarf, I would have just carried on writing historical film scripts that nobody wanted. It is because I found myself facing the reality of death, of oblivion, in the eyes of someone who watched me from the day I was born, as I grew up, bared my arse, pinned naked women to my bedroom walls, provoked, fell in love, liberated myself, got beaten up, learned, picked myself up, started over ... that I had to write. I had to write fast; I had to write to record the face of my dear uncle in history. I owed him that much, after all. I owed it to him to smash Khomeini's skull in with a hammer. To let him know that I had not forgotten any of it.

As long as there are readers, as long as we aspire to raise our heads and look beyond ourselves, there will be men of imagination who are capable of overthrowing tyranny. As long as there are words. That is what art (and literature in particular) does for us: it opens the floodgate of the mind, confronts us with other feelings, other voices, other eternities.

Despite all the attacks—despite all the steps backward and the relentless desire of the Beards to imprison women in a feminine essence that is just a fantasy, born out of the fear of being robbed of their imaginary manhood—they will never win. There are too many desires, too many perspectives, too many borders, too many wars, too many little girls who want to learn to read, too many women being silenced, too many books. And there is Sade. The possibility of a future will always exist in the words of Sade, there will always be some forgotten book in a library, a book found in a landfill site, a novel lost along the way. Beards of all kinds might carry on imprisoning speech, forbidding the flesh, locking up knowledge; all it takes is one shout, one 'No', one flash of courage. Point and laugh at them, and they will no longer exist. My convictions and my tears, my provocations and my whores, my words and Sade will not be in vain. They will be taken up by other little girls, other women and even men who refuse the Beards and who will stand up as free men to continue the fight. A fight that encourages me every day to get up and write. A fight that started with my arse, and which continues with my friendships and my loves, my relationship with others, my daily life. All the time. I will never give up because I have too much past, too much memory, too much childhood. I will not give up because the Beard has not yet been born who will make me bow my head and keep quiet. Keeping quiet is surrendering.

What will be left of my anger and my hope? Words. Words and my arse. What will be left of my convictions and my provocations is my father, smiling wisely at the freedom that was always mine for the taking and which he so lovingly supported. What will be left of my convictions is my belief in the Enlightenment; my belief in a past that dethroned kings and toppled the clergy. There is no power more absolute than that of men and women who know that no man or woman is superior to them in law. And when the day comes when all the Beards are gone, when all women will be proud to be women, the fight will go on. It has to go on, to keep the Beards far away from power. It has to go on, because there is nothing more tenacious than badly trimmed Beards and moustachioed Crows. There will always be Beards and Crows who are as convinced of their beliefs as I am of mine, lurking beneath smiles and waiting—so patiently ... eternity is theirs—for the slightest hint of complacency, to come back with their prohibitions and their prisons the size of my childhood; they will come back even more self-assured, even stronger.

Khomeini will never die. I know that now. I no longer suffer because of it. It is no longer as important. I have accepted that he is immortal. But what he doesn't know is that I am too. There will always be a little girl who is just dying to bare her naked arse. Another little girl who will be lucky enough to have a father like mine. Khomeini can come back all he wants. The little girl will be there. And Sade will never leave her, as long as she discovers him. He will always be there. With his dirty words and his unwavering strength as a free man. For a very long time to come.

Contents

Notes

1   *Philosophy in the Boudoir*, Marquis de Sade D.A.F.
    Penguin Classics Paperback (2006).

2   http://wikiislam.net/wiki/Qur'an,_Hadith_and_
    Scholars:Women#cite_note-12

3   http://2pm.co/demo/2500/12/28/

4   *My Apprenticeships & Music-Hall Sidelights*, Colette.
    Penguin (1967).

5   *Rameau's Nephew*, Denis Diderot (1805). A Project
    Gutenberg of Australia eBook (2007).

6   *Thérèse the Philosopher: and, The Story of Mrs Bois-
    Laurier*, Jean-Baptiste de Boyer Marquis d'Argen. Locus
    Elm Press (2014).

7   *The Life and Adventures of Father Silas*, by Anonymous.
    Erotic eBooks (2014).

8   *Le portier des Chartreux; ou, Mémoires de Saturnin*,
    Gervaise de La Touche, Jean Charles (1715–1782);
    English translation © Charlotte Coombe 2015.

9   *Venus in the Cloister, or the Nun in her Smock.* Birchgrove Press (2010) Kindle Edition.

10 *Le rideau levé ou l'éducation de Laure*, Comte de Honoré-Gabriel de Riquetti Mirabeau (1786); English Translation ©Charlotte Coombe 2015.

11 *Philosophy in the Boudoir*, Marquis de Sade D.A.F. Penguin Classics Paperback, Penguin (2006).

12 *Friend or Foe: A History of France*, Alistair Horne. Orion (2012).

13 *Letter on the Book Trade*, Arthur Goldhammer and Denis Diderot, in Daedalus.

14 Extracts from *La traversée des sens*, Nedjma. Plon (2009); English translation ©Charlotte Coombe 2015.